Synchronized Factories

Juan S. Blyde
Editor

Synchronized Factories

Latin America and the Caribbean in the Era of Global Value Chains

Springer Open

Editor
Juan S. Blyde
Integration and Trade Sector
Inter-American Development Bank
Washington, DC, USA

ISBN 978-3-319-09990-3 ISBN 978-3-319-09991-0 (eBook)
DOI 10.1007/978-3-319-09991-0
Springer Cham Heidelberg New York Dordrecht London

Library of Congress Control Number: 2014947872

Printed on acid-free paper

Springer is part of Springer Science+Business Media (www.springer.com)

Prologue

Until recently, most international trade between industrialized nations and developing countries—the so-called North-South trade—consisted of an exchange of Northern manufactures for Southern raw material and primary goods. Meanwhile, most trade between industrialized nations consisted of exchanges of different manufacturing goods or of similar goods with different qualities or varieties. This scenario changed dramatically when the production of manufactures in the North became fractionalized into various stages and geographically dispersed to plants across the globe. Today many countries, including several developing countries, are manufacturing and trading fragments of goods that they did not produce before. In the last three decades, this fragmentation of production has been one of the main factors behind the current unprecedented level of world trade as a share of world GDP.

Besides providing opportunities to diversify production and trade, participation in global value chains allows countries to capture some of the rents associated with the good manufactured in the chain without having to develop proficiency in all of its stages of production. There is a general perception, however, that most countries in Latin American and the Caribbean have not been able to capitalize on these new trends in production fragmentation.

In this report we undertake an extensive analysis of the prospects of Latin America and the Caribbean to participate in global value chains. The study is part of a broader research effort at the Inter-American Development Bank to examine the region's trade agenda beyond traditional trade barriers. The report first presents a comprehensive picture of the extent to which the region's countries participate in global value chains vis-à-vis other regions. Second, it examines the main factors behind the rates of participation observed. The analysis concludes with a series of policy prescriptions.

The report shows that with the emergence of global value chains, countries must address a series of challenges, some of which are already well known by policymakers, and others that have been relatively overlooked.

Antoni Estevadeordal
Manager, Integration and Trade Sector, IDB

Purpose of the Report

Production processes have grown increasingly fragmented worldwide. Many goods are now made in a multi-country process in which different production stages are carried out in plants in different parts of the world, in industries as diverse as electronics, transport equipment, garments, and food products. Frequently cited examples are the iPod and iPhone. Less technologically intensive, but still involving multiple countries, is the production of the Barbie doll.

The new patterns of international organization of production have attracted the attention of researchers, businessmen, and policymakers, who have invented a whole new lexicon to describe them: international fragmentation of production, global value chains, offshoring, international production networks, slicing the value added chain (Krugman, 1995), disintegration of production (Feenstra, 1998), delocalization (Leamer, 1996), globalization of production and trade (Gereffi, Humphrey, & Sturgeon, 2005), and the great unbundling (Baldwin, 2006), among others.

For firms in developing countries, the international fragmentation of production presents opportunities to participate in activities that formerly were virtually closed to them. Without international production networks, emerging economies would have to master entire production processes to effectively compete in world markets. By joining global supply chains, however, firms in developing countries can participate in one or a few phases involved in the production of a final good. Such participation provides countries with new opportunities to diversify trade and production, an issue of particular importance for countries in Latin America and the Caribbean whose export base is highly concentrated in a few industries, and particularly in natural resource-intensive sectors. In addition to providing market outlets, global value chains can also open access to knowledge and technology. Participation in international supply chains has been frequently associated with rapid learning, technology transfers, and knowledge spillovers.

Before continuing further it is worth pausing to ask whether there is anything really new about the emergence of global supply chains that deserves a fresh look, particularly as regards policy issues. Despite the sometimes sumptuous terminology, are we merely witnessing the continuing trajectory of an ever more integrated world that can be examined through the lenses of conventional trade models?

As such, are the relevant policy implications already well established? As the following pages will show, today's global supply chains are indeed new. A quick look at the issues suggests that the increasing hype might be justified at least on two grounds, one theoretical, the other practical.

Take, for instance, the conventional trade models in which international trade flows are explained in theory by differences in factors endowments. These models were based on the notion that international competition occurred between sectors in different countries, which made it easy to predict which sectors and which factors of production would gain or lose after trade was liberalized. But in today's fragmentation of production, competition from abroad now occurs at a more disaggregated level—like a bundle of tasks—making it more difficult to measure the general equilibrium effects of increased international competition. Assume that two of the four tasks that a worker performs in a factory are moved offshore. The overall demand for her job falls, and thus, in principle, her wage. But now the worker is focusing on the tasks that she can do better, and since her compensation is associated with her productivity, her wage must rise in accordance with her higher average productivity. These opposite forces make it harder to predict the impacts of opening to trade when offshoring is allowed.[1] In fact, the new trade models with offshoring frequently highlight the notion that relocating fragments of production abroad is analogous to technological progress in which productivity gains might be shared by all sectors of the economy (Grossman and Rossi-Hansberg, 2008).

From the practical point of view, the emergence of international production networks also warrants a fresh look at policy issues. For example, many trade flows are purely market transactions that take place among unrelated parties or at arm's length. However, the trade of specific inputs often associated with global supply chains increasingly occurs under contractual relationships. This is because suppliers may need to customize their production to the specifications of particular buyers, and the parameters governing such specifications are typically established in contractual agreements. So, even if trade is liberalized, firms in developing countries might not automatically gain access to some international production networks, for instance, if they are governed by a few buyers who require very particular contractual guarantees.

Therefore, from the outset, it seems that the evolving trends we are witnessing warrant a closer look at how firms and countries participate in international production networks. This is the objective of this report. In particular, the report examines the extent to which countries in Latin America and the Caribbean participate in global production networks and describes the drivers of such participation. The aim is to identify policies that would allow countries to improve their insertion in regional and global production networks.

The report consists of five chapters. The first chapter describes international production networks, including why firms engage in cross-border production sharing, how this process has evolved over time, the different strategies firms use to fragment

---

[1] This result does not imply that trade in tasks does not follow factor price differences across countries.

production internationally, and the consequences that joining global supply chains have on a country's development.

In Chap. 2 we present a series of measures that establish the region's status in terms of global value chain participation. While there is a general notion that Latin American and Caribbean countries participate less in international production networks than those of other regions, there is a lack of systematic evidence supporting this perception. The main reason for this information deficit is the difficulty of measuring participation in global supply chains. For instance, global production networks were initially built through what is known as vertical foreign direct investment (FDI), the creation of linkages between affiliates providing inputs to parent companies in other countries. But FDI data do not normally differentiate whether affiliates are vertically linked to parent companies or whether they are merely producing the same good abroad, which is known as horizontal FDI. Likewise, trade data by themselves do not convey enough information to precisely measure the extent to which a country is participating in international supply chains. To overcome these shortcomings, new methodologies have been developed in recent years to proxy participation in production networks. Chapter 2 presents various indicators, including aggregated measures of value added in trade flows based on international input-output tables and measures that employ more disaggregated datasets. The chapter's aim is to present a battery of indicators that provides a broad picture of the extent to which Latin America and the Caribbean participates in global supply chains and how this participation compares to that of other regions.

In Chap. 3 we turn to the drivers of global value chain (GVC) participation: the factors that explain the differences in GVC participation between Latin America and the Caribbean and other regions. While the list of potential factors can be quite extensive, we look at areas that seem most relevant due to the availability of theoretical and analytical work, and also because of the potential for policy action. First, we look into the role of transportation and logistics services, including communication and information technology. Then, we examine the impact of trade agreements and of trade policy in general. The issues of contracting institutions and contract enforcements are analyzed as regards firms' offshoring strategies. While most of the chapter is devoted to international fragmentation related to the production of goods, the last section presents empirical exercises that look at the drivers behind the offshoring of services.

While Chap. 3 is mostly based on analyses that compare data across countries and industries, Chap. 4 moves the discussion closer to the ground to examine micro-level data on the experiences of firms participating in production networks. This micro approach allows us to study additional aspects of global supply chain participation that are difficult to analyze with cross-country regressions. The core of the discussion in this chapter is on the capabilities firms must acquire to access global supply chains. First, we employ firm-level data to compare the performance of firms in international production networks with the performance of other firms. The analysis shows that firms participating in GVCs typically have superior skills and capabilities. We then move even closer to the ground, using insights derived from case studies to highlight a set of empirical regularities among the firms participating in international supply chains. We discuss what these empirical regularities reveal about difficulties Latin American firms face in attaining adequate levels of capabilities and quality standards due to factors such as information and coordination problems. The chapter then discusses policy options for dealing with such challenges.

In this way, the report moves progressively from the most macro evidence, including the measures of GVC participation from international input-output tables in Chap. 2; through the cross-country and cross-industry analyses of Chap. 3; and finally to the more micro evidence of firm-level data and case studies of Chap. 4. This combination of analyses and levels of aggregation is intended to present a rich picture of the prospects for Latin American countries to share in cross-border production and with other regions. Each chapter offers policy prescriptions; the main policy implications are summarized in Chap. 5.

A final word is in order regarding the report's content. Even though the theoretical and empirical analyses behind the notion of global value chains are relatively new, writing on this subject is already very extensive. Different aspects of GVCs have been examined, among them, financial institutions, innovation systems, diasporas, and the exchange rate. This report does not intend to cover them all. Rather, this analysis focuses mainly on the trade-related aspects of GVCs, with the primary aim of providing information that the countries in Latin America and the Caribbean can use to formulate their trade and integration strategies. In addition, we hope that this publication will fuel further discussions and analyses in the region in the other many areas related to this multifaceted topic.

Acknowledgments

Synchronized Factories: Latin America and the Caribbean in the Era of Global Value Chains is part of a series of flagship publications developed by the Trade and Integration Sector (INT) of the Inter-American Development Bank (IDB). This report was produced under the direction of Juan Blyde, Lead Trade and Integration Economist, based on internal policy research prepared by Juan Blyde, Christian Volpe, and Danielken Molina. Kun Li and Jeremy Harris provided key inputs to Chaps. 2 and 3, respectively.

The report also benefited from case studies provided by the following external collaborators: Thiago Alves Ribeiro, Tiago Andreotti e Silva, Flor Brown-Grossman, Fabrizio Cafaggi, Lilia Domínguez-Villalobos, Lucila Gabriel de Almeida, Andrea González, Juan Carlos Hallak, Luana F. Joppert Swensson, Marcela Meléndez, Ricardo Monge-González, Clarissa Piterman Gross, Ronaldo Porto Macedo Jr., Peter K. Schott, Tatiana Soria Genta, Maria José Uribe, and Sandro Zolezzi.

Timothy Sturgeon, Senior Research Associate of the Industrial Performance Center of the Massachusetts Institute of Technology, was the external technical advisor for the case studies.

The report would not have been possible without the intellectual and institutional support of Antoni Estevadeordal, INT's Sector Manager, and Santiago Levy, Vice-President for Sectors and Knowledge. Mauricio Mesquita Moreira, INT's Sectoral Economic Principal Advisor, oversaw the content of the document.

We are thankful for the many comments and suggestions from our two external peer reviewers, Peter K. Schott, Professor of Economics at Yale School of Management, and Juan Carlos Hallak, Professor of Economics at Universidad de San Andrés, and from our internal reviewer, Carlo Pietrobelli, Private Sector Development Lead Specialist.

The report benefited from conversations with many individuals, including Facundo Albornoz, Roberto Alvarez, Koen de Backer, Richard Baldwin, Emily Blanchard, Meng Bo, Eduardo Boreinstein, Luis de la Calle, Ricardo Carciofi, Ralph S. Carter, Maggie Chen, Ana Corbacho, Rafael Cornejo, Marcela Cristini, Flavio Díaz, Gabriel Duque, Karina Fernandez-Stark, Michael Ferrantino, Renato da Fonseca, Teresa Fort, Alan K. Fox, Paulo G. Franklin de Abreu, Brigette Gage,

Pablo García, Gary Gereffi, Paolo Giordano, Anabel González, Ana Carolina González, Isaías González, Jaime Granados, Luis Amadeo Hernández-Situ, Satoshi Inomata, Alejandro Izquierdo, Beatriz Leycegui, Maria del Pilar Londoño-Kent, Andrés Lopez, Ernesto Lopez Córdova, Sébastien Miroudot, Virgilio Mota, Nanno Mulder, Lindsay Oldenski, Fabrizio Opertti, Andrew Powell, William Powers, Roberta Rabellotti, Andrés Rebolledo, Maryse Robert, Carolyn Roberts, Gabriel Sanchez, Diego Saravia, Huberth Scaith, Georg Schaur, Ernesto Stein, Sherry Stephenson, Tim Sturgeon, Jonathan Thorpe, Alberto Trejos, Raúl Urteaga, Marcel Vaillant, Guillermo Valles, Johannes Van Biesebroeck, and Reinhard Waehlen.

We would also like to thank Nathan Nunn of Harvard University for kindly providing measures of industry contractibility used in Chap. 3; Natalia Volkow, Lázaro Trujillo, and José Francisco Cuiriz from the Instituto Nacional de Estadística y Geografía of Mexico for their assistance with the IMMEX census and for kindly running our statistical and econometric codes in their computers; Will Bonasin and Amanda Schrauth of Dun & Bradstreet for their dedicated support with the Worldbase dataset; and Kristen S. Corwin from the US Census Bureau for her support with the US Related Party Trade database. Julieth Santamaria, Alejandro Graziano, Rubén Irvin Rojas, and Gabriela Schmidt provided excellent research assistance.

Roger Hamilton was the general editor and Ingrid Carolina Barreto oversaw all the editing process.

The opinions expressed in this publication are those of the authors and do not necessarily reflect the views of the IDB or its board of directors.

Contents

1 Preliminaries: Concepts, Trends, and Frameworks 1
Supply Chains 1
Offshoring Strategies 2
Why Do Firms Fragment Production Internationally? 3
What Do Countries in Latin America and the Caribbean Stand to Gain? .. 6
Immense Opportunities but also Potential Risks 9
Rationale for Public Policy 10

2 The Participation of Latin America and the Caribbean in International Supply Chains 13
Evidence from Intra-industry Trade Indexes 13
Evidence from Trade in Value Added 15
Evidence from FDI Data 23
Evidence from Trade in Services 26
Recapitulating 28

3 The Drivers of Global Value Chain Participation: Cross-Country Analyses 29
Synchronizing Trade: The Role of Transportation, Communication, and Logistics Infrastructure 31
Policy Issues 39
Production Disintegration and Market Integration: Deep Integration Agreements at Work 44
Policy Issues 47
Production Unbundling and Firm Boundaries: Foreign Affiliates or Local Suppliers? 54
Policy Issues 62
Service Offshoring: Grasping the Intangibles 66
Policy Issues 70

4 What It Takes to Join an International Value Chain: The Firm-Level Evidence ... 75
No Ordinary Firms ... 75
Empirical Regularities from Case Studies ... 79
Empirical Regularity 1: Prior Exposure to International Practices and/or Markets ... 80
Empirical Regularity 2: Targeting of Market Segments Based on Some Form of Comparative Advantage ... 81
Empirical Regularity 3: Painstaking Accumulation of Capabilities and Use of Certifications as Evidence of Proficiency ... 81
Empirical Regularity 4: Firms Leveraged Resources and Collaborated with Other Peers to Address Common Challenges ... 82
Empirical Regularity 5: Continuing to Learn and Improving Capabilities Even After Joining a GVC ... 82
Policy Lessons from the Empirical Regularities ... 83
Local Linkages ... 94
Exploit Synergies Through a Coordinated Approach ... 104

5 Conclusions ... 105

Appendix A ... 111
Trade in Value Added and Set of Countries ... 111
FDI Dataset ... 112

Appendix B ... 115
Specification for the Model of Vertical FDI and Logistics Infrastructure ... 115
The Effects of Economic Integration Agreements: Estimation and Data Sources ... 116
Specification for the Model of Intra-firm Trade ... 121
Specification for the Model of Service Offshoring ... 124

Appendix C ... 127
Specification for Measuring the Performance of Vertically Linked Affiliates ... 127

References ... 131

Chapter 1
Preliminaries: Concepts, Trends, and Frameworks

This chapter presents background that will provide context for the rest of the report, including key concepts and frameworks, recent trends in the emergence of production sharing, and a discussion on the potential benefits and risks of joining global supply chains.

Supply Chains

A supply chain is normally defined as a group of economic units that provide a range of tangible and intangible value-adding activities needed to bring a good or service from its conception, through the different production phases, to final delivery to consumers. The supply chain often includes a lead unit that specifies what is to be produced by whom and when. This lead unit typically exercises some control over the chain even if it doesn't have ownership of it.[1] As such, the units tend to work in tandem such that the different inputs are produced according to the right specifications, and distributed in the right quantities, to the right locations, and at the right time. Throughout, the goal is typically to minimize costs for the total system.

It is common to use the term *supply chain* to refer to the network of a particular firm, such as Nike's supply chain. The term *value chain* is more commonly used in a broader context to refer to the industry, as in the footwear value chain. Increasingly, however, both terms have been employed indiscriminately, as we do in this report. When a supply chain encompasses establishments that are located in different countries, the term *global supply chain* is used.

[1] The coordinating role can be exercised by a firm but also by other units, such as a trader, a wholesaler, or a supermarket.

J.S. Blyde (ed.), *Synchronized Factories: Latin America and the Caribbean in the Era of Global Value Chains*, DOI 10.1007/978-3-319-09991-0_1

While a global supply chain is basically a group of establishments working together from the design to the distribution of a product, data are often lacking that would enable economists to know whether the observed trade transactions are effectively part of an international production network. This is why economists have been using broader definitions to measure participation of countries in global supply chains. In Chap. 2 we introduce some of these definitions as well as the measures applied to them.

The term *value chain* suggests that the production process moves in a linear manner, from upstream to downstream stages, a configuration sometimes likened to that of a snake. But production processes can have quite different configurations. For instance, they can take the form of spiders, in which parts from different locations arrive in a central location for final assembly; or of complex combinations of spiders and snakes (Baldwin & Venables, 2013). Moreover, intermediate inputs can bend back, as country A imports an intermediate good from country B that itself uses other inputs from country A (Bhagwati, 2013). In our analysis we follow the convention in the literature and continue to use *value chain* even when referring to these more complex production configurations.

Offshoring Strategies

Firms follow different strategies to unbundle their production processes. One is to delegate part of the production process to an affiliate in another country. This is normally referred to as *vertical FDI*—in other words, a vertically linked affiliate produces an input that will be used downstream in the multinational's supply chain.[2] Another strategy is to outsource part of the production process to an entirely independent firm in the other country. This is known as *foreign outsourcing*.

The term *offshoring* is then used in the literature to refer to the international fragmentation of production that takes place through either vertical FDI or foreign outsourcing. We will follow the same convention here and use the term *offshoring* when there is no need to make an explicit distinction between vertical FDI and foreign outsourcing.

Each strategy—vertical FDI or foreign outsourcing—has advantages and disadvantages. For instance, one advantage of vertical FDI is that it potentially eliminates the need for costly renegotiations of a contract after an agreement has been reached. On the other hand, foreign outsourcing eliminates the fixed incurred costs of opening an affiliate.

[2] A different motive for FDI is to replicate the entire production process in another country, typically to save on transportation and other costs and to avoid tariffs. This is referred in the literature as horizontal FDI.

The decision to use vertical FDI or foreign outsourcing is known as the *internalization decision*. The factors involved in making this decision are addressed in Chap. 3 when we examine what the internalization decision and its determinants imply for the strategies of the Latin American countries regarding accessing GVCs: should countries in the region promote links between local suppliers and global buyers? Or should they seek to attract vertically linked affiliates to their shores?

Why Do Firms Fragment Production Internationally?

We are all familiar with the wine-for-cloth example used by David Ricardo in the early 1800s to illustrate his theory of comparative advantage. Even if Portugal could produce wine and cloth with less labor than England, both countries would gain by specializing in the good that they could produce more efficiently—that is, the good in which they had a comparative advantage. While Ricardo was thinking about final goods, the same concept applies to tasks performed in making those goods. For instance, if making clothes requires two tasks, and at a certain point in time those tasks could be separated geographically, the country producing cloth would gain by offshoring the task in which it has the least advantage while keeping the other task at home. This is true even if the country has an advantage in both tasks. In this way, offshoring allows home workers to focus on the tasks that they do relatively better.

While the theory of comparative advantage has been around for two centuries, the international fragmentation of production and the emergence of global supply chains—at least on its current scale—is a relatively recent phenomenon. One could then ask, why didn't firms engage more in cross-border production sharing in the past? The short answer is that until recently, a number of factors limited the degree to which the production of a good could be unbundled. Many of these limitations, however, have receded in recent years in response to certain trends. In this report we will examine the importance of many of these trends; nevertheless, at this point we can offer some preliminary conjectures regarding which trends have facilitated the surge in cross-border production sharing.

Reduction in trade costs. Traditional barriers, such as tariffs, have been falling worldwide, particularly since the Uruguay Round of multilateral trade negotiations about 20 years ago. While the present Doha Round has progressed very slowly, many tariff barriers have continued to fall in several parts of the world, particularly in response to the more than 160 regional trade agreements that have come into force since 2000. Figure 1.1, for example, shows world simple averages for ad valorem MFN-applied rates and for the percentage of dutiable imports in three different years. Today, most countries have ad valorem tariff rates below 10 %, and the percentage of dutiable imports tends to be below 70 %. Of course, there are still many sectors and countries with high trade barriers, but there is no doubt that in most parts of the world today those tariff barriers are significantly lower, providing critical incentives for trading blocks of fragmented production across borders.

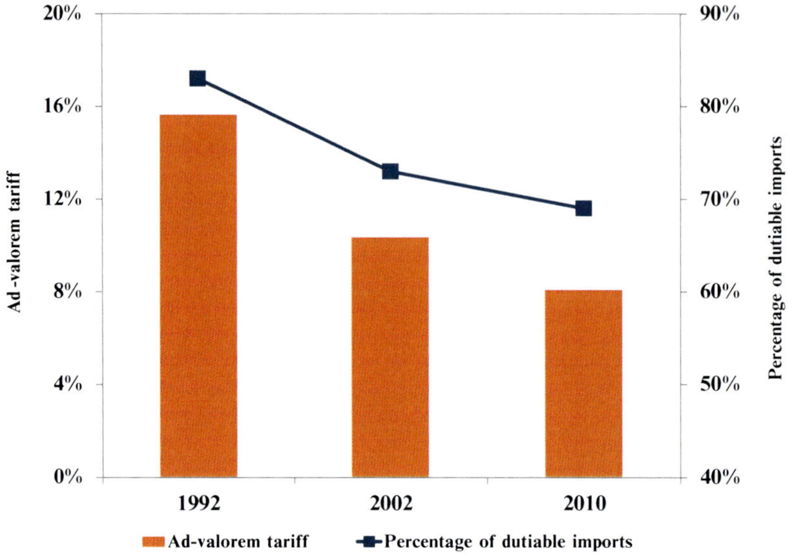

Fig. 1.1 Measures of Import Restrictions, World Averages *Note*: The ad valorem tariff rates and the percentage of dutiable imports are calculated as simple averages across countries. *Source*: Authors' calculations based on data from TRAINS

Reduction in transportation costs. The cost of transporting intermediate inputs is also a factor discouraging the geographical relocation of production bundles, particularly in distant locations. Transport costs have been falling since the introduction of the steamship and the steam locomotive in the late 1700s and the early 1800s. But recent developments have accelerated this trend. For instance, bigger vessels and aircraft capable of exploiting larger-scale economies are continuously being introduced in the transport industry; cargo is increasingly containerized, and competition on commercial shipping routes has intensified in recent years. As a result, transport costs have continued to fall. Figure 1.2, for example, shows the average ad valorem freight rates associated with the exports of 135 countries to the US in 1974 (vertical axis) and 2006 (horizontal axis). Most points are located above the diagonal line, indicating that transport costs have sharply declined in most parts of the world. The reduction in freight rates therefore adds to the decline in traditional barriers such as tariffs, making total trade costs in most parts of the world a fraction of what they were in the past.

The emergence of logistics companies. The number of logistics companies in the world has increased rapidly since the 1970s. Data from Dun & Bradstreet, for example, indicate that between 1970 and 2011, supply chain management firms and freight forwarders have multiplied by three and eight times, respectively. Logistics companies offer a wide range of services—from the preparation of documents, such as commercial invoices and bills of lading, to support activities, such as freight consolidation, warehousing, shipping, and distribution. All these services facilitate the movements

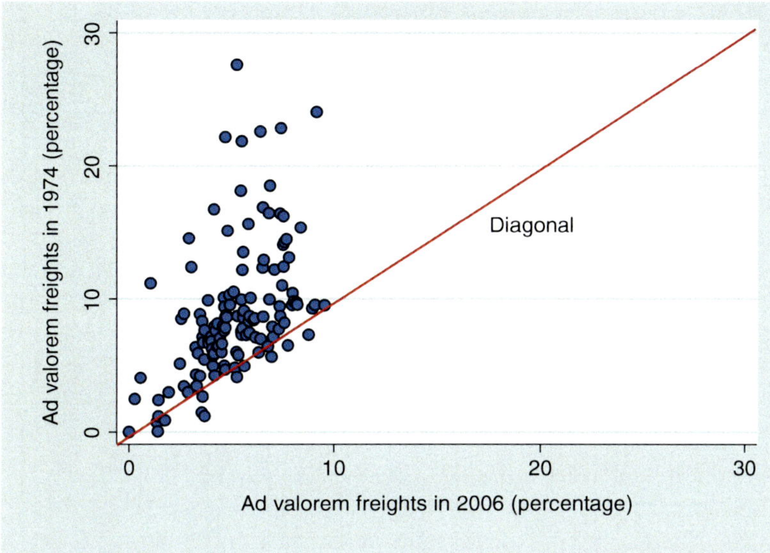

Fig. 1.2 Ad Valorem Freight Rates of Exports to the US, Country Averages *Note*: The figure shows fitted ad valorem rates derived from country regressions that control for changes in the mix of products traded over time. See Hummels (2007). *Source*: Authors' calculations based on *U.S. Imports of Merchandise* of the U.S. Census Bureau

of goods across borders. The surge of logistics companies has also been accompanied by attempts by a few firms to become truly globally oriented. For instance, in 2012, UPS, a major logistics company based in the US, announced the acquisition of TNT Express, a Dutch logistics firm with a strong presence in Europe; the move was designed to fill a gap in UPS's Europe operations.[3] The rise of these global logistics companies and the ever-growing worldwide network of places that they serve have greatly helped firms propel their supply chains around the world. Support for this claim can be found in the words of Victor Fung, chairman of Li & Fung, the well-known garment company and world leader in buyer-driven supply chains:

> There is absolutely no way we could conduct our business today without the growth of people like UPS, who describe what they do as synchronized commerce. With this logistical support to move products and components, you are able to achieve faster turnaround times…[4]

The surge of specialized logistics services and platforms has intensified in recent years to meet the demand of many firms for assistance in creating seamless supply chains.

---

[3] According to *The Economist*, March 24, 2012.

[4] Speech by Victor Fung to the Executive Committee of the Federation of Indian Chambers of Commerce and Industry, Bangalore, October 11, 2011.

Reduced information costs and improved communications. In the last two decades, production processes, international trade, and commerce in general have been impacted by vast increases in computerization power, the Internet, massive growth in the network capacity of optical fiber, and a range of inexpensive information transmission capabilities. There have been major improvements in the quality, capacity, and reliability of communication technologies, including faxes, emailing, and videoconferencing. Before these developments, proximity was necessary to keep the costs of coordination low (Baldwin, 2012). But today, the transmission of information and communication over vast distances is fast, accessible, and accurate. The result has been lower costs for coordinating and monitoring blocks of production at a distance, which facilitates the unbundling of production to distant locations. Additionally, improved information technology has also been very helpful in facilitating the transmission of previously tacit knowledge through codification and industry-level standards (Sturgeon, 2008).

Contract enforcement and intellectual property rights. Global production networks necessarily entail contracting relationships between agents in different countries with different legal systems and contracting institutions. Uncertain and ambiguous practices in contract enforcement can undermine international transactions. The problem can be particularly acute in international supply chains because they tend to involve significant relationship-specific investments. Likewise, weak intellectual property rights can undermine the delegating of links of the value chain to other parties for fear of intellectual property infringement and the unauthorized use of technical and production knowledge by the other party. Recent trends in contract enforcement and property rights have reduced these fears. For instance, the costs of enforcing contracts have consistently declined worldwide, particularly in the industrialized countries.[5] The world has also seen a remarkable improvement in the protection of intellectual property rights, particularly with the recent conclusion of the WTO agreement on Trade-Related Aspects of Intellectual Property Rights, or TRIPS (Maskus, 2012). Such developments have improved the willingness of firms that engage in international fragmentation of production to engage with foreign suppliers and their countries' institutions.

What Do Countries in Latin America and the Caribbean Stand to Gain?

Global value chains provide countries with opportunities to industrialize at a faster pace than in the past. Many of today's industrialized countries developed by building entire supply chains within their own territories, with all the challenges, costs,

[5] Based on comparisons between 2003 and 2012 from Doing Business data on enforcing contracts.

and time that this entails (Baldwin, 2012). The emergence of GVCs, however, is allowing nations to industrialize much more rapidly by joining international production networks rather than by building entire supply chains at home. Fragmentation and vertical specialization are enabling countries to participate in world markets by eliminating the need to master all the aspects involved in the production of a final good (Baldwin, 2011). This has been the path to industrialization taken by some Asian countries and, more recently, by some Eastern European countries as well.

The gains from participating in global value chains can also be measured in terms of increased trade opportunities that did not exist in the past. The fragmentation of production and the relocation of slices of the value chain across various countries opens up new opportunities for trade diversification, an issue of particular importance for Latin America and the Caribbean. The export base of our region is highly concentrated in natural resource-intensive sectors, a trend that has intensified during the last decade with the emergence of China. While specialization in the region's factor-abundant sectors provides the basis for important gains from trade, complete specialization in natural resources could also have negative consequences. The literature referring to these risks is long and well known. Some examples are the notion that natural resource-intensive goods might produce too much instability in the economy due to their high price volatility, which, in the absence of appropriate hedging opportunities, can hurt growth (Larrain, Sachs, & Warner, 1999). Negative consequences can also be related to the familiar concept of Dutch disease (Corden, 1984) or to the notion that natural resource-rich countries concentrate their resources in land, crops, and extractive equipment, leaving minimal incentives to invest in human capital which, in turn, inhibits diversification towards more technology-intensive, higher-return activities, with the result of undermining future growth (Leamer, Maul, Rodriguez, & Schott, 1999).

Beyond the issue of natural resources, export diversification per se has been justified on other grounds. For instance, a diversified export base can help to protect countries from sector-specific shocks and their negative effects on export revenue, income, and growth. Countries that expand their exports beyond a limited number of products also lower their risks of worsening their terms of trade (see, e.g., Hummels & Klenow, 2005). Other arguments are based on a direct link between export variety and growth that result from productivity gains arising either from learning by exporting or from having a better resource allocation (see, e.g., Feenstra & Kee, 2004; Lederman & Maloney, 2003).

Participation in global production networks has also been associated with other benefits, including learning, technology transfers, and knowledge spillovers. Evidence of successful cases of learning within the chain can be found in many sectors, such as apparel (Gereffi, 1999), motorcycles (Fujita, 2011), agroindustry (Cafaggi et al., 2012), and the computer industry (Kawakami, 2011). In some cases, knowledge and skills that first-tier suppliers absorb from global players also diffuse to other firms (Poon, 2004).

Learning from interaction with global actors might confer different benefits, such as improving production processes, attaining consistent and high quality, and/or increasing the speed of response (Humphrey & Schmitz, 2000).

In this way, the acquisition of various forms of knowledge, including technical and managerial, and the further diffusion of this knowledge, constitute additional benefits from accessing international supply chains. Box 1 shows an example in which the

Box 1: Chili Pepper and Knowledge Transfer in Global Supply Chains

How knowledge is transferred from a lead firm to its supplier can be illustrated with the case of a Colombian firm, Hugo Restrepo y Cía's. The example is interesting for at least two reasons. First, the transfer of knowledge occurred in the agribusiness industry instead of the often discussed high-tech industries, showing that learning from global players can occur in traditional sectors. Second, the knowledge transfer was not limited to the core technology of the agribusiness industry but also included managerial aspects.

Hugo Restrepo y Cía's is the main provider of chili pepper paste for the Tabasco brand owned by the American firm McIlhenny Company. Large-scale hot sauce makers frequently outsource the production of chili pepper paste to growers in relationships that require continuous interactions to guarantee the quality of the chilies that go into the production process.

The relationship between McIlhenny and Hugo Restrepo began in the late 1970s with a few chili pepper seeds provided by McIlhenny and a great deal of trial and error on the part of Hugo Restrepo. Both firms agreed on a business model in which McIlhenny would provide expertise to Hugo Restrepo in exchange for exclusivity for the next 15 years, during which Hugo Restrepo could not produce for other clients. The relationship was established by a long-term agreement based on contracts that were renewed every 2 years.

At the beginning of this relationship, the quality of the chili pepper paste produced by Hugo Restrepo was low, so McIlhenny sent an experienced agronomist to Hugo Restrepo twice a year to check on the crop and advise on technological innovations. As a result, over the next 15 years, Hugo Restrepo acquired key technical knowledge on crop management and production, and its agronomists developed expertise. After the exclusivity period ended, the firm no longer needed the technical assistance from McIlhenny.

Armed with its new technical knowledge, Hugo Restrepo ventured out on its own and expanded its business. It entered into many relationships with small farmers of chili pepper in Peru as well as in Colombia, providing them with technical knowledge originally acquired from McIlhenny and with seeds. As such, Hugo Restrepo applied lessons learned from McIlhenny to guarantee itself a stable supply of high-quality chili pepper through permanent technical support and appropriate and long-term agreements based on contracts renewed every 2 years. Meanwhile, Hugo Restrepo focused its attention on other activities in the supply chain, such as packaging and logistics.

In this way, Hugo Restrepo acquired not only key technical knowledge from a global buyer but also a successful business model that the firm was able to replicate with growers that eventually became its own suppliers.

Source: Based on material from Meléndez and Uribe (2012).

learning of a Colombian supplier from a global firm comprised the transfer not only of technical capabilities but also of managerial skills needed to conduct a business. Additional benefits from participating in global production networks are associated with market access and the distribution channels developed by a brand leader.

Immense Opportunities but also Potential Risks

While the potential gains and benefits from joining global supply chains seem remarkable, there are also limitations and risks. For instance, evidence indicates that benefits from GVCs may only materialize under specific conditions related to the nature of inter-firm relationships, the level of absorptive capacity of the supplier, or the technology used in the supply chain, among others (Gereffi, Humphrey, & Sturgeon, 2005; Pietrobelli & Rabellotti, 2007, 2011; Schmitz, 2006).

Firms joining global supply chains not only must meet conditions but also face potential risks. We mentioned that global supply chains offer the potential for rapid learning, which seems to be supported by several analyses. However, the literature also highlights some of the limitations to acquiring knowledge from global players. One is that the learning process might be quite narrow in scope. For instance, research on the footwear supply chain shows that the contribution of the lead firms to their suppliers tends to be exclusively related to production; suppliers learn little about non-production activities, which tend to be part of the buyer's main functions, such as design and marketing. Findings generally show that knowledge is transmitted to the suppliers as long as the learning does not trespass on the lead firm's core competences (Humphrey & Schmitz, 2000).[6]

A related concern is that rapid learning from global buyers may lead to short-term gains but also long-term disadvantages. The hypothetical scenario is that of a small producer in a developing country that receives all the necessary instructions to supply a good to a particular buyer, but does not necessarily acquire a broader knowledge about how to break into the buyer's market on its own if the relationship with the global firm came to an end (Humphrey, 2004).

Finally, offshoring decisions regarding the location of a lead firm's suppliers can rapidly change. Many firms that fragment production internationally are constantly evaluating their sourcing strategies, including the option of reshoring. Some recent studies have indicated that between 15 % (MIT, 2012) and 20 % (Hackett Group, 2012) of US manufacturing firms engaged in offshoring are engaged in reshoring initiatives. Other studies have suggested that offshoring is diminishing (KPMG, 2012). Changes in offshoring strategies can certainly be quite damaging to the countries of the suppliers. A supplier sometimes must make specific investments to participate in a production network, such as tailor-made and customized inputs. If supply chain relationships end, suppliers in developing countries could be left with machinery and capital goods with little or no alternative use.

[6] It is also been argued that more mutually beneficial interactions are expected to occur when knowledge is more tacit (Giuliani, Pietrobelli, & Rabellotti, 2005).

In this way, joining international production networks can entail risks that potential participants should not ignore. Nevertheless, some of these risks can be manageable. For instance, even though lead firms are normally less willing to transfer knowledge in activities related to their core competences, suppliers can still tap into many segments that are not part of these core competences. For example, research on a horticulture chain showed that suppliers of supermarkets not only took part in production activities but eventually started operating in other areas, such as quality certification, packaging, and a range of logistics activities (Dolan & Humphrey, 2000).

Regarding the very real risk of being locked within the narrow knowledge of one buyer, there is ample evidence of firms that apply skills and capabilities acquired in one market to serve new markets and customers (Meléndez & Uribe, 2012; Navas-Alemán, 2011; Tewari, 1999). Some of these firms eventually develop their own brands (Cafaggi et al., 2012; Poon, 2004). Regarding reshoring, it is important to note that recent trends do not necessarily signal the end of offshoring. According to a recent study, most firms are still sending more production to other countries than the amount they are bringing back home (Hackett Group, 2012). Moreover, recent reshoring trends might just be a shift from a global sourcing strategy to a more regional sourcing strategy: Chinese firms serve those of other Asian countries, firms from Eastern European countries serve those of Western Europe, and firms in the US, Mexico, or elsewhere in Latin America serve firms in the Americas (MIT, 2012). Nevertheless, it is important to bear in mind that the mere possibility that offshoring strategies could reverse at any time should be a powerful reminder to potential suppliers that participation in global value chains is not only about entering into the network, but also about sustaining the capabilities that made the entry possible in the first place.

Rationale for Public Policy

As stated above, joining global value chains can provide many benefits to a country's economy, such as creating opportunities for trade diversification or providing access to technical/managerial knowledge. But the rationale for public policies cannot be based solely on the existence of potential gains and benefits. Public interventions should be justified on the basis of market failures such as externalities, coordination failures, or the inability of the market to provide a public good.

In this report we will present cases where public policy is required to address market failures that limit participation of firms in GVCs. For instance, in Chap. 3 we will show that the likelihood of joining international production networks may depend on the provision of certain public goods, such as transport infrastructure, or specific types of regulation, such as contract enforcement. In other cases, coordination among firms and the public sector may be necessary to provide collective goods, such as airport storage facilities. Coordination among firms may also be necessary in the case of industries related through backward and forward linkages. For example, an assembly plant might be unable to start operations in a given location because there are no local suppliers of a particular component; but at the same time, a potential supplier of that component might not initiate production because there is no local downstream demand for that product and exporting is costly (Trindade, 2005).

Sometimes, the public intervention might be justified on the basis of externalities. For example, information generated by a supplier's successful search for international buyers may spill over to other suppliers. In particular, once a supplier has obtained a contract with a lead firm and establishes a good track record (showing in the process that the country as a whole is capable of delivering a good product), it is easier for other suppliers in the sector to follow without incurring the same costs as the initial supplier. In so doing, the followers obtain important benefits from the first supplier's initial investments (and simultaneously devalue the initial supplier's potential benefits from its searches). The private returns from establishing relationships with the buyer would accordingly be lower than the corresponding social returns, and thus the investment in developing those relationships would be suboptimally low. This provides a rationale for public intervention. Spillovers can also take place among the buyers. For example, the "discovery" by a buyer of a well-qualified local supplier may also benefit other buyers, and thus the private returns associated with any investment to assist that supplier in developing its skills and capabilities may be lower than the social returns. This gap between private and social returns also provides a rationale for intervention.

Therefore, there are many instances in which the existence of market failures could provide a rationale for public intervention in the area of GVCs. However, identifying specific market failures can be challenging. For instance, measuring the existence of spillovers might be difficult because they by no means occur automatically (see Blyde, Pietrobelli, & Volpe, 2014). Notwithstanding these challenges, countries should seek to substantiate as much as possible their interventions in GVCs on the basis of market failures.

Chapter 2
The Participation of Latin America and the Caribbean in International Supply Chains

As mentioned in the previous chapter, the concept of international supply chain is typically understood as a group of firms in different countries that work together—from the design to the distribution of a product—under the coordination of a lead firm that seeks to minimize total system costs. Unfortunately, very few existing trade or foreign direct investment databases provide enough information to verify that the cross-border transactions that economists observe conform to this definition. Therefore, short of working with case studies, empirical research in this area has relied primarily on proxies to measure value-chain participation.

No single measure is likely to address all the nuances related to offshoring, and no single method is immune to some form of criticism. Therefore, in this chapter, rather than relying on a single indicator we gather various types of datasets on trade and FDI to construct a battery of alternative measures. The goal is to present as comprehensive a picture as possible of the participation of Latin America and the Caribbean (LAC) in international production networks. The various indicators provide a very consistent picture of how LAC fares relative to other regions regarding participation in global supply chains.

Evidence from Intra-industry Trade Indexes

The first measure relies on intra-industry trade indexes (see Fukao, Ishido, & Ito, 2003; Jones, Kierzkowski, & Leonard, 2002; Kimura, 2006). This measure is based on the premise that global supply chains are associated with sequential production links in which countries may import intermediate goods, add value, and export them to another country. As such, production linkages involve trading related goods at different stages of production. In this way, intra-industry trade can be a proxy for these processes, provided that this trade is measured at sufficiently high levels of

J.S. Blyde (ed.), *Synchronized Factories: Latin America and the Caribbean in the Era of Global Value Chains*, DOI 10.1007/978-3-319-09991-0_2

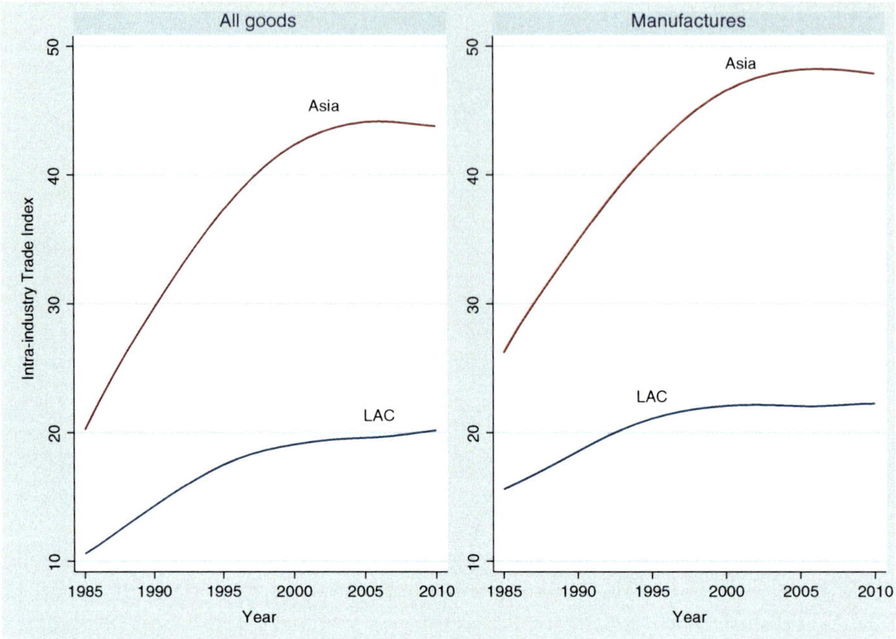

Fig. 2.1 Intra-industry trade indexes, regional averages. *Source*: Authors' calculations based on data from Comtrade

aggregation. For this reason, the measures of intra-industry trade constructed here are based on four-digit SITC data.[1] The use of intra-industry trade measures does not come without limitations, however, since they also capture horizontal trade in the same goods, which does not necessarily reflect participation in global supply chains. Nevertheless, it is reassuring that in our results, the countries that have experienced the largest increases in intra-industry trade between 1985 and 2010 are China, Indonesia, Malaysia, Mexico, Philippines, and Thailand, all of which are highly integrated in global supply chains.

Figure 2.1 depicts the evolution of the average intra-industry trade for countries in the Asia-Pacific region and for LAC (see appendix A "Trade in Value Added and Set of Countries" for the list of countries in each region). The figure shows how intra-industry trade boomed in the Asia-Pacific region in the period 1985–2010 while increasing relatively slowly in Latin America, particularly in manufactures. This is the case whether we use all goods or only manufactures. The overall levels are also

[1] In particular, we use the Grubel-Lloyd index.

very different, with an average measure of intra-industry trade in the Asian region twice that of Latin America. The result is in line with the general notion that the Asian countries are far more engaged in vertical specialization and cross-border production sharing than the countries in LAC.[2]

Evidence from Trade in Value Added

Another way to measure the participation of countries in global supply chains is to trace the value added of each source country in a globally integrated production network. Studies have applied this approach to specific goods, such as the iPod and iPhone (Dedrick, Kraemer, & Linden, 2008) and the Barbie doll (Tempest, 1996). The information in these case studies is very rich, showing which countries participate in the supply chain of a particular good and how much value they add to its production. The studies have revealed, for example, that even though China exports the iPod, and the trade statistics report the full value of this product, the country only contributes to 3.8 % of the value added, because many other countries also participate in the production. This case-by-case examination of specific international supply chains is very revealing, but the approach is so data-demanding that it would be impossible to examine every such supply chain in which a country participates. For this reason the technique is impractical for measuring the participation of countries in GVCs.

A new group of analyses are taking a different, more practical approach to tracing the value added of a country's trade flows: combining input-output tables with bilateral trade statistics (e.g., De La Cruz, Koopman, & Wang, 2011; Hummels et al., 2001; Johnson & Noguera, 2012a, 2012b; Koopman, Wang, & Wei, 2008, 2014; Miroudot & Ragousssis, 2009). The literature has evolved rapidly and has produced an array of indicators that help quantify the extent to which countries participate in cross-border production sharing.

[2] The advantage of using intra-industry trade indices is their simplicity: they only require data on international trade flows. Other approaches that only require trade data use the description of trade line classifications to pick up terms like "parts and components" as proxies for trade in intermediates. The main idea is to measure the percentage of trade in intermediates in total trade. These methods have been used, for instance, in Yeats (2001), Ng and Yeats (1999), and Fung, Garcia-Herrero, and Siu (2009). A related approach is to employ a United Nations classification that separates goods according to their use. The classification is called the Broad Economic Categories (BEC), http://unstats.un.org/unsd/tradekb/Knowledgebase/Intermediate-Goods-in-Trade-Statistics. This method has been employed, for instance, in Baldwin and Taglioni (2011). A shortcoming of these two methods is that they tend to rely on subjective criteria on what constitute an intermediate good (see Hummels, Ishii, & Yi, 2001). We nevertheless compare Asia and Latin America in terms of the share of intermediate inputs in total trade as measured by Fung et al. (2009). The results are in line with the findings from the intra-industry trade indexes. For instance, in 1990, exports of parts and components as a share of total manufacturing exports was on average at around 31 % for Asia and 16 % for Latin America. Two decades later, in 2010, this share increased to 40 % in Asia and declined slightly to 14 % in Latin America.

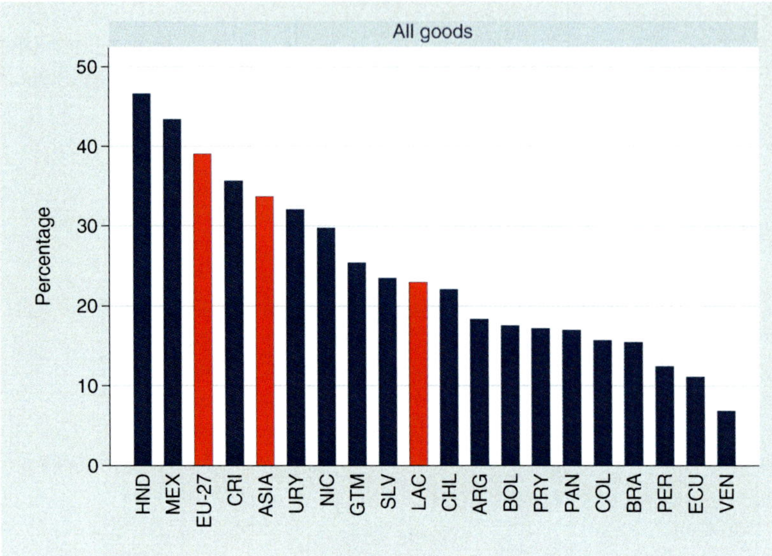

Fig. 2.2 GVC Participation through upstream linkages: foreign value added as a percentage of total exports, average 2003–2007. *Source*: Authors' calculations based on data from GTAP 7 and 8

In this literature, the insertion of countries in GVCs is measured with indicators that seek to capture the extent to which countries participate in a sequential chain of production activities that crosses many borders. The first indicator, called import content of exports, introduced by Hummels et al. (2001), is based on the notion of vertical specialization. Vertical specialization refers to the use of imported inputs to produce goods that are later exported, a notion that precisely captures the idea of various countries linked sequentially to produce a final good. More recently, the concept of foreign value added in exports is being used to measure vertical specialization by emphasizing value added from other countries embodied in a country's exports (Koopman et al., 2014). Foreign value added of exports is nowadays a common measure of the participation of countries in vertically fragmented production through upstream linkages.

Figure 2.2 depicts the foreign value added of exports for various Latin American countries. The measure reflects the share of foreign value added in each country's total exports. Appendix A "Trade in Value Added and Set of Countries" explains in detail the methodology and data used to develop this measure.[3] The figure also shows simple averages for two comparator groups: the Asian countries and the EU-27.

[3] There are publicly available datasets in which similar measures of trade in value added have already been constructed for many countries in the world. These include the World Input-Output Table, funded by the European Commission and developed by the University of Groningen, and the "Trade in Value Added (TiVA) indicators," a joint OECD-WTO initiative. The coverage of Latin American countries in these databases, however, is very limited, making them unsuitable for this report.

We can see that in general, the participation of Latin America in GVCs averages less than the participation of the comparator regions. The exports originating in Asia and in the EU use more intensively imported intermediate inputs than Latin America's exports. In particular, the exports of Asia and the EU use 12 and 15 % points more foreign value added, respectively, than the exports of Latin America; this suggests that the countries from these two regions are more involved in sequentially linked production processes than the countries in the LAC region.[4]

At first it might seem surprising that a small, low-income country such as Honduras exhibits a measure of foreign value added that is higher than that of Mexico, given the latter country's extensive production linkages with North American firms in motor vehicles, electronics, aeronautics, and other industries. Clearing up this apparent anomaly provides a good opportunity to further explain what Fig. 2.2 is measuring. A foreign value added of, say, 45 % indicates that this portion of the value of a country's exports comes from other nations. This value is independent of the number and/or type of industries participating in global value chains. In the case of Honduras, for example, more than a third of the total exports of the country are in textiles, predominantly T-shirts. Eighty percent of the value added in these exports are yarns, fibers, and other inputs that originate in other countries, which include the US, Mexico, China, and South Korea. This explains the high value of foreign value added for Honduras.

The example of Honduras clearly shows that global supply chains should not be associated exclusively with high-tech industries. Some countries participate in value chains of high technological content, while others, due to their comparative advantage, participate in value chains of low technological content. The issue of technological content becomes clearer when we separate the foreign value added embodied in countries' exports by the sectors generating such value added. The results, which are presented in Fig. 2.3, were calculated on the basis of the OECD classification of manufacturing sectors according to their technological content,[5] which is depicted by the two graphs on the top of the figure. We complete the picture by including foreign value added generated by the primary sector (bottom left figure) and from services (bottom right figure). Note that for each country, the sum of the numbers in the four figures equals the value in Fig. 2.2.

Through this analytical lens, Mexico has much higher foreign value added generated by high and medium-technology sectors than does Honduras, while the reverse remains true for low and medium low-technology sectors. This further supports what we mentioned earlier: Honduras' exports, mainly of textiles and apparel, use mostly foreign inputs of low technological content, that is, fibers and yarns, with

[4] Note that there is some ambiguity in measuring GVC participation in this way. For instance, while the high value of foreign value added that is observed in Mexico certainly corroborates the insertion of this country in many international production networks, the common concern in Mexico is how to continue participating in many of these supply chains with more Mexican value added (see Box 3, Chap. 4), a trend that will lower this country's share of foreign value added of exports.

[5] OECD (2005).

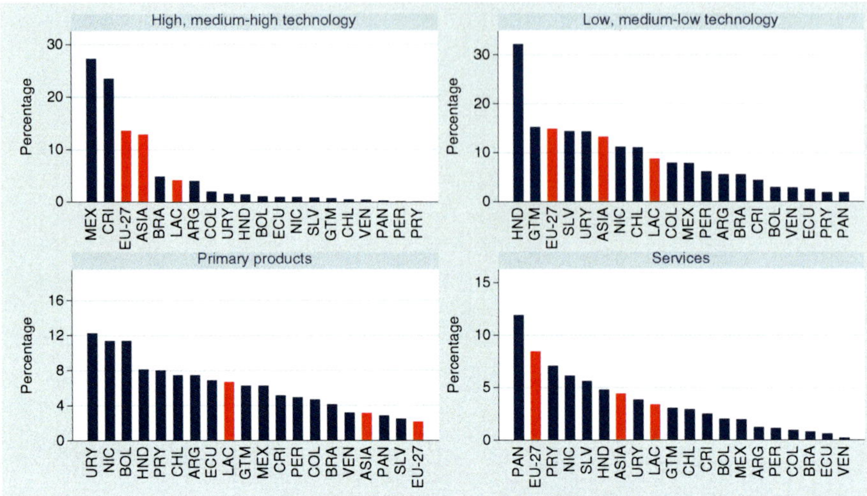

Fig. 2.3 Sector generating foreign value added in exports, average 2003–2007. *Source*: Authors' calculations based on data from GTAP 7 and 8

very little inputs from high-technology sectors, while the exports of Mexico largely depend on high- and medium-technology intermediate inputs.

Figure 2.3 can also be used to compare the status of Latin America as a whole with that of our comparator regions. For instance, the average values for the EU and Asia are higher than for LAC in the manufacturing sectors and in services, but the reverse is true for the primary sector. In other words, Europe and the Asia-Pacific countries are more involved than Latin America in the co-production of goods that largely utilize manufacturing sector inputs, as well as those from services; Latin America, on average, is more involved in the co-production of goods in which the main inputs come from the primary sector.

Returning to Fig. 2.2, another interesting finding is the high degree of heterogeneity that exists within Latin America, with Mexico and the countries in Central America showing the largest shares of foreign value added of exports and the countries in South America showing the smallest. This heterogeneity is in part related to differences in the patterns of specialization across the LAC region. The production of primary goods and related products tends to require fewer imported inputs than the production of many manufactures. As production processes in South American countries are typically biased toward primary products, the foreign value added of these countries' exports is particularly low.

Countries specializing in primary products are most likely to participate in the early stages of supply chains, providing inputs to other countries downstream rather than receiving inputs from abroad. To examine the extent to which the exports of a country are linked to vertically fragmented production downstream in the chain, we calculate what is known as indirect value added. This is a measure of the degree to which a country provides value added by exporting intermediate inputs that are later

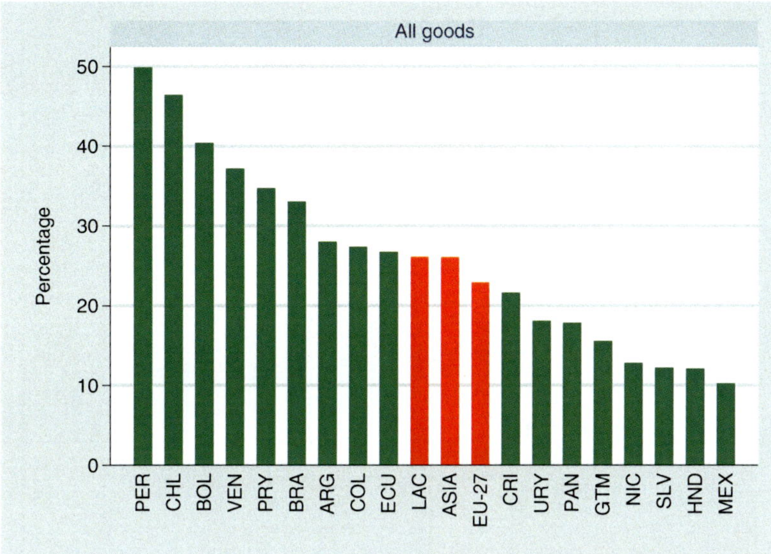

Fig. 2.4 GVC participation through downstream linkages: domestic value added used in third countries' exports, average 2003–2007. *Source*: Authors' calculations based on data from GTAP 7 and 8

utilized in the exports of other countries.[6] This measure, which is shown in Fig. 2.4, indicates the percentage of a country's exports used as inputs in the exports of third countries. Note now that the countries in South America tend to have higher values of this measure than the countries in Central America. Note also that the average for the Latin American region is higher than for the EU and Asia. This suggests that the LAC region, on average, participates more than the EU or Asia as a supplier of value added downstream in the chain. But this is only true for the value added generated from the primary sector (as shown in Fig. 2.5), which decomposes the measure by value added generating sectors.[7] This figure clearly shows that the average for Latin America is higher than the average for the EU and Asia in the primary sectors (bottom left figure), while the reverse is true in the manufacturing sectors (top figures). In other words, on average, Latin American countries participate more than Europe and Asia in international value chains as suppliers of primary inputs, while Europe and Asia participate more than Latin America as suppliers of manufacturing inputs with high, medium, or low technological content.

[6] Technically, indirect value added is measured as the country's value added embodied as intermediate inputs in third countries' gross exports, as a percentage of the country's gross exports (see Koopman, Wang, & Wei, 2010).

[7] Note that the sum of the four values for each individual country in Fig. 2.5 is equal to the value in Fig. 2.4.

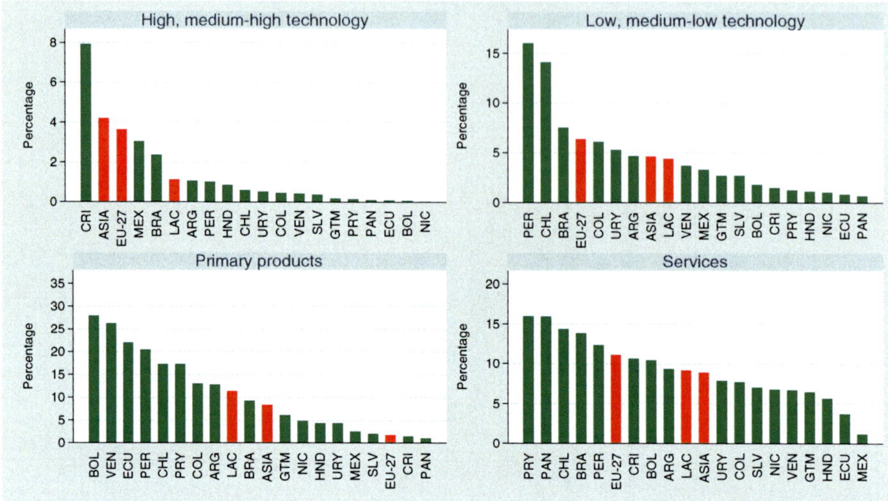

Fig. 2.5 Sector generating domestic value added used in third countries' exports, average 2003–2007. *Source*: Authors' calculations based on data from GTAP 7 and 8

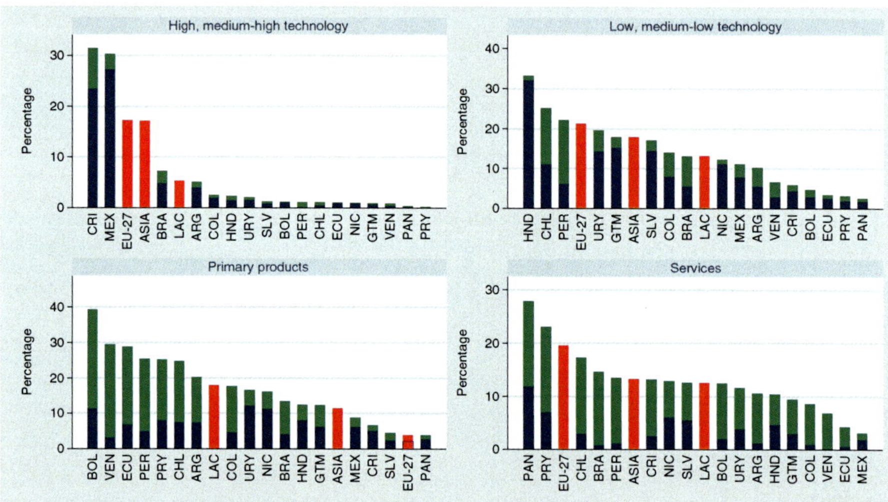

Fig. 2.6 Foreign value added (*blue*) and domestic value added used in third countries' exports (*green*), by the value added generating sector, average 2003–2007. *Source*: Authors' calculations based on data from GTAP 7 and 8

One way to present a combined measure of value chain participation is to add the measure of foreign value added of exports and the measure of value added used in the exports of third countries (see Koopman et al., 2014). This reflects participation through linkages both upstream and downstream. The measure calculated by the value added generating sector is shown in Fig. 2.6. Examining the averages for Latin America and the comparator regions clearly shows that our region in general participates less than the EU and Asia in the manufacturing (and service) segments of the global value chains, while it tends to participate more in the segments associated with the primary sector.

It is also possible to see once again how countries in Latin America differ in their participation. Costa Rica, Mexico, and Honduras, for example, participate more as recipients of foreign value added (blue segments tend to be longer than green segments), while Chile, Peru, and Bolivia participate more as providers of value added downstream in the chain than recipients (green segments tend to be longer than blue segments). Therefore, beyond the general comparison of Latin America with Europe and Asia, Latin America emerges as a region with large heterogeneity in value chain participation. On the one hand, we have countries—primarily Mexico and Central America—that process lots of foreign inputs that are incorporated in the export of goods close to their final production stages, so these countries tend to be positioned closer to the end of the supply chain. Meanwhile, the South American countries are more specialized in natural resources; they provide inputs to other countries' exports and thus are positioned more at the beginning of the supply chain.

We can construct a general measure of the position of the country in the chain by dividing the indirect value added and the foreign value added measures (see Koopman et al., 2014).[8] The higher this value, the more upstream the country's position in the chain. Figure 2.7 shows the results. It is interesting to see, for

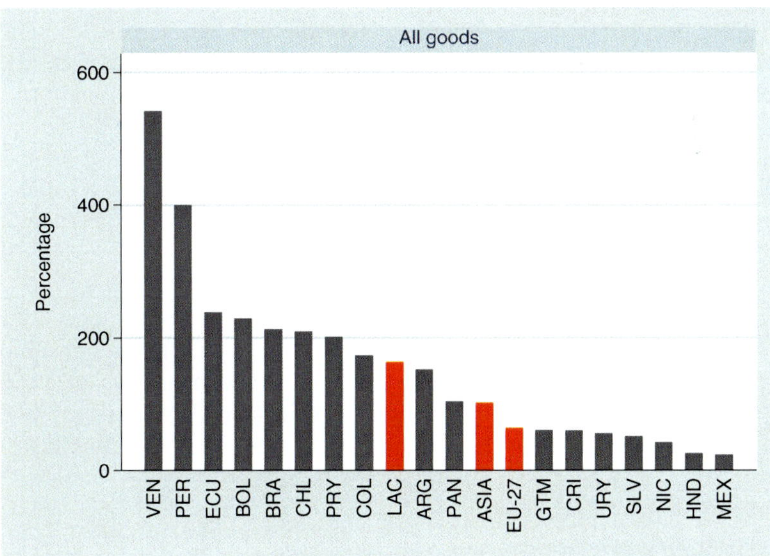

Fig. 2.7 Global value chain position, average 2003–2007. *Source*: Authors' calculations based on data from GTAP 7 and 8

[8] This measure is the percentage of a country's exports used as inputs in the exports of other countries, divided by the foreign value added of the country's exports.

example, that the value added from Peru used as inputs in third countries' exports is four times greater than the value added from other countries employed in Peruvian exports. Figure 2.7 shows clearly the heterogeneity within the region that we mentioned before, with Mexico and Central America more at the end of supply chains and South America more at the beginning. Latin America as a whole is positioned more upstream in global supply chains than the comparator groups due to the average specialization of the region towards natural resource intensive sectors.

Summarizing the results, there is considerable heterogeneity within Latin America, in which Central American countries and Mexico participate more in downstream segments of global value chains while South American countries are relatively more active in upstream segments, mainly due to their specialization in primary sectors. Even within the group of countries participating in downstream supply chain segments, some economies specialize in value chains of low technological content while others focus more on high-technology segments. In general, however, the various indicators confirm the general perception that Latin America tends to participate less than other regions in global value chains, particularly in value chain segments related to the manufacturing sector.

Two obvious questions arise from these findings: Can countries in the region increase their participation in global value chains? And can they participate in segments of higher value added? Note that these questions do not necessarily imply that the countries should target industries of high technological content, such as electronics. Instead, the questions point to the potential even for countries with comparative advantages within certain industries to identify segments of high value that have not been exploited. For instance, Honduras has traditionally been linked to the low-technology global value chain in which the production of T-shirts is one of the main staples. Today, Honduras can use knowledge developed through the supply chains of exporting T-shirts to enter new export segments of the textile industry, such as parachutes. The same can be said for the primary sector. Abundance of natural endowments and specialization in primary goods does not preclude countries from adding value in natural resource-related supply chains. These are without doubt important issues for the Latin American region that we will address in later chapters of this report.

We can also use this methodology to examine the contribution of the different world regions to global value chain participation. The idea is to see how much participation in value chains occurs among countries of the same region and how much takes place with countries in other regions. For instance, do countries in Europe engage in international supply chains mostly with other European countries? Or are their production networks spread evenly across the globe? Figure 2.8 shows that the participation in international production networks is more intense among countries of the same region than with other regions. The within-region participation in the EU, Asia-Pacific, and LAC is 51 %, 47 %, and 29 %, respectively. In each case, the within-region participation is always the highest. This result suggests that global value chains do not cope well with vast distances, an issue that will recur in the rest of this report.

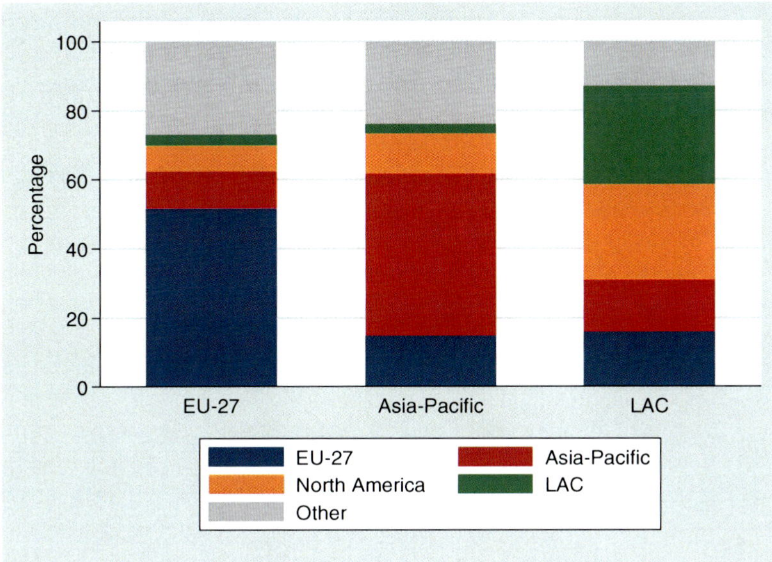

Fig. 2.8 Regional contribution to foreign value added, average 2003–2007. *Source*: Authors' calculations based on data from GTAP 7 and 8

Evidence from FDI Data

An alternative way to examine the participation of countries in global supply chains is to look at data on FDI. True, many companies offshore part of their production processes through independent suppliers and not through FDI. Nevertheless, multinationals still play an important role in many global production networks, and looking at their locations gives us an additional opportunity to analyze the extent to which Latin American countries take part in cross-border production sharing.

We employ the Dun & Bradstreet (D&B) Worldbase dataset, which covers more than 200 countries and territories and has been used in academic studies for various purposes.[9] For each firm in this dataset there is information on an array of variables, including location (city/country), industry of production, and family tree (the firm's parent and other related parties). We follow Alfaro and Charlton (2009) in identifying

[9] For instance, the comparison of size and diversification patterns of foreign investment in North America (Caves, 1975), the development of microdata sets on enterprises (Lipsey, 1978), the effect of bank credit availability and business creation (Black & Strahan, 2002), the relationship between financial development and vertical integration (Acemoglu, Johnson, & Mitton, 2009), the patterns of intra-industry and inter-industry FDI (Alfaro & Charlton, 2009), and the relationship between foreign ownership and establishment performance (Alfaro & Chen, 2011).

whether the relationship between a parent company and its subsidiary is horizontal (the parent and the subsidiary produce the same good), vertical (the subsidiary produces an input for the parent), or complex (the relationship is both horizontal and vertical). The methodology compares the industry codes (at the four-digit SIC level) of both parents and affiliates to examine whether they produce the same good and/or whether the affiliate is a supplier to its parent. The latter is determined by using the industry codes in combination with an input-output table to identify whether the industry of the subsidiary corresponds to an upstream industry of the parent's output.[10] One potential shortcoming of this approach could be uneven coverage of a worldwide company dataset, particularly in developing countries where information is harder to obtain. Appendix A "FDI Dataset", however, provides details about the extensive checks and quality controls used by D&B to gather information and presents a test that appears to validate the coverage of the data.

Figure 2.9 shows the network of parents and their vertically linked subsidiaries around the world. The size of the circles in each country indicates the total number of parent companies located in that country that own vertically linked subsidiaries in other countries. The thickness and color intensity of the lines represent the number of bilateral vertical subsidiaries between each parent country and a corresponding host country. Several interesting insights emerge from this figure. First, most multinational parent companies are located in industrialized countries, and a very large number of their foreign affiliates are also located in the industrialized world. This is consistent with the general finding in the literature that most FDI is of the North-North type. This is also consistent with recent evidence indicating that what had been thought to be horizontal FDI flows among developed nations are actually vertical FDI flows (Alfaro & Charlton, 2009). Our evidence is also consistent with results from a US survey: data from Fortune 1,000 companies show that more than 60 % of all the offshoring of these companies is conducted in industrialized economies (Sturgeon, Nielsen, Linden, Gereffi, & Brown, 2012).[11]

On a regional level, well-defined supply chain networks in Europe are led by Germany, those in Asia are led by Japan, and networks in North America are led by the US, which also has very strong links with the EU and Asia. With the exception of Mexico and possibly Brazil, LAC—like Africa—remains pretty much on the sidelines when it comes to participating in production networks led by multinationals.

---

[10] Similar to Alfaro and Charlton (2009) we use the Bureau of Economic Analysis 1987 benchmark input-output table and employ alternative thresholds of the input-output total requirements coefficient.

[11] It has been noted that supply chains have been prevalent among nearby high-wage countries, such as the US and Canada, or Germany and France. The trade in these supply chains is typically based on exploiting scale economies rather than on wage gaps. For instance, a firm in a developed country dominates the market of a particular input through continuous learning-by-doing and scale economies. This has been referred to as "horizontal specialization" (Baldwin, 2012).

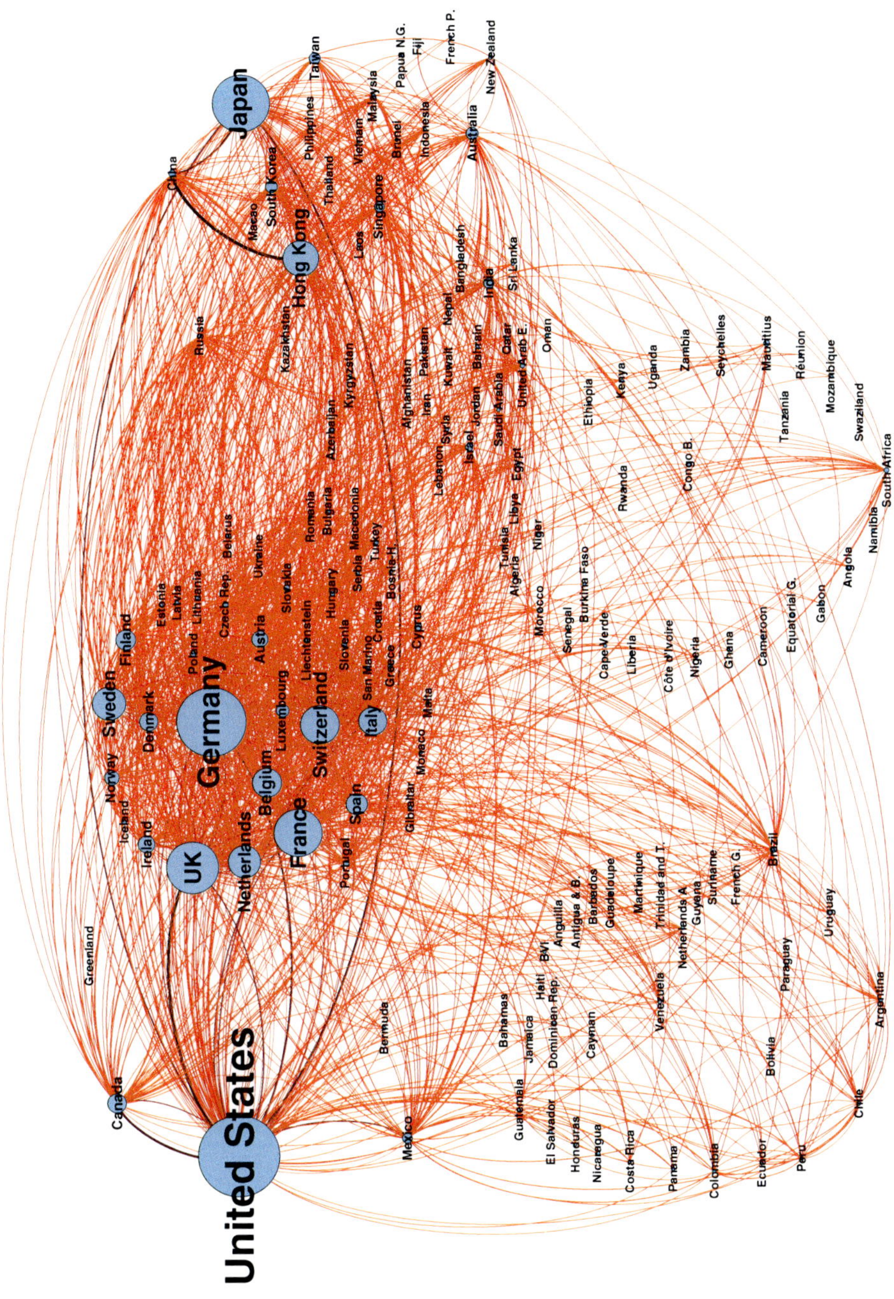

Fig. 2.9 Vertically linked foreign subsidiaries and their parents. *Source:* Authors' calculations based on data from Dun & Bradstreet

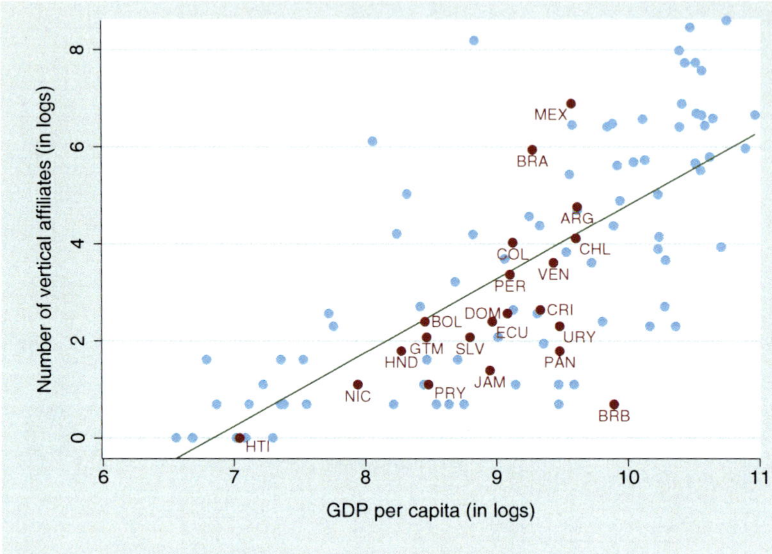

Fig. 2.10 Number of vertically linked foreign subsidiaries and income. *Source*: Authors' calculations based on data from Dun & Bradstreet

Figure 2.9 only provides crude evidence on the location of vertical FDI and does not control for factors such as differences in the level of development. One could expect, for instance, that more developed countries would host more foreign subsidiaries than less developed countries. In controlling for differences in per capita income, Fig. 2.10 indeed shows that there is a clear positive relationship between the level of income of the country and the number of vertical subsidiaries that it hosts. However, most countries in Latin America fall below the trend line, indicating that the number of foreign subsidiaries is lower than what should be expected from their level of development. In other words, even after accounting for differences in income per capita, the participation of most countries in the region seems to be low.

Evidence from Trade in Services

International trade in services is a growing trend in global commerce. In particular, the offshoring of business functions such as accounting or IT services is part of the same phenomenon of international fragmentation in which firms decide to locate part of their production of components and/or services in different countries.[12]

[12] Note that the offshoring of services does not involve all trade in services. Some trade in services might not be related to the fragmentation of production.

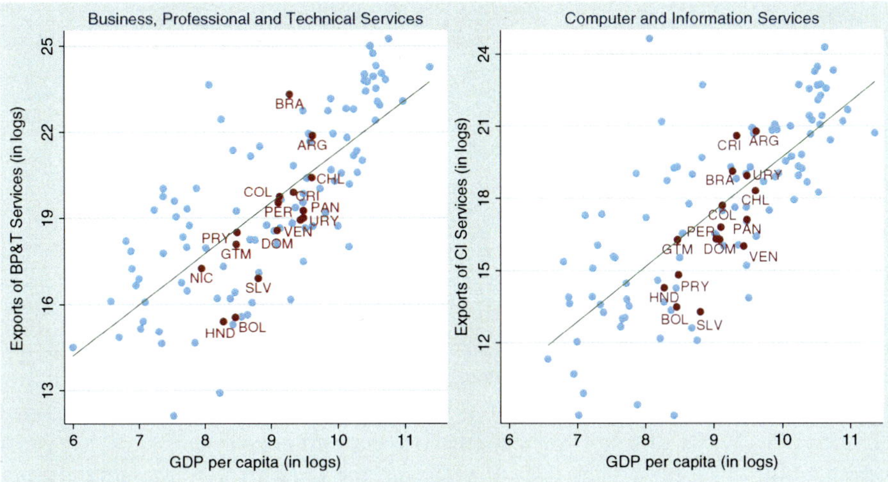

Fig. 2.11 Exports of selected offshoring services and income. *Source*: Authors' calculations based on the UN's Service Trade Database

We will now examine the level of Latin America's participation in the offshoring of such services and compare it with the participation of other regions.

We will make this comparison through an analysis of two service categories that are intrinsically related to global supply chains: "computer and information services" and "miscellaneous business, professional, and technical services."[13] The second category includes services related to business process outsourcing and knowledge process outsourcing.[14] The data are taken from the UN's Service Trade Database.

Figure 2.11 shows the positive relationships between exports of these services and the countries' GDP per capita: more developed countries tend to export more of these services. Also clear from the figure is that most countries in the region underperform the respective trend lines, suggesting that Latin American countries tend to export less of these services than would be expected given their level of economic development. In the next chapter, we present a model that indicates the potential factors behind this subpar performance.

[13] The categories are part of the Extended Balance of Payment Classification, which is commonly used in the service trade databases of the UN, OECD, and IMF.

[14] This category includes the following: legal services; accounting, auditing, bookkeeping, and tax-consulting services; business and management consultancy and public relations services; advertising, market research, and public opinion polling; research and development; architectural, engineering, and other technical services; and other business services.

Recapitulating

Most of the indicators we used to examine the participation of LAC in global value chains present a similar picture: LAC's participation generally tends to be low relative to other regions. However, there is also significant heterogeneity within the region. For instance, Mexico and countries in Central America are more engaged in production networks, particularly with North America, and tend to participate in the final stages of production networks. For their part, countries in South America typically enter supply chains in the early stages. A set of clear factors explain at least some of these differences. For instance, proximity to the US makes Mexico an ideal recipient of offshoring activities. Likewise, the sheer abundance of natural resources in South America biases countries to participate in more upstream stages of supply chains. Proximity, the endowments of natural resources, and the relative abundance of different classes of labor are obvious drivers behind the levels and types of participation in supply chains. But they are not the only drivers. The next chapter uses a more rigorous analysis to identify a more complete spectrum of factors behind the region's relatively subpar participation in international supply chains.

Chapter 3
The Drivers of Global Value Chain Participation: Cross-Country Analyses

Building on the work of Jones and Kierzkowski (1990), economists have been writing models that describe how firms are increasingly fragmenting production processes into various stages or tasks and moving them to more advantageous locations (e.g., Deardorff, 2001a, 2001b; Findlay & Jones, 2001; Grossman & Rossi-Hansberg, 2008; Jones & Kierzkowski, 2000, 2001). Most of the models in this literature draw on findings from an earlier literature on FDI, namely that firms will fragment production or tasks across different countries to arbitrage international differences in factor prices (Helpman, 1984; Helpman & Krugman, 1985).[1] The rationale behind most models of fragmentation can be stated in simple terms: in traditional production processes, inputs are organized and combined to generate final outputs in the same location. Where there are many inputs, coordination is normally necessary and proximity helps to lower the costs of coordination and transportation. But if firms could separate the production process into different production blocks and relocate them in places with lower factor prices, the total costs of production could be further reduced. Therefore firms will unbundle their production processes, as long as the resulting reduction in production costs would more than compensate for the additional costs of coordinating remotely located production blocks and moving these production blocks around.

[1] This class of models, called the vertical model of FDI, was developed in parallel with the horizontal model of FDI. In the latter model, the motive behind the multinational corporation (MNC) is to save on trade costs associated with exporting by setting up foreign subsidiaries producing similar goods to those produced at home (Horstmann & Markusen, 1987; Markusen, 1984). Later on, the knowledge-capital model was developed, which allowed for simultaneous horizontal and vertical motives for FDI (Markusen, 1997). The new models of fragmentation are generally not exclusively limited to the study of multinationals. The main predictions of these new models tend to apply to companies that fragment production internationally, regardless of whether this is done within the boundaries of the firm or through independent suppliers. Another strand of the literature examines the more specific issue of whether the fragmentation of production occurs within the boundaries of the firm or through an independent supplier (Antràs, 2003; Antràs & Helpman, 2004, 2008). This is called the internalization decision.

J.S. Blyde (ed.), *Synchronized Factories: Latin America and the Caribbean in the Era of Global Value Chains*, DOI 10.1007/978-3-319-09991-0_3

This model highlights the main forces behind the international unbundling of production: on the one hand, there are comparative advantage considerations, such as differences in factor prices that make offshoring attractive. But on the other hand, additional costs related to offshoring need to be factored in. Therefore, the unbundling of production will take place if the lower marginal costs of production more than offset these extra costs related to offshoring.[2]

This reasoning helps explain why some countries, such as China, are attractive destinations for offshoring: when the marginal costs of production are very low they almost always compensate for the extra costs related to offshoring. By the same token, however, countries with mid- to high-factor prices have a greater need to avoid the extra costs of offshoring to become attractive destinations.

Different offshoring costs have been highlighted in the literature. For instance, high transportation costs are likely to discourage the movement of intermediate inputs between countries. Similarly, inadequate telecommunication services would make it harder for a firm to coordinate with production units located abroad (Jones & Kierzkowski, 1990). In addition, tariff barriers and costly custom clearances will drive up the prices of imported inputs, especially if they cross international borders many times. Finally, high costs of dealing with legal procedures in another country in the event of a breach of contract would likely limit offshoring decisions in that country (Jones & Kierzkowski, 2001). As shown in Chap. 1, many of these obstacles have been declining in recent years.

In this chapter we analyze the impact of reducing some of these costs on offshoring decisions. The aim is to identify potential avenues by which countries in Latin America and the Caribbean could improve their participation in production networks. To add nuance to the analysis, the discussion is divided into four sections. The first section looks at the role of transportation and logistics services, including communication and information technology. The second section analyzes the impact of trade agreements and trade policy in general. In the third section we examine the factors behind the decision to fragment production through vertical FDI versus foreign outsourcing, which naturally leads to the subject of contract enforcement. Finally, section "Service Offshoring: Grasping the Intangibles" studies the determinants of service offshoring. As mentioned in the introduction, the list of potential drivers behind the formation of global supply chains can be quite extensive. In this chapter we look into areas that seem most relevant in terms of insights contained in the literature and opportunities for public policy solutions.[3]

---

[2] There is a parallel and influential literature on GVCs that depend less on general or partial equilibrium economic models and more on the typologies of linkages in GVCs and the characteristics of the units that participate in them (see, for instance, Gereffi, 1999; Gereffi, Humphrey, & Sturgeon, 2005; Humphrey & Schmitz, 2000). In this literature the analysis is mostly focused on the governance dimension of the value chain. In other words, central to this literature is the study of power relations across the units of the value chains and how these relations affect issues such as transfer of knowledge or learning. We will address some of these aspects in Chap. 4 of this report.

[3] In the next chapter we take a much closer look at the issue of the supplier's capabilities.

Each section presents recent relevant empirical studies that address specific issues behind the drivers of offshoring. While each model is tailored to the particular determinant being addressed, they are all estimated in ways that control for other elements that may impact offshoring decisions.

Synchronizing Trade: The Role of Transportation, Communication, and Logistics Infrastructure

Firms that fragment production internationally incur risks. One is the possibility of delays in the arrival of components, which can result in shutting down entire production lines until the necessary inputs have arrived. Firms can address this uncertainty by maintaining large inventories of components. However, modern supply chain practices are increasingly moving towards so-called "lean production" strategies, which involve keeping low inventories to cut costs. Accordingly, firms fragmenting production internationally are likely to look for locations with adequate transport and logistics infrastructure to reduce disruptions in the supply chain, inventory-holding costs, depreciation costs, and handling costs. In this section we present empirical evidence on the link between logistics infrastructure and the international location of fragmented production. The objective is to measure the extent to which deficiencies in Latin America's logistics infrastructure are standing in the way of the region's greater participation in global supply chains.

We will begin by comparing Latin America with other regions in terms of logistics infrastructure indicators that measure three dimensions relevant for the location of fragmented production. The first two dimensions are the quality of the port and airport infrastructures; improvements in these facilities are associated with declines in transport costs, waiting times, and handling costs (Clark, Dollar, & Micco, 2004; Limão & Venables, 2002; Micco & Serebrisky, 2006). Accordingly, countries with adequate port and airport infrastructures should be attractive locations for companies seeking to locate part of their production processes abroad while minimizing transportation costs and potential disruptions in the supply chain.

The third infrastructure dimension that we examine is the logistics required to coordinate production across space. As mentioned in Chap. 1, information and communication technology (ICT) infrastructure is crucial for providing firms the ability to move information over long distances quickly, cheaply, and reliably, and in this way lower the costs of coordinating production blocks across borders. The development of readily available and good quality ICT is needed to provide instant access to information for the numerous stakeholders in a global value chain, e-commerce for consumers, and logistics management. Therefore, countries need adequate ICT infrastructures to be attractive destinations for firms fragmenting production internationally.

Detailed data on port and airport efficiency are hard to find. In this chapter we use a combination of hard data and survey indicators for our estimations. First, we obtain hard micro data on port and airport characteristics to construct hard measures of port and airport availability at the country level. Following Clark et al. (2004), we use this data to construct a measure of seaport infrastructure that captures the country's ports that have adequate leverage capacity.[4] Similarly, following Micco and Serebrisky (2006), we construct a measure of the availability of airports with runways capable of serving the air cargo industry.[5] With respect to communications, we combine a series of hard indicators utilizing the core measures on ICT infrastructure suggested by The Partnership on Measuring ICT for Development.[6,7] As mentioned above, we combine these hard data indicators with survey data from the Global Competitiveness Index, 2011, of the World Economic Forum. Specifically, we employ the "quality of port infrastructure," the "quality of air transport infrastructure," and the "quality of ICT infrastructure" indexes. We then normalize each of the hard data and survey indicators to take values between 1 and 100.

Figure 3.1 compares the average of each of these indexes for the Latin American region, the EU, and Asia. The results speak for themselves. LAC, on average, clearly has less adequate logistics infrastructure (port, airport, and ICT infrastructure) than the other two regions, regardless of which measure we use.[8] The relevant question then becomes the extent to which these shortcomings in logistics infrastructure reduce Latin America's ability to attract fragmented production.

We examine this question by performing an analysis of global data on multinationals using the Worldbase dataset that we introduced in Chap. 2. In our analysis we assess whether countries with inadequate logistics systems attract fewer vertical affiliates. We start by showing a very simple association between the share of countries'

[4] Our port infrastructure variable consists of the number of ports in the country that have lifts with leverage capacity of at least 50 tons (squared), normalized by the country's population. The data on port characteristics come from the World Port Index, 2011, prepared by the US National Geospatial-Intelligence Agency. In an alternative version we normalized by using the country's employment, which yielded similar results.

[5] The measure consists of the number of airports with paved runways at least 2,000 m long and 40 m wide (squared), divided by the population of the country. This choice of runway dimension is based on the minimum requirements of aircraft typically used in the air cargo industry (see Micco & Serebrisky, 2006). The data on airport characteristics come from the ST3400 Database, 2011, of Sandel Avionics. In an alternative version we normalized by the country's employment, which yielded similar results.

[6] This partnership was created in 2003 by ITU, OECD, UNCTAD, UNESCO Institute for Statistics, UNECA, UNECLAC, UNESCAP, UNESCWA, the UN ICT Task Force, and the World Bank, to work towards defining and collecting a set of common ICT indicators and assisting developing countries in their efforts to produce information statistics. The data come from the ITU World Telecommunication/ICT Indicators 2011.

[7] The core indicators are fixed telephone lines per 100 inhabitants, mobile cellular telephone subscriptions per 100 inhabitants, terrestrial mobile wireless subscriptions per 100 inhabitants, dedicated mobile data subscriptions per 100 inhabitants, fixed (wired) Internet subscriptions per 100 inhabitants, fixed (wired) broadband Internet subscriptions per 100 inhabitants, and the international Internet bandwidth per Internet user.

[8] This is not a new result. Evidence that countries in LAC have lower port and airport productivity measures than other regions has been shown, for example, in Moreira, Volpe, and Blyde (2008) and Pages (2010).

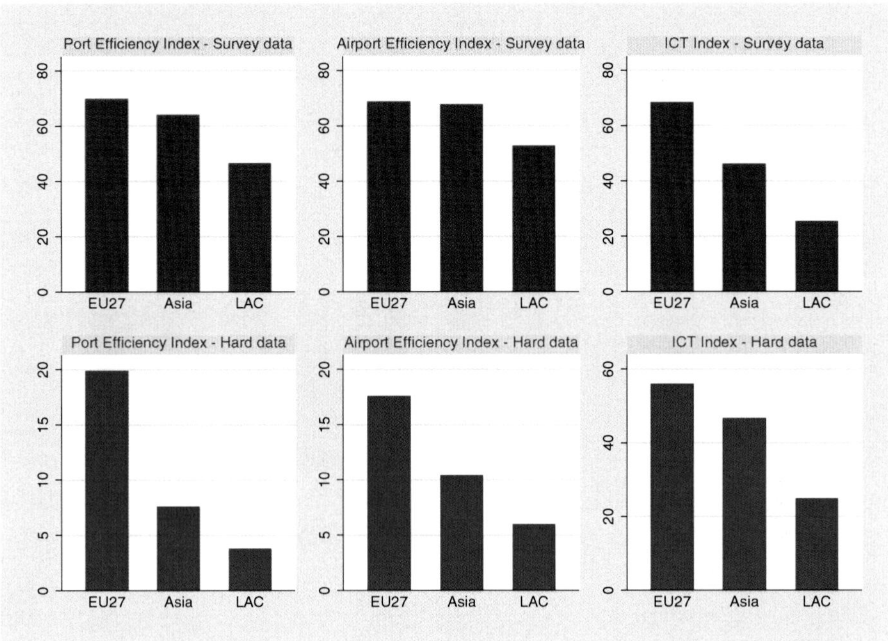

Fig. 3.1 Measures of logistics infrastructure, efficiency indexes, 2012. *Source*: Authors' calculations

vertical affiliates and the quality of their logistics infrastructure. For the latter we first create sub-indexes that combine the hard data and the survey data for each of the three infrastructure dimensions, and then we take the average of these three sub-indexes.[9] Figure 3.2 divides the countries in the sample into four groups (or quartiles) according to the quality of their logistics infrastructure. The first quartile corresponds to the countries with the least adequate logistics infrastructure, and the fourth quartile corresponds to the countries with the best quality infrastructure. It is immediately clear that the higher the quality of logistics infrastructure, the larger the share of vertical affiliates. For instance, the countries in the fourth quartile have 75 % of the vertical affiliates in the entire sample, while the countries in the first quartile have less than 1 %.

We can gain further insights by examining the dependence of industries on good logistics services. We can see, for example, that some industries are more sensitive to shipping times than others (Hummels & Schaur, 2012), particularly for the

[9] We create a port infrastructure index that consists of the average of the port measure constructed with the hard data and the port measure constructed with the survey information after each measure is normalized to take values from 1 to 100. Similarly, an airport infrastructure index and an ICT infrastructure index are constructed by combining their corresponding hard data and survey indexes. Finally, an overall logistics index is constructed that consists of the average of the three sub-indexes.

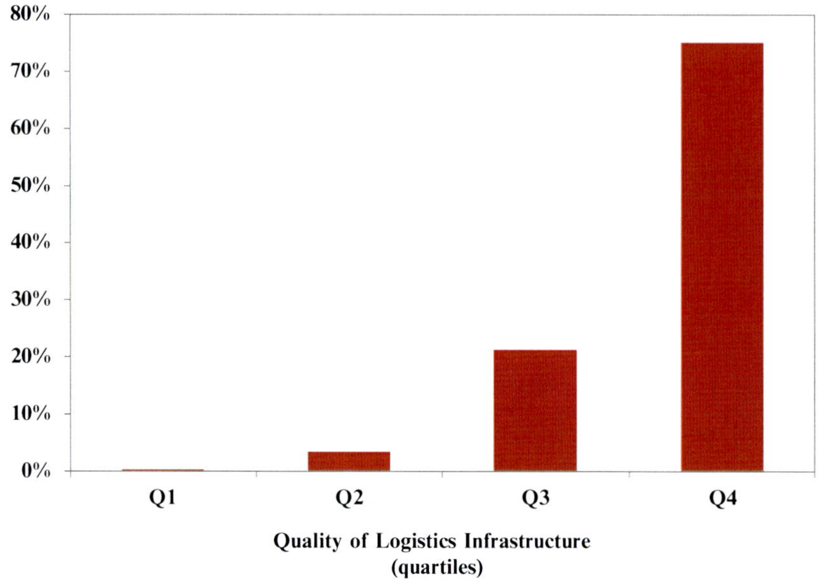

Fig. 3.2 Share of vertical affiliates by quality of logistics infrastructure. *Source*: Authors' calculations

movement of intermediate inputs in a global supply chain. For example, a major challenge for a supply chain for computer components is their rapid depreciation; therefore, components in such production networks must move rapidly along the chain, which requires logistics systems that can handle fast deliveries. A recent study on offshoring found that rapid supply of local markets was the most important decision driver in the development of a manufacturing sourcing strategy in the consumer electronics industry (Hackett Group, 2012). According to the study, highly dynamic industries with short product life cycles and high levels of demand variability base their decisions about where to locate on the quality of transportation and logistics. However, the study found that rapid delivery of components is much less important in the supply chains of less dynamic but highly price-sensitive industries, such as furniture manufacturing. For these industries, raw material and component costs are much more important factors driving the location decision than the quality of the logistics infrastructure.

To proxy for the dependence of the industry on logistics services, we employ a measure of industry sensitivity to shipping times constructed by Hummels and Schaur (2012). The rationale is the idea that rapid delivery requires good logistics infrastructure; therefore, industries that are sensitive to shipping times are also sensitive to good logistics services. The measure is based on the premium for air shipping that firms in an industry are willing to pay to avoid an additional day of ocean transport.[10] It is interesting to note that since the measure is constructed to be agnostic regarding

[10]The measure is calculated for more than 1,000 products at the four-digit level of the Harmonized System (HS).

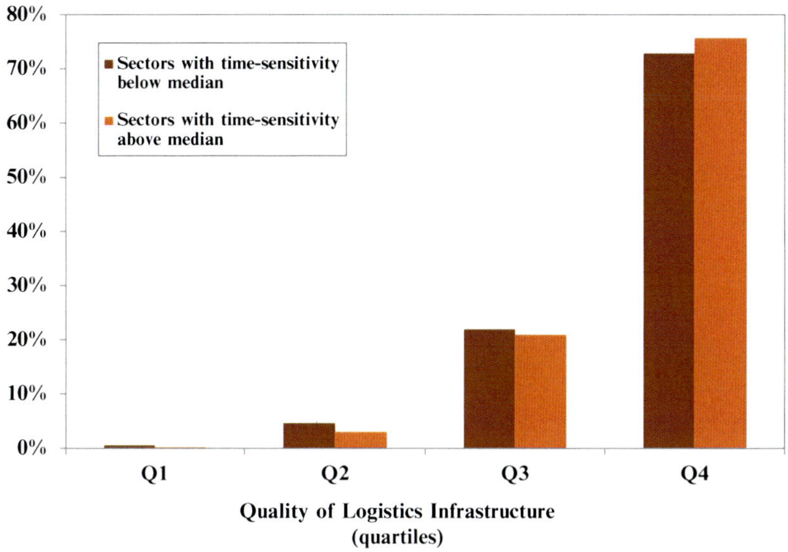

Fig. 3.3 Share of vertical affiliates by quality of logistics infrastructure and dependence on logistics services. *Source*: Authors' calculations

the importance of speed, it can capture dependence on logistics services for a variety of reasons for rapid deliveries—such as the use of perishable goods, goods with short life cycles, or those with high demand variability—and in cases where uncertainty and potential disruptions in the supply chains must be minimized.[11]

Figure 3.3 shows the distribution of vertical affiliates for countries with different levels of logistics infrastructure (as in Fig. 3.2), but in this case the sample is split between vertical affiliates in sectors with values of time sensitivity below the median and sectors with values of time sensitivity above the median. The first aspect to note is that similar to the previous figure, countries with better logistics infrastructure attract more vertical affiliates than countries with inadequate logistics infrastructure. This is observed regardless of the sector: i.e., both sets of columns increase across the quartiles. Another interesting finding is that while both shares of vertical affiliates increase from the first to the fourth quartile, the share in sectors with time sensitivity above the median increases relatively faster. For instance, while countries in the second quartile own more vertical affiliates in non-time-sensitive industries, the opposite is true for the countries in the fourth quartile. This result is interesting because it is telling us that countries with better logistics infrastructure attract not only more vertical affiliates overall, but also, particularly, affiliates in sectors that are more dependent on logistics services.

---

[11] For instance, Hummmels and Schaur (2012) and Evans and Harrigan (2005) examine the link between speed of delivery and uncertainty due to rapid fluctuations in demand. Clark, Schaur, and Kozlova (2012) show that firms tend to switch to more expensive air shipping when uncertainty in ocean shipping increases.

Table 3.1 Expected relationship between bilateral vertical FDI and its determinants

Determinants	Expected sign
Common border	(+)
Common language	(+)
Common colonial origins	(+)
Distance	(−)
Free trade agreement	(+)
Skill differential between parent and host country	(+)
Quality of logistics infrastructure parent country	(+)
Quality of logistics infrastructure host country	(+)

Figures 3.2 and 3.3 support the notion that countries with adequate transport and logistics infrastructure attract more vertical affiliates. But while these results are suggestive, they are far from definitive. Countries with good logistics infrastructure could offer additional benefits that would be attractive to vertical FDI. There is also the issue of causality: improvements in logistics infrastructure might attract vertical FDI, but FDI might also spur investments in logistics infrastructure. Therefore, to make a statement on the relationship between logistics infrastructure and international production networks, we need an econometric model that isolates the effect of logistics infrastructure from other factors while simultaneously addressing the issue of causality. For this purpose we employ an augmented version of the empirical workhorse model in international trade, the gravity equation.

A complete description of the model and its estimation is provided in Appendix B "Specification for the Model of Vertical FDI and Logistics Infrastructure". Here we present the basic intuition of the quantitative analysis. Table 3.1 summarizes the expected signs of all the variables included in the model. In essence, vertical FDI, and thus trade of intermediate inputs between a subsidiary and its headquarters, should be larger between countries with common borders, a common language, common colonial roots, shorter distances, lower trade barriers, larger skill differentials, and higher-quality logistics infrastructures in both countries.[12] The analysis also employs techniques that control for additional variables at the country and sector level that might influence vertical FDI but are not observed by the econometrician.[13]

The dependent variable in the model is the number of vertical affiliates located in host country i from parent country j and sector k. The dataset is for the year 2012. One interesting aspect of the empirical analysis is that we also formally test the proposition that countries with adequate logistics systems may attract more vertical

[12] We proxy the skill differential by the ratio of the parent country's skill to the host country's skill, where country skill is the average years of schooling in the population of age 25 and above. Alfaro and Charlton (2009) also use the average years of schooling to proxy for human capital abundance.

[13] These are country and sector fixed effects. See appendix B "Specification for the Model of Vertical FDI and Logistics Infrastructure".

FDI in industries that are more dependent on logistics services, as suggested by Fig. 3.2.[14] The outcomes of the regression are consistent with the expectations. Even after controlling for the effect of alternative factors, the results indicate that countries with better logistics infrastructure attract more vertical affiliates, particularly in industries that are more dependent on logistics services. As shown in the appendixes, this result holds under alternative estimation techniques and control variables.[15] The magnitude of the effect is economically meaningful. We find, for instance, that a change from the first quartile to the third quartile of the distribution of logistics infrastructure is associated with an average increase in the number of vertically integrated affiliates equivalent to 15 %.

We also explore whether the importance of logistics infrastructure tends to increase with distance. One can reasonably assume, for instance, that differences in time sensitivity across industries might be less relevant for countries that are very close to each other, because products can be delivered quickly. But when countries are far apart, these differences should matter more. Results in Table B.1 (in Appendix B "Specification for the Model of Vertical FDI and Logistics Infrastructure") confirm this assumption: the importance of adequate logistics infrastructure, particularly for logistics-sensitive industries, increases with distance. In other words, for distant countries to attract more vertical FDI, issues such as improving port or airport efficiency are likely to be more important in offsetting the impact of distance than for nearby countries. This result is relevant for Latin American countries. For example, the average bilateral distance across all the East Asian + ASEAN countries is about 2,400 km, while the average distance across the countries in Latin America is 3,000 km. If we include the US and Canada, the distance across the Americas is 3,200 km, or 30 % more than in Asia. In the case of the EU-27, the average bilateral distance is a mere 1,400 km. Therefore, geography imposes a challenge when countries in Latin America seek to join distant supply chains in Asia or Europe, or even to develop supply chains within their own region. What the econometric results suggest is that the issue of logistics infrastructure should be, if anything, relatively more important for Latin America than for other regions, whose countries tend to be closer to each other.

---

[14] Indeed, this test addresses the potential causality issue mentioned earlier. In particular, the test implies examining a cross-country, cross-sector interaction effect, the so-called difference-in-differences estimation. The estimation seeks to alleviate the potential endogeneity problem associated with cross-country regressions. The difference-in-differences estimator would suffer from reverse causality if the FDI flow of a given sector compared to those of other sectors had a causal effect on the overall level of logistics infrastructure. This seems much less likely to be the case than in the more common cross-country regressions, in which total FDI flows could have a causal effect on the overall level of logistics infrastructure investment.

[15] In particular, Appendix B "Specification for the Model of Vertical FDI and Logistics Infrastructure" shows that the main finding holds under least squares and negative binomial estimations, as well as after the inclusion of parent, subsidiary, and sector-fixed effects, and under the more stringent parent-subsidiary, sector-fixed effects. In a longer version of this analysis we also show that the results are sufficiently robust to explicitly include additional covariates in the model; see Blyde and Molina (2013).

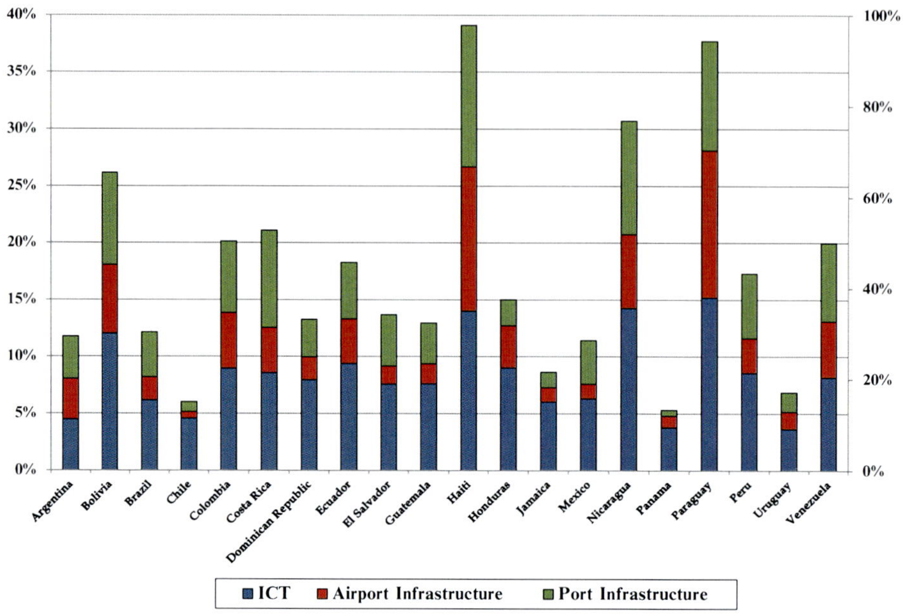

Fig. 3.4 Simulated change in the number of vertical affiliates from improving logistics infrastructure to the EU-27 average. *Note*: The values for Haiti are represented on the *right* axis. *Source*: Authors' calculations

We now use the results from the estimations to simulate the impact of improving the quality of logistics infrastructure in the region. In particular, we ask by how much the particular measure of value chain participation would increase if a country in LAC improves the quality of its logistics infrastructure to the average level in the EU-27. We do this for each of the infrastructure dimensions that comprise the overall index: port, airport, and ICT infrastructure. The results for the number of vertical affiliates are shown in Fig. 3.4.[16] Since most countries have important gaps in all three infrastructure dimensions, closing any of these gaps generates noticeable surges in vertical FDI. On average, the number of vertical affiliates would rise by around 20 %; countries with more important shortcomings in logistics infrastructure, such as Haiti or Paraguay, would experience much larger increases.

The results in Fig. 3.4 presented the average increase in the number of vertical affiliates across all the sectors of the economy. Figure 3.5 shows the results of the same simulation when we look only at the sectors with time-sensitivity above the median. The figure indicates that the number of vertical affiliates in these sectors increases even more than before, with an average of 28 % for the entire region.

[16]We use the results from column 3 in Table B.1 (see Appendix B "Specification for the Model of Vertical FDI and Logistics Infrastructure").

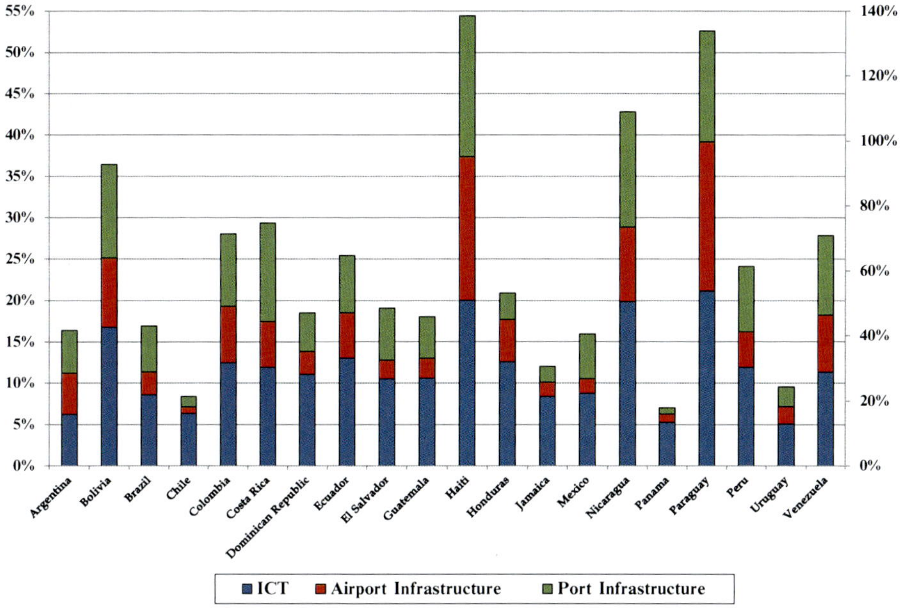

Fig. 3.5 Simulated change in the number of vertical affiliates in sectors with time-sensitivity above median from improving logistics infrastructure to the EU-27 average *Note*: The values for Haiti are represented on the *right* axis. *Source*: Authors' calculations

Policy Issues

Improving a country's transportation and logistics systems requires that an array of issues be addressed, from the quality of the infrastructure to the efficiency of related services. While a detailed description of the required policies is beyond the scope of this work, a few general issues of particular importance for production networks should be stressed. Box 1 further provides specific examples from case studies in Latin America in which logistics has been fundamental for enabling firms to join or develop supply chains.

With respect to maritime transportation, countries in Latin American and the Caribbean have come a long way since the days of heavy state intervention. Cargo reserves for state-owned shipping companies have been mostly eliminated, and maritime shipping services have generally been liberalized. In addition, many national ports and terminals have granted concessions to private port operators. One result has been to trigger a wave of modernization in many port infrastructures, including the installation of gantry cranes for faster loading and unloading and electronic tracking of containers to reduce waiting and turnaround time for ships. Although these improvements have been a critical factor for many supply chains, the productivity of Latin American port infrastructure remains far from world-class. A rare dataset available for a selected group of ports, for example, shows that when

Box 1: The Role of Logistics

This box presents two case studies in which logistics policies facilitated the spread of global supply chains.

Bombardier Querétaro. During the 1970s, the world aeronautic industry was vertically integrated, with only about 20 % of the typical aircraft manufacturer's total value being outsourced. Today, that outsourced share is close to 80 %. Mexico is taking advantage of this trend by spurring the development of an aeronautic cluster, mainly centered in the state of Querétaro. The aim is to attract global firms and support linkages between them and Mexican suppliers.

One of the foreign firms attracted to Querétaro was Bombardier, the Canadian aircraft manufacturer. Cost advantage, proximity to the US and Canada, and the free trade agreement among Mexico, Canada, and the US (NAFTA) were among the pull factors for Bombardier. But these incentives were complemented by a series of logistics developments, such as large investments in the Querétaro airport. With specialized warehouse services and one of the longest runways in the country, the airport sits at the convergence of Mexico's road, rail, and telecommunications network, thereby facilitating multimodal operations and allowing Bombardier to ship parts to Wichita and Toronto for assembly much more quickly than if they had been produced in China. In fact, Bombardier's plant is located within the perimeters of this airport.

Bombardier was attracted to the cluster by the massive transport infrastructure investments made by the state government. Nevertheless, a number of logistics issues also needed to be addressed to guarantee smooth operations of the company's supply chain. For instance, when Bombardier started its operations in Mexico, the federal customs office was located in downtown Querétaro, not at the airport. The authorities initially insisted that every component be brought from the airport to downtown for customs clearance, and then shipped back to the airport, where the Bombardier factory is located. This extra step increased time and costs for customs clearance. Eventually, the federal government established a customs area at the airport.

Another soft policy measure was the signing of the Bilateral Aviation Safety Agreement with the US, which allows Mexico's civil aviation authority to certify parts and components produced in Mexico. This development essentially eliminated one step in the supply chain, which considerably reduced costs and time because components and parts no longer had to be inspected in the US before being shipped off to the assembly locations.

Basso. Since the 1990s, the automotive industry has become more global with the growing importance of FDI in developing countries during recent years. This shift in global production resulted from a significant organizational change in which the Ford model was replaced by the Toyota model, which prioritizes production flexibility, quality, and speed. Assemblers started delegating more design responsibilities to component suppliers, urging the latter to supply them with efficient technological solutions.

(continued)

Box 1: (continued)

One of these component suppliers is Basso, a producer of combustion engine valves, located in Rafaela, Argentina. The firm makes valves for automakers (e.g., Peugeot, Ferrari, and Ford), motorcycle producers (Harley Davidson), and farm tractor producers (John Deere).

Basso has been able to compete globally due to its high-quality customization of products and a strict commitment to provide just-in-time delivery services, the demanding mode of production that became widespread with the emergence of the Toyota model. Logistics is key to the firm's business, and its just-in-time delivery service—which coordinates storage, transport, and inventory—is one of the firm's main distinguishing features.

Complying with just-in-time shipment commitments is not easy, however, particularly when about half of the company's clients are located more than 8,000 km away. Basso orchestrates a logistical system that makes customers feel that such long distances are not relevant.

One change that was fundamental to the company's ability to fulfill its delivery commitments was the creation of an Argentine customs office in the city of Rafaela, a move that resulted from joint action by businessmen and city officials. The new customs office enables Basso to clear every export and import operation in Rafaela without the need to do so at the Port of Buenos Aires. Since the valves that are shipped from Rafaela already have customs verification and approval, delivery is much more rapid.

Despite these advances, the company must still plan for possible logistics problems, such as roadblocks or strikes at the ports. For example, the firm maintains a permanent stock of goods on ships and in warehouses, a practice that increases its inventory costs. As such, while the firm benefits from facilitated customs clearance, it incurs other costs in dealing with uncertainty in logistics.

The examples of Bombardier and Basso illustrate that creating an adequate logistics system is not only about big physical infrastructure works, but also about the less visible but perhaps equally important soft policies related to logistics.

Sources: the story of Bombardier is based on material from Brown-Grossman and Domínguez-Villalobos (2012) and remarks by Michael R. McAdoo, Vice-President of International Trade, Bombardier, at the 2012 World Economic Forum on Latin America. The case of Basso is based on material from González, Hallak, Schott, and Soria (2012).

measured in terms of TEU per meter of quay,[17] the average productivity for ports in South East Asia is almost three times higher than the average productivity in Latin American ports (Drewry, 2010).

[17] The maritime literature frequently uses this performance indicator for container terminals. The measure means the number of 20-ft-equivalent unit containers handled per running meter of quay per year.

Latin American countries seeking to participate in global production networks must therefore continue to pursue reforms that improve the productivity of their port infrastructure and increase the efficiency of their ancillary services, such as cargo handling, storage, and warehousing.

In addition to the liberalization of the industry and the decentralization of port operations, there are many other areas in which the government should play an active role. For instance, government must create effective regulations that assure proper market contestability to prevent anticompetitive practices by carriers and shipping companies (Sanchez & Wilmsmeier, 2009). In addition, government must make investments, such as channel dredging, to enable larger vessels with lower operating costs to enter a port; such investments might not take place without government intervention. Increasingly larger vessels that travel at higher speeds are constantly being introduced. The largest vessels currently in use (average 13,000 TEUs) are expected to start serving the region within the next 5–8 years (CEPAL, 2012). Accommodating these vessels may require new plans and strategies for port industries and related activities in many countries of the region (CEPAL, 2012). An important step in this direction is the expansion of the Panama Canal. Completion of the new set of locks and ancillary projects (dredging and widening), will enable the canal to handle containerships of 13,000 TEUs.

As with port infrastructure, airport efficiency has improved as a result of a gradual shift from the traditional public ownership model to arrangements that include alternative privatization schemes and concession contracts. With the exception of a few services, such as meteorological services, most commercial and handling operations can be provided on a competitive basis. Airport privatization throughout the world has generally led to improvements in efficiency, but privatization in Latin America has proceeded at a slower pace than in many other parts of the world, particularly in the Asia-Pacific region and in industrialized countries (ACI, 2008). Additionally, transfer of ownership has not always resulted in improved efficiency, due to lack of market contestability. Governments in the region must enact regulatory frameworks that ensure competitive conditions for ancillary services (Serebrisky, Schwartz, Pachón, & Ricover, 2011).

Meeting the demands of global supply chains also requires a liberalization of the region's international air services. In other parts of the world, many firms engaged in production networks can choose among multiple carriers because of more open air transport markets. For example, an airline's right to carry cargo from its own country to a second country, and from that country to a third country—the so-called "fifth freedom"—is instrumental for many supply chains. With manufacturers demanding inputs from multiple suppliers, the fifth freedom gives carriers the needed flexibility to serve multiple nodes.

In Latin America and the Caribbean, air services are still restricted by old bilateral agreements that put stringent limitations on market access. For example, while many agreements grant fifth freedom rights, there are usually maximum capacity thresholds, and passengers generally receive preference over cargo.

Efforts should be made to remove these maximum thresholds. At a broader level, the region must do more to move in tandem with liberalization efforts in other parts of the world, most of which have been carried out through open skies agreements. For example, it has been shown that open skies agreements signed by the US have reduced air transport costs by around 9 % while increasing the share of imports arriving by air by 7 % (Micco & Serebrisky, 2006). A movement towards a regional open skies agreement in Latin America and the Caribbean would certainly lower the costs of connecting suppliers and buyers in various points of the region's supply chain.

Policy issues also must be addressed to improve the region's ICT infrastructure. Prior to the waves of privatization during the 1990s, prices in the telecommunication sector did not reflect the true costs for providing the services; there were no incentives for innovation, and services were generally of low quality (Razo & Rojas Mejia, 2007). The privatization of the state monopolies brought about more innovation and generally increased efficiency in the provision of services (Aguerro & Mastrini, 2009; De Laiglesia, 2007). However, the liberalization did not automatically result in increased competition. Many countries, for example, granted exclusivity periods to allow companies to invest in infrastructure upgrading and installation so as to consolidate their position in the market. Such exclusivity periods strengthened the dominant position of the incumbent firms and created incentives to set high prices and prevent access to new services (Razo & Rojas Mejia, 2007). The long periods of exclusive operation granted to the initial investors significantly delayed the entry of new providers and obstructed the creation of competitive markets.

Furthermore, the ICT legal frameworks and regulatory agencies that were put in place years ago have not proved themselves capable of encouraging competition and dealing with the challenges of the sector. For example, firms today commonly offer packages that combine different types of services. This new trend creates a challenge for the regulator, who must determine the relevant market definition on which to base judgments about anticompetitive behavior (Aldana & Vallejo, 2010; Rozas, 2002). The main challenges in the telecommunication sector today are to reduce the high levels of market concentration and create conditions for the development of competitive markets. The constant evolution of the sector requires the regulator to continuously adapt to deal with these challenges.

The econometric exercise in this section explicitly modeled the role of critical air, maritime, and ICT infrastructures. However, although these infrastructures are important pieces of a country's logistics system, they are not the only ones. Supply chains also require more efficient customs services and streamlined security clearance processes (see Box 1 and also the next section). Likewise, inadequate internal transport-related infrastructure, including the low density and poor quality of many road networks in Latin America, have been shown to negatively impact the region's trade performance. In this area, important policy issues range from placing a new priority on these long-neglected investments to improving regulation of the domestic transport industry. These important subjects deserve to be addressed in separate reports (see, for instance, Mesquita Moreira, Blyde, Volpe, & Molina, 2013).

Production Disintegration and Market Integration: Deep Integration Agreements at Work

How do economic integration agreements affect the formation of international supply chains? Under what conditions do they support production networks among countries? Are trade agreements, and trade policy in general, partly responsible for the lack of participation of Latin American countries in global value chains? This section seeks to provide some answers to these important questions.

Casual evidence and regional studies often suggest that many global supply chains are affected by agreements and/or arrangements between nations. For instance, before the 1965 US–Canada Auto Agreement, trade in auto parts between these two countries practically did not exist. After the agreement was signed and tariff barriers were reduced to 0, a US–Canada auto supply chain was created and auto trade soared (Hummels, Rapoport, & Yi, 1998).[18]

It is self-evident that tightly integrated countries are more likely to share international production networks. To begin with, crossing borders is always associated with additional costs, such as the tariff duties, which are commonly removed in trade agreements. The impact of removing tariff barriers can be proportionally larger for a production process that crosses borders many times—often the case for many supply chains—than for a final good that crosses borders only once.[19] Beyond the issue of tariffs, establishing production networks across countries may involve a mix of flows related to trade, investment, and technical knowledge, whose maximization requires the close collaboration of the parties involved. For instance, offshoring from an affiliate involves making cross-border investments that might not take place without adequate investment rules in the host country. Similarly, engaging in contract manufacturing with local suppliers typically requires a flow of knowledge that some lead firms may be reluctant to provide without adequate intellectual property rights. Rapid delivery of products, a feature of particular importance for many industries (as observed in the last section), might require harmonizing and streamlining customs and security procedures among the parties involved. In short, complex cross-border activities tend to demand complex rules (Baldwin, 2012).

[18] Likewise, Curran and Zignago (2012) show that after the expansion of the European Union in 2004, the new members became a much more important source of intermediate inputs for the old members of the union. Similarly, Karkkainen (2008) shows that flows of FDI from the old EU members to the new members increased to unprecedented levels in the run up to the expansion. The main FDI recipients were Hungary, the Czech Republic, and Poland, the three countries that since then have become crucial parts of the European supply chain. In Asia, the initial growth of production networks may have induced a rising demand for the harmonization of certain national policies across jurisdictions and generally deeper integration, to enable cross-border production networks to operate more smoothly (WTO, 2011).

[19] This notion is formally developed by Ishii and Yi (1997), who show that tariff reductions have a proportionately greater effect on vertical trade involving goods produced sequentially in multiple countries relative to goods produced entirely in one country.

In this regard, deep integration schemes may be associated with more cross-border production sharing because they tend to incorporate disciplines beyond the simple reduction of tariff rates. These disciplines include, among others, rules in investment policy, intellectual property rights, or the harmonization of management techniques in customs procedures to expedite clearance of goods. In short, deep integration agreements tend to create conditions that are likely to be important for global supply chains.

In this section we analyze the proposition that economic integration agreements facilitate the process of fragmentation. In particular, we examine the notion that deep agreements provide greater incentives for the formation of global supply chains than shallow agreements. If integration agreements, particularly deep ones, are closely associated with the formation of international supply chains, two general issues emerge for the countries of Latin America. On the one hand, the prospects of improving the region's participation in extra-regional production networks governed by the countries' respective agreements are likely to remain limited unless membership in those agreements is expanded or their rules of origin are made more flexible; we will examine this issue later in this section. The other issue is related to the multiple trade agreements in Latin America. The countries in LAC are not integrated in one regional trade agreement but share memberships through a complex web of multiple agreements that are likely to restrict the scope of production fragmentation across the region. We will also examine this issue later in this section.

We will first analyze the impacts on GVC participation that one could expect from trade agreements. For this purpose, we use an econometric model that examines the effects of economic integration agreements on a measure of offshoring based on the FDI data introduced in Chap. 2, specifically, the vertically linked subsidiaries. The model estimates the impacts of economic integration agreements on the number of vertically integrated foreign subsidiaries in a pair of host–parent countries in a particular year during the period 1980–2005. It includes a series of variables that control for time-invariant country-pair characteristics (such as bilateral distance) as well as for host and parent characteristics, such as GDP, that vary over time. Details of the model and the data employed can be found in Appendix B "The Effects of Economic Integration Agreements: Estimation and Data Sources".

The results (shown in Fig. 3.6) indicate that economic integration agreements have a positive and significant impact on the number of vertically linked subsidiaries hosted by partner countries. The first bar shows that countries with trade agreements have 8 % more subsidiaries than countries with no trade agreements. The next three bars present the results of an exercise that examines the premise that deep forms of integration induce more cross-border production sharing than shallow trade agreements. For the sake of simplicity, we have grouped the agreements into three types: preferential trade agreements (PTA), free trade agreements (FTA), and deep integration agreements, which cover customs unions (CU), common markets (CM), and economic unions (EU). The figure shows that preferential trade agreements do not have a significant effect on cross-border production sharing. Countries with free trade agreements, however, have 9 % more subsidiaries than countries with no free trade agreements. Finally, countries with deep trade agreements,

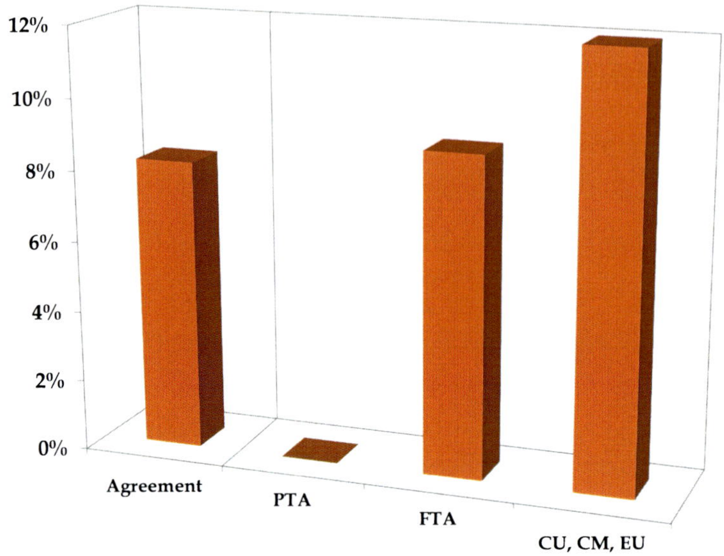

Fig. 3.6 Estimated impact of trade agreements on vertical FDI. *Source*: Authors' calculations

such as common markets or economic unions, have 12 % more subsidiaries than countries without deep trade agreements. These findings support the notion mentioned earlier that deep integration agreements provide more incentives for the formation of global supply chains than shallow agreements, because they tend to incorporate measures beyond the simple reduction of tariff rates. In so doing, they address a number of dimensions that tend to be important for well-functioning supply chains.

We can probe more deeply into the relationship between trade agreements and vertical FDI by exploring the channels by which trade agreements increase the number of vertically linked affiliates. In our analysis, we wish to determine whether the total increase in the number of subsidiaries is due primarily to an increase in the number of subsidiaries opened by parent companies or to an increase in the total number of parent companies opening subsidiaries. Likewise, we investigate whether the increase in the number of subsidiaries corresponds to an expansion of the number of subsidiaries in the same sectors or an expansion in new sectors. The results (shown in Fig. 3.7) suggest two things: first, the increase in production fragmentation is primarily due to an increase in the total number of parent companies opening subsidiaries; and second, the increase mainly occurs due to a greater diversification of sectors in which these plants operate.

One issue regarding integration agreements and production networks is that while such agreements may induce the formation of production networks, existing production networks might also generate demand for integration agreements. Such a demand for deeper integration, for example, could take the form of the elimination of technical barriers to trade, which tend to be costly for offshoring (Lawrence, 1996).

In Asia, for example, many regional production networks were developed prior to the acceleration of Asian integration under the ASEAN Free Trade Area and

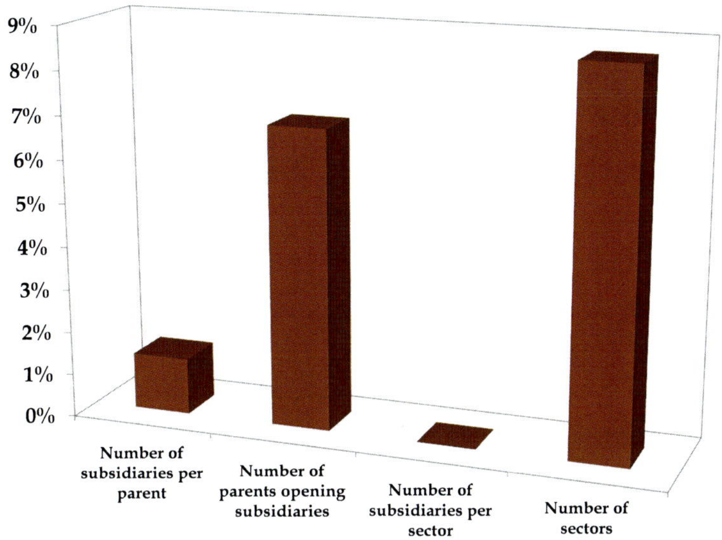

Fig. 3.7 Estimated impact of trade agreements on vertical FDI, by channels. *Source*: Authors' calculations

under the ASEAN+1 FTAs (Kimura & Obashi, 2011). Still, many pro-trade and investment policies implemented in Asia may have contributed to this early growth of regional supply chains, such as the aggressive moves to attract FDI that started in the late 1980s, the unilateral trade liberalization periods, the establishment of export processing zones, and, particularly, the low levels of protection for the imports of intermediate inputs, which we will discuss later.

Generally, however, the potential causality from GVCs to trade agreements could introduce a bias in the estimations we presented above. Therefore, we performed a series of tests to examine the possibility of reverse causality. For instance, we included both lagged and lead values of the agreement variable. While the lag values were significant, the lead values were not. In addition, we conducted a placebo exercise by examining whether there was a correlation between current production linkages and future agreements; we found no evidence of such a correlation (see Appendix B "The Effects of Economic Integration Agreements: Estimation and Data Sources" for details). These results indicate that the potential causality from production networks to agreements is unlikely to explain the results presented above.

Policy Issues

While deep integration schemes are associated with GVCs, it is clear that the multilateral approach would be the optimal way to foster global production networks. As regional trade agreements continue to multiply, a firm seeking to participate in production networks spanning various trade agreements will be hard pressed to keep track of all the differences in the governing rules. Similarly, as the production of a good is sliced up across more and more countries, barriers between third countries upstream or downstream become as important as the barriers between the two main partners; they might better be addressed together. But the evolution of the multilateral system has not kept up with modern trends of production fragmentation, and it has yet to provide the policy environment at the global level that international supply chains need to thrive. Instead, countries have used bilateral and regional trade agreements to fill this void.

Trade agreements (TAs), however, can be associated with the well-known problem of trade diversion, the situation in which trade is shifted from a more efficient producer that does not belong to the agreement to a less efficient producer within the agreement.

Another potential risk of TAs is that sometimes they set stringent limits regarding the scope of activities within the supply chain in which the member countries can engage. This was the case with the Caribbean Basin Initiative (CBI), in which the member countries exporting textiles to the US enjoyed tariff-free status in the US, but only for the most basic assembly operations of the textile and apparel industry, mainly sewing. Eventually, the CBI was expanded into the Caribbean Basin Trade and Promotion Act (CBTPA), but even at this point the tariff rate fell to 0 only on products in which the local value added consisted of cut, make, trim, and finishing operations. Not until CAFTA went into effect in 2005 could every aspect of the production process in this supply chain of textiles and apparel, including the use of local yarns, fibers, and other raw materials, be performed in the Central American countries (Pipkin, 2011). This example shows that even though some TAs can open up new prospects for developing countries to participate in cross-border production sharing, this participation may be limited to only a few segments of the supply chain, a practice that could eliminate potentially important opportunities.

TAs may also discourage the utilization of cheaper parts and materials from third countries due to their rules of origin (RoO). This is particularly the case if these parts and materials are used to produce final goods that are later exported to other members of the agreement. In this sense, RoO could increase production costs to the point where the cost of compliance exceeds the benefit of the preferences conferred by the agreement (Estevadeordal & Suominen, 2006, 2008). This can be especially problematic for Latin American countries seeking to participate in extra-regional supply chains, particularly in North America, the EU, and Asia.

Of course, RoO are critical parts of many TAs because they establish the conditions that a product must satisfy to be deemed eligible for preferential access in the member countries. They are primarily used to prevent trade deflection—that is, to prevent products from non-participating countries reaching a high-tariff TA partner via the transshipment of the product through a low-tariff TA member. But RoO can severely narrow the choices that firms have for locating slices of their production abroad.

TAs also require that firms deal with the potential complexity associated with keeping track of multiple RoO. When an exporter produces only one good and most intermediate inputs are sourced domestically, the costs of complying with multiple RoO might not be too large. But when an exporter produces more goods, and the sourcing involves many countries, the costs of dealing with multiple origins can be substantially greater. These costs may increase even more if the suppliers are not wholly owned affiliates but rather independent firms in other countries. In this case, transparent channels for conveying the supplier's origin information, such as pricing and other sensitivity issues, are less likely to exist. For instance, suppliers might lack sufficient incentives to provide their clients with complete sourcing information for fear that this might jeopardize their relationship; the client might then make direct contact with the subcontractor and cut the supplier out of the chain (Staples & Harris, 2009).

The question is how to better align the legitimate practice of curbing trade deflection with the reality of GVCs. The constraints generally presented by RoO, can be reduced through the use of various mechanisms, such as higher de minimis levels, allowing for duty drawback, or flexible cumulation rules.

De minimis rules, for example, allow for the use of a specified percentage of non-originating products in the production process without affecting the origin status of the final product. Duty drawback is used to return the payment of applicable duties to the non-originating material employed in the production of a final product that is subsequently exported to other members of the agreement.

Finally, cumulation generally means that inputs from trading partners can be used in the production of a final good without undermining the product's origin. Practically all TAs permit bilateral cumulation, meaning that materials originating in any one member country are considered as originating in the partner country and vice versa. In agreements among more than two countries this is sometimes called diagonal cumulation. Full cumulation means that any operation performed in any of the partner countries can be counted, whether or not the processing is sufficient to confer originating status upon the materials themselves. Full cumulation is particularly beneficial to the formation of regional value chains, as it allows the various contributions to the final product to be accounted and combined to establish its origin. Additionally, there is a growing trend to employ expanded cumulation to allow three or more countries with separate but overlapping trade agreements to effectively merge their individual bilateral treaties so that inputs can be sourced anywhere within the network. This approach could be the most effective strategy for "multilateralizing" RoO across trade agreements.

Ample empirical evidence suggests that some of these mechanisms can ease constraints imposed by RoO and generate larger trade flows. The evidence is particularly strong for the role of cumulation schemes (Augier, Gasiorek, & Tong, 2005; Estevadeordal & Suominen, 2008; Hayakawa, 2012; Park & Park, 2009).[20]

[20] The evidence is based on different identification techniques. For instance, Estevadeordal and Suominen (2008) and Park and Park (2009) look at the difference in trade flows across groups of country pairs (i.e., differences between members of agreements with diagonal cumulation and members of agreements without diagonal cumulation). Augier et al. (2005) compare trade flows in the same country pairs before and after the introduction of diagonal cumulation. Hayakawa (2012) compares trade flows between the same two countries but under two kinds of schemes—one with bilateral cumulation and another with diagonal cumulation.

All of these analyses show positive and significant trade effects of more flexible cumulation schemes. For instance, Augier et al. (2005) and Hayakawa (2012) show trade creation effects on the order of four to 15 % associated with diagonal accumulation. Even larger effects, on the order of 30–100 %, are found when comparing members in full cumulation schemes to those in bilateral cumulation schemes (Estevadeordal & Suominen, 2008; Park & Park, 2009). Therefore, there is a compelling argument in favor of expanding the cumulation of RoOs to reduce the implicit costs faced by active and potential participants of international production networks.

There are signs that countries in many parts of the world are growing more aware of the importance of flexible sourcing schemes. For example, over the nearly 20 years of NAFTA's operation, the agreement has gone through four rounds of changes in RoO that have become progressively more permissive of materials from outside North America. This is clearly good news for other countries in Latin America aiming to enter production networks within the North American hub. Other agreements have similar mechanisms for amending their RoO over time, although as other agreements also learned from the NAFTA experience, they have tended to negotiate less restrictive rules in the first place.

The evidence also shows that reforms have been made that deal with issues such as cumulation. As mentioned before, the existence of multiple and overlapping trade agreements can impose limits on the fragmentation of production across borders. Countries are becoming more aware of the need to eliminate those frictions. Perhaps the most substantial experiment in the expansion of cumulation involved the Pan-Euro-Med cumulation zone. The mechanism that went into effect in 1997 harmonized the RoO provisions of more than ten bilateral EU agreements and enabled cumulation among all of the partners.

One notable Latin American experience of cumulation involved Central America and Mexico. Between 1995 and 2001, Mexico had signed separate agreements with Costa Rica (1995), Nicaragua (1998), and the "Northern Triangle" of El Salvador, Guatemala, and Honduras (2001). These agreements did not provide for cumulation among all six countries and thus had the effect of segmenting value chains that tied the Central American countries to Mexico. For example, chocolates from Costa Rica would not encounter tariff charges in Mexico as long as they were produced entirely in Costa Rica, but the same chocolates would pay a tariff duty if they used cocoa paste from Honduras. In 2011, however, the countries signed a new agreement that enables full cumulation across all six countries under a single set of RoO agreed upon by all parties, giving firms much more flexibility regarding where to source their various inputs. While the Mexico–Central America example is a step in the right direction, a more systemic approach is needed. One bold move would be to promote cumulation of origin across the many bilateral and regional trade agreements in LAC. As a result, firms would be better able to take advantage of the differences in factors prices across locations, resulting in more cross-border production sharing within the region.

In other regions, two negotiations are underway that could have profound effects on the ability of companies to form sophisticated GVCs. The first is the Trans-Pacific Partnership (TPP), which joins 14 countries in a single agreement; members include the NAFTA countries, Japan, Peru, Chile, Australia, New Zealand, and four ASEAN countries. Negotiating texts published thus far do not make it clear how the countries intend to structure the cumulation provisions, but it is vital that the structuring be done as broadly and inclusively as possible. If complete cumulation, including all members of the agreement for all products, is not a feature of the TPP, its eventual value will be significantly undermined, especially for supporting the formation of GVCs. Furthermore, since the TPP will include two of the three GVC hubs—Japan and the US— cumulation is needed to exploit complementarities between these hubs.

The second negotiation is the Trans-Atlantic Trade and Investment Partnership between the US and the EU, which aims to eliminate tariffs and seeks regulatory harmonization between the world's two largest economies. In matters of preferential market access, both the US and the EU have large networks of trade agreements with third countries in all regions of the globe. The elimination of bilateral tariffs would erode those preferences. While there is no obligation to mitigate preference erosion, this could be accomplished by explicitly including mechanisms for expanding cumulation to these third parties. Such mechanisms would allow third countries to participate in the GVCs operating in these economies, gaining benefits instead of being sidelined. On this issue, however, LAC countries have very little influence. Nevertheless, where both the US and the EU have already granted duty-free access to materials from many countries in the region, it would seem particularly unreasonable to exclude them from bilateral value chains.

There is also the issue of harmonization of RoO across agreements. Since harmonizing the rules themselves might be quite difficult, countries instead may want to focus on harmonizing the methods of calculating regional value content, as well as on the procedures for certifying and verifying origin. The evidence suggests that differences in these mechanisms and procedures have caused tremendous problems for firms seeking to take advantage of trade agreements. Therefore, the bulk of the gains from RoO harmonization are likely to be in this area.

Another and more general issue regarding trade policy is related to the protectionist bias that remains in many parts of the world. As we mentioned above, certain trade agreements have been designed to limit the participation of developing countries to only a few segments of the supply chain. This is only a manifestation of a more endemic practice called the tariff escalation problem, in which countries impose low duties on raw materials but higher duties on higher value-added segments of the supply chain. This problem is not as severe as in the past (WTO, 2008), but it still exists. Box 2 shows a very simple example of the MFN tariffs imposed by the countries of the European Union on various segments of the automotive industry. The existing scheme clearly generates disincentives to move beyond the supply of raw materials and into higher value-added segments of the automotive supply chain. Table 3.2 shows that the practice of tariff escalation is not restricted to the automotive sector but rather is widespread across many industries.

Many countries, including developing nations, engage in tariff escalation. However, since the industrialized world leads most of the international supply chains, tariff escalation is particularly harmful for developing countries' participation in

Box 2: Tariff Escalation in the Automotive Industry

Following is an illustration of how tariff escalation in developed countries generates disincentives in Latin American countries to upgrade in international supply chains.

Figure 3.8 shows the EU's simple average MFN-applied tariffs for selected products used in the automotive industry, including aluminum ore, a raw material produced in large quantities in the region and used in many vehicle components. A Latin American exporter of aluminum ore would pay no duties to enter the European market. However, a firm in Latin America that uses that aluminum ore to produce pistons for engines faces a duty of 2.7 % to export its pistons to Europe. If instead the firm decides to produce not only the pistons but the entire engine, the European tariff rate will rise to 4 %, and if that engine is mounted to a chassis, the tariff increases to 9.1 %, and so on. This example illustrates how progressively higher tariffs in the automobile supply chain generate disincentives to move beyond the supply of raw materials and into other segments downstream in the industry.

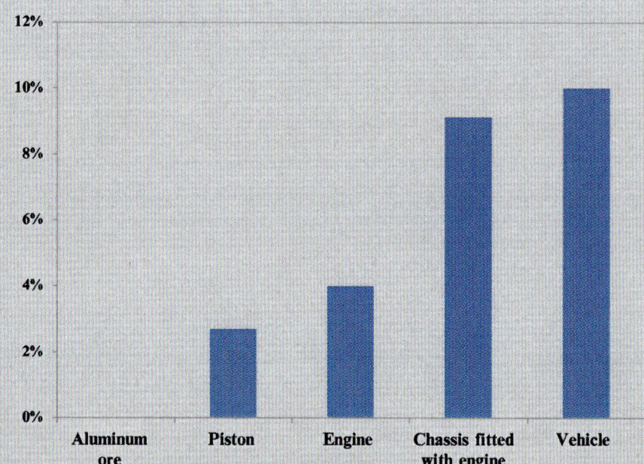

Source: TRAINS.

Fig. 3.8 EU average unweighted MFN applied tariff, selected products

supply chains when the practice is employed in the industrial world. This is clearly an obstacle for many firms in Latin America seeking to move beyond the simple provision of raw materials and into other segments of the industrialized world's supply chains.

Another issue related to trade policy concerns the capacity of local firms to complement their production with high-quality inputs from other countries. The emergence of international production networks has indeed strengthened the economic case against import protection, because firms inserted in global supply

Table 3.2 Average unweighted applied MFN tariffs, 2011

	European Union			United States		
	Raw materials	Semi-finished	Finished	Raw materials	Semi-finished	Finished
Fish and fish products	9.33	12.50	14.31	0.41	1.65	3.36
Fruit and vegetables	6.69	10.30	15.44	5.37	7.04	10.85
Coffee, tea, mate, and cocoa	3.07	8.73	9.46	0.58	0.00	5.96
Mineral products and precious metals	0.12	2.19	3.14	0.33	0.84	3.38
Metal ores	0.00	1.57	2.81	0.09	1.18	2.00
Wood, pulp, paper, and furniture	0.00	0.59	0.62	0.00	0.12	0.63
Textiles and clothing	2.98	6.57	9.73	3.47	9.40	8.52
Leather, rubber, and footwear	0.07	2.43	6.00	0.00	2.02	5.60

Source: TRAINS
Note: The table shows the average unweighted applied MFN tariffs in the EU and the US for various categories of products. The tariffs are shown in MTN (Multilateral Trade Negotiation) categories

chains source inputs not only from their own countries but also from other parts of the world. The capacity to export successfully in international markets increasingly depends on the capacity to import efficient inputs. Constraining access to high-quality inputs from abroad through high levels of protection may increase production costs and damage the ability of potential suppliers to provide adequate and reliable products in downstream segments of international supply chains. Local content and trade balance measures—the so-called performance requirements—also force firms (in particular multinational corporations, MNCs) to draw their intermediate inputs from local production, thus limiting their freedom to use imported supplies.[21] Countries in Latin America will have more opportunities to participate in international production networks when access to foreign intermediate inputs becomes more liberalized.

We will conclude this section by reflecting on the potential scope for developing international production networks as countries become more integrated. The econometric results shown above provide evidence that countries engaging in deep forms of integration tend to share more production processes. But this does not necessarily imply that the production networks must originate exclusively in the countries party to the agreement. Regional integration could also help attract production from outside the region that is subsequently sliced and shared among the countries of the agreement. Hard proof of this argument is difficult to find, but casual evidence suggests that such processes occur more often than expected. An example is found in research by Hiratsuka (2011) and Sturgeon and Florida (2004), who show how multinationals

[21] Local content requirements specify the percentage or the absolute value of inputs that must be acquired from local sources or produced domestically. Trade balancing requirements normally limit the imports of the firm to some proportion of the value of its exports.

in the automobile industry source their inputs. Traditionally, subsidiaries of major multinationals located in different countries sourced most of their inputs domestically, except for key components like engines or transmissions, which were supplied by their parent countries. However, this practice has been changing rapidly, and nowhere is this more evident than among the ASEAN countries. Highly incentivized by the ASEAN Free Trade Area, assembly plants located in the ASEAN countries trade large quantities of inputs among themselves. A plant (and its suppliers) in each country tends to specialize in the production of specific components of the car; then each plant exports these components to the other plants of the multinational while importing from them the inputs that are not produced there. Therefore, multinationals from Japan and the US are effectively slicing the production of their cars across various ASEAN countries, taking advantage of their highly integrated space.

This suggests that more regional integration need not be viewed solely as an instrument to develop supply chains originated in Latin America. More regional integration can also attract firms from outside the region and encourage them to establish their supply chains among the Latin American countries.

Production Unbundling and Firm Boundaries: Foreign Affiliates or Local Suppliers?

Firms planning to fragment production internationally must decide on the degree of control that they want to exercise over the process; as mentioned in Chap. 1, this is called the internalization decision. In this classic make-or-buy decision, the firm chooses either to outsource the procurement of its inputs to non-affiliated suppliers or to engage in foreign direct investment (FDI) and import intermediate inputs from its affiliates. This issue is important for countries wishing to know whether the optimal strategy for improving their participation in production networks should be based on attracting affiliates of multinationals or relying on their local suppliers.

At the heart of this issue is the basic question of why some firms decide to offshore part of their production process to external suppliers while others prefer to employ affiliated plants. Nike, for instance, subcontracts part of its production to independent factories in several countries and keeps only stages, like design and marketing, within the boundaries of the firm. An example of the second form of offshoring is illustrated by General Motors Corporation, which relies on GM affiliates located in different countries to produce specific vehicle components: GM Powertrain-Kaiserslautern in Germany for manufacturing engines, GM Delphi Interior Systems in Mexico for airbags, or GM Strasbourg in France for carburetors, pistons, rings, and valves (Alfaro & Charlton, 2009).

It could be possible that the type of offshoring that firms choose is an arbitrary decision not based on a particular determinant. However, empirical analyses demonstrate some industry patterns in how firms choose to offshore production. For example, Bernard, Jensen, Redding, and Schott (2010) show that trade between affiliates and headquarters of the same firm (intra-firm trade) accounts for more than 70 % of US imports in industries such as vehicle engines and medical equipment and instruments, suggesting that most of the offshoring in these industries occurs through vertical FDI. However, in the rubber and plastic footwear industries, the share of intra-firm trade is only 2 %, indicating that offshoring in this case takes place mostly among firms in the US and independent contractors in other countries. The existence of industry patterns suggests that the internalization decision does not occur at random, but is rather a process determined by the interplay of various factors.

If the decision is not random, countries in Latin America should know what these determinants are in order to design strategies to maximize their chances of joining international production networks. For instance, if offshoring in certain industries occurs mostly through affiliates of MNCs, then countries seeking to join production networks in those industries may need to focus on attracting multinationals. But if joining a supply chain is more likely to occur through linking with independent suppliers, as in the case of Nike, then countries should provide support to existing local plants. The general questions then are: Under what conditions should countries wishing to participate in global production networks seek to attract vertical FDI? And under what conditions should they foster their domestic suppliers? This section provides some insights into this important question.

Analysis of this issue requires information on whether offshoring occurs between lead firms and their affiliates in other countries, or between lead firms and independent suppliers. Unfortunately, there are practically no international trade data on transactions identifying the relationship between the supplier and the buyer. A rare exception is the US Related Party Trade database compiled by the US Census Bureau. These data distinguish whether each international trade transaction in the US occurs between affiliated parties or between independent firms. We employ this data in this section. Appendix B "Specification for the Model of Intra-firm Trade" provides more details regarding this dataset as well as the estimations presented in this section.

A cursory look at these data across industries reveals considerable variation in intra-firm imports among industries. Some industries are largely traded between affiliated parties, while others are mostly traded between independent firms. Fig. 3.9, for instance, shows that while imports of electrical equipment, transport equipment, or computer and electronic products exhibit intra-firm shares higher than 50 %, the equivalent figures for livestock, leather, and fish products are close to 10 %. The results are very similar regardless of whether we consider the imports of all goods or the imports of intermediates only, which is a closer proxy to the goods traded in international production networks.[22]

[22]To eliminate the exports of final goods from the total flows of exports we employ the Bureau of Economic Analysis (BEA) 2002 Import Matrix and Input-Output table, which is disaggregated at the six-digit NAICS level. This information shows the share of imports that is used as intermediate inputs and the share of imports that is used for final consumption for each import at the six-digit NAICS level. We multiply the share of imports that is used as an intermediate with the flows of related and non-related party trade to eliminate the exports of final goods in each category. Then, we recalculate the ratio of related to total (related + non-related) exports. The use of I-O tables to separate intermediates and final goods has gained favor in recent years because it avoids the arbitrariness of classification schemes that divide goods into intermediate and other categories, as stressed by Hummels, Ishii, and Yi (2001).

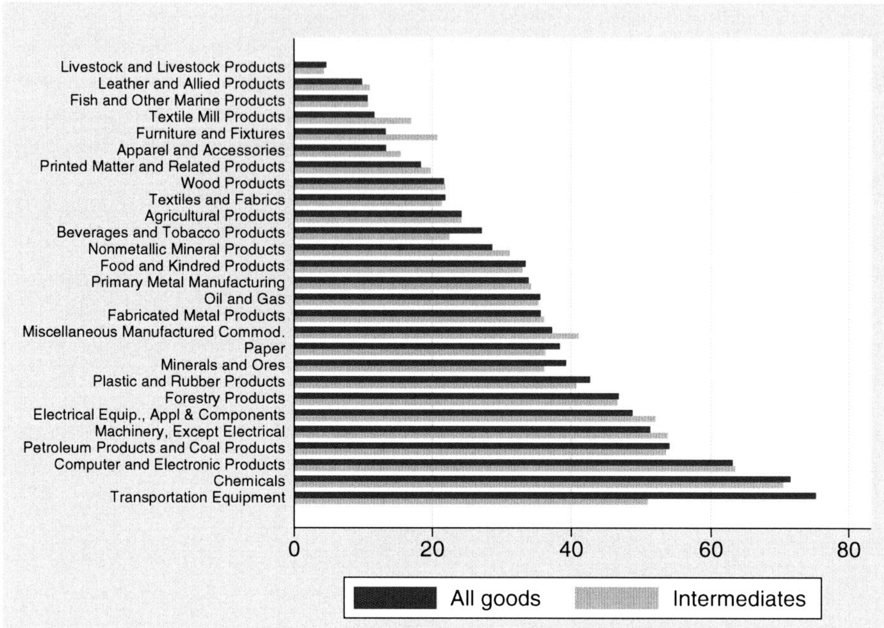

Fig. 3.9 Share of US imports that is intra-firm, by industry (three-digit NAICS), 2010. *Source*: Authors' calculations based on the Related Party Trade dataset from the US Census Bureau

While the results from Fig. 3.9 suggest that industry characteristics play an important role in the mode by which firms select to offshore their production, other factors might also drive the final outcome. However, it is possible that these other factors are masked by the averages for each industry. In Fig. 3.10, for example, we present an example for a particular industry: electrical equipment, appliances, and components (NAICS 335). Even though in Fig. 3.9 this industry has, on average, a share of intra-firm imports of around 50 %, the results from Fig. 3.10 indicate that the share associated with each exporting country varies from 0 to 100 %. A similar finding is observed in many other industries. This implies that the mode of offshoring is not completely determined by the industry characteristic. Some country characteristics of the supplier are also likely to play a role.[23]

The evidence presented in Figs. 3.9 and 3.10 indicate two groups of factors that determine the optimal mode of offshoring: those that are intrinsic to the production process (or the industry) and those that are related to country characteristics. Regarding product (or industry) characteristics, it is argued, for example, that the more standardized or codified the knowledge, the greater the chances that the offshoring will occur through independent contractors. Conversely, in highly knowledge-intensive sectors, and in industries where knowledge tends to be tacit

[23]Antràs (2014) also shows that US intra-firm shares vary (i) greatly across exporting countries within narrowly defined products and (ii) across products within exporting countries.

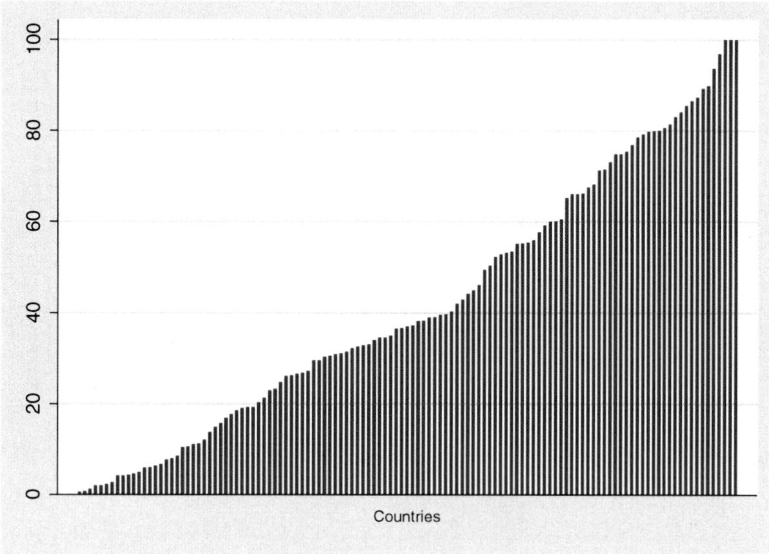

Fig. 3.10 Share of US imports of electrical equipment, appliances, and components that is intra-firm, by country of export, 2010. *Source*: Authors' calculations based on the Related Party Trade dataset from the US Census Bureau

and difficult to transfer, vertical FDI is more likely to occur. With respect to country factors, it is often argued, for example, that the capacity of the host country to enforce contracts plays an important role in the FDI vs. outsourcing decision. The prevailing view is that if contracts in host countries are hard to enforce, then multinationals have an incentive to internalize activities via vertical FDI to ensure that the parties abide by their obligations. But when the contractual environment strengthens, then outsourcing with external suppliers is more likely to occur.

In the last decade, a growing body of studies has analyzed this particular decision of whether to offshore through affiliates or independent contractors (Antràs, 2003; Antràs & Helpman, 2004; Antràs & Helpman, 2008; Costinot, Oldenski, & Rauch, 2011). A key feature from this literature is that there is indeed a tradeoff between employing independent contractors and opening affiliates, which depends on a complex interaction of factors, some of which are related to intrinsic characteristics of the industry and others to host country-specific factors.[24]

A brief summary of the key aspects of this literature can provide helpful insights. One industry-related aspect that affects the choice between vertical FDI and outsourcing is the factor intensity of the industry. The argument is based on the notion that local suppliers tend to have superior knowledge for hiring and managing local workers.

[24] The theory reviewed here is not the only one developed to explain the boundaries of multinational corporations (see, for instance, Buckley & Casson, 1976). Nevertheless, we focus on the most recent literature dealing with this issue, and particularly related to global supply chains.

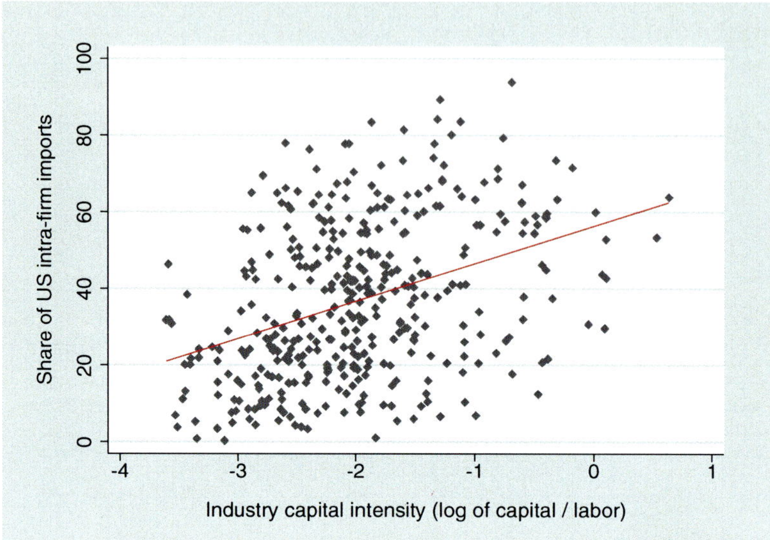

Fig. 3.11 Intra-firm trade and industry capital intensity. *Source*: Authors' calculations

Therefore, in labor-intensive industries, local management is important, and outsourcing tends to be the preferred choice for offshoring. In comparison, managing workers is a much less challenging proposition in capital-intensive industries, making the importance of local management less relevant. Therefore, in capital-intensive industries, vertical integration is more likely to occur. Figure 3.11 provides some support for this prediction. As shown by the trend line, the share of intra-firm trade is positively correlated with the degree of capital intensity of the industry.

Another factor that affects the choice between vertical FDI and outsourcing emanates from the first aspect and is related to country characteristics. Comparative advantage theory states that capital-abundant countries tend to specialize in capital-intensive industries. If vertical integration is the preferred arrangement for capital-intensive industries, as mentioned above, then capital-abundant countries are more likely to engage in intra-firm trade than capital-scarce countries. Figure 3.12 shows again some support for this prediction. Capital-abundant countries are more likely to engage in intra-firm trade, a positive relationship that is clearly visible in the figure.

Another important factor that influences whether or not offshoring will take place through vertical FDI or through independent firms is related to the nature of the contract between the parties involved. In general, if the product is easily "contractible," then firms fragmenting production internationally can turn to independent suppliers to source their inputs through outsourcing. When the product is not contractible, vertical FDI is favored because multinationals tend to internalize all production activities to ensure that all obligations are met. Again, this is shown in the data. Following Nunn and Trefler (2008), the proxy we use for the difficulty of writing contracts is the proportion of each sector's intermediate inputs that are not traded on organized exchanges or have reference prices; these conditions are likely to give rise to contracting problems. Figure 3.13 indeed shows that industries that

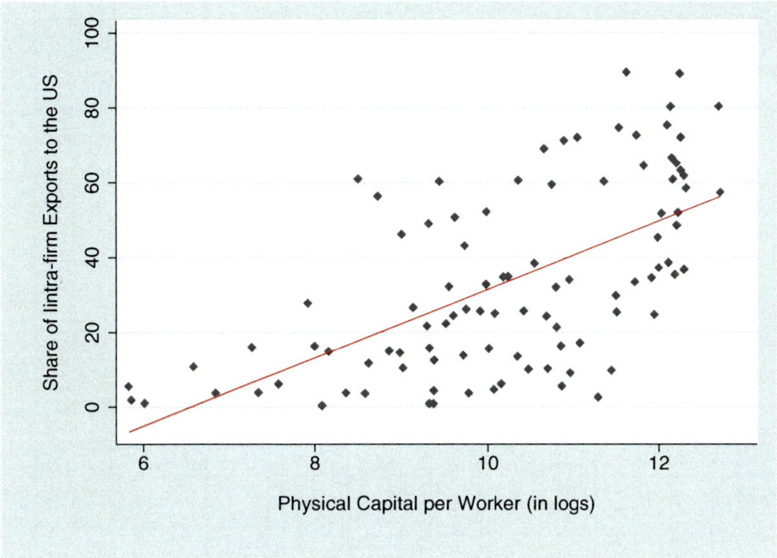

Fig. 3.12 Intra-firm trade and country physical capital. *Source*: Authors' calculations

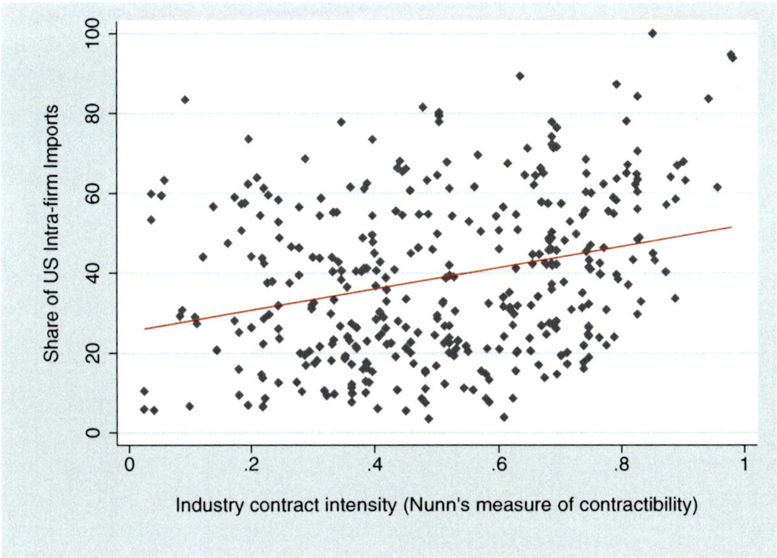

Fig. 3.13 Intra-firm trade and industry contract intensity. *Source*: Authors' calculations

are more contract intensive (and where contracting problems are more likely to be present) tend to have larger shares of intra-firm trade. In other words, in industries that are more susceptible to potential contracting problems, offshoring tends to occur between affiliated parties and less between independent firms.

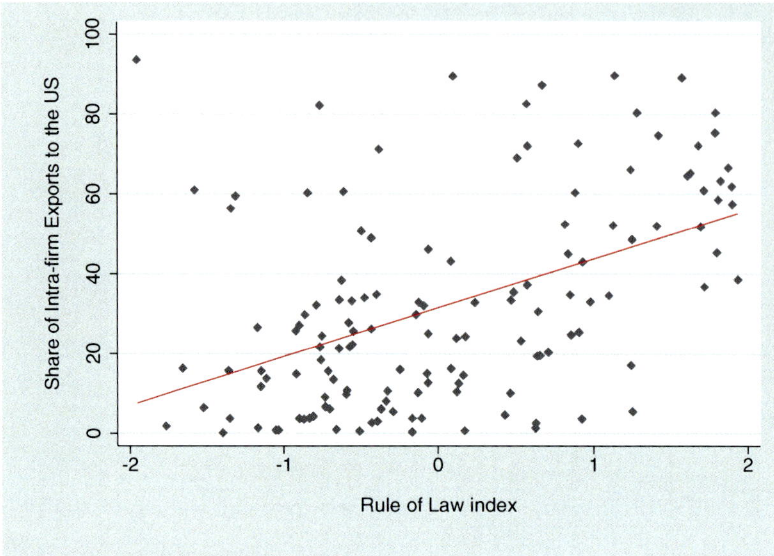

Fig. 3.14 Intra-firm trade and quality of contracting institutions. *Source*: Authors' calculations

It is important to note that the concept of contractibility depends not only on the characteristics of the good but also on the characteristics of the contracting institutions in the countries. In the first case, a product is contractible when its characteristics make it is easy to write a contract and verify the investments made by the parties. This is the industry-related aspect of contractibility.[25] In the second case, a product is contractible when it is easy to comply with a contract because the institutions in the country are adequate for doing so; this is the country-related aspect of contractibility.

The general view of the so-called transaction costs literature (e.g., Williamson, 1975, 1985) on this issue is that improvements in the contractibility environment of a host country tend to trigger an increase in outsourcing instead of FDI, because multinationals can rely more on the local legal system to ensure compliance with the contracts.

In Fig. 3.14 we show the relationship between intra-firm trade and a measure of the quality of the host country's contracting institutions. The figure suggests that countries with better contractual environments export more to the US through intra-firm transactions, which in principle goes against the prevailing view that vertical FDI is the most popular choice to deal with problems of weak contracting institutions. The results of the figure, however, do not test the transaction costs theory, because this

[25] Note that changes in technology might impact the contractibility of a product. For instance, it has been argued that many electronics manufacturing processes previously done by hand became automated due to a technological shift. This facilitated the transmission of otherwise complex information and contributed to the rise of contract manufacturing in the electronics industry (Sturgeon, 2002).

correlation might be affected by other factors. As we will show below in a more rigorous analysis, the relationship between the quality of contracting institutions and the mode of offshoring is not as linear as this graph suggests.[26]

While the results presented in Figs. 3.11, 3.12, 3.13, and 3.14 are suggestive, they are far from a thorough examination of the factors affecting the trade-off between vertical FDI and outsourcing. A more formal analysis (presented in Appendix B "Specification for the Model of Intra-firm Trade") is based on a recent body of empirical analyses that examine the drivers of the internalization decision (see Bernard et al., 2010; Carluccio & Fally, 2012; Corcos, Delphine, Mion, & Verdier, 2009; Tomiura, 2007). It is worth highlighting several findings from this analysis. First, the results show that, in general, industries that are capital intensive, skill intensive, and not easily contractible tend to be offshored more through vertical FDI, whereas labor- and unskilled-intensive industries as well as industries that are easily contractible are more likely to be offshored through outsourcing. Country characteristics also play a role. For instance, vertical FDI tends to be favored in countries with large physical capital endowments, large size, and adequate market access. These findings tend to support the evidence shown in the above figures.

The second result that should be stressed is that industry characteristics and country factors interact—sometimes in complex ways—to determine the final outcome regarding how offshoring is carried out. We can see this in the issue of contractibility. We have noted, for example, that in industries in which it is more complicated to set up contracts, vertical FDI is more likely to occur, and those industries thus exhibit higher shares of intra-firm trade. This is indeed the prediction of our econometric model, which is indicated in Fig. 3.15 by the positive slope of the blue line. However, as the red line of the figure also shows, the slope decreases in countries with better contracting institutions. In other words, even though vertical FDI is more likely to occur in industries where it is more complicated to set up contracts, this is less the case in countries with good governance. The reasoning is that multinationals can rely more on the local judicial system for compliance with the contracts. The result suggests that offshoring in industries susceptible to contracting problems might initially take the form of vertical FDI, and as contract enforcement improves, local suppliers may become more involved.[27]

[26] In principle, it could be argued that the results in Fig. 3.12 support the notion developed recently by Antràs and Helpman (2008) that a better contracting environment in the host country reduces the need to outsource to incentivize foreign suppliers to comply with contracts, thus tilting the balance towards vertical integration. As mentioned in the text, however, the correlation shown in the figure can be affected by many other variables. Therefore, a proper econometric exercise, such as the one shown in appendix B "Specification for the Model of Intra-Firm Trade", is needed to isolate the particular impact of the quality of contracting institutions on intra-firm trade.

[27] For industries not likely to experience contracting problems, the model predicts that the share of intra-firm trade will be higher in countries with good governance. That is, for industry contract intensity below 0.2, the red line is above the blue line. But even starting from small values of contract intensity, it is still the case that increasing the level of contract intensity of the industry raises the share of intra-firm trade less in countries with good governance than in countries with weak governance.

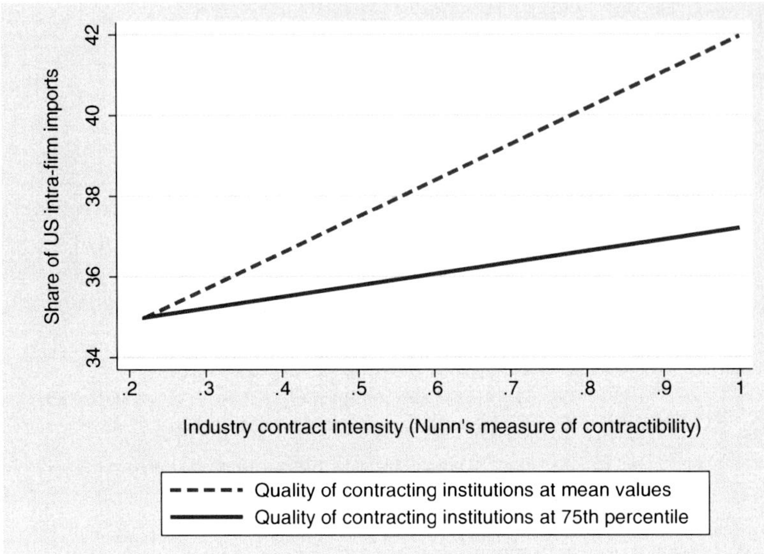

Fig. 3.15 Predicted relationship between intra-firm trade and contract intensity. *Source*: Authors' calculations. *Note*: The figure shows the predicted relationship between intra-firm and contract intensity according to the model estimated in column 2 of Appendix B "Specification for the Model of Intra-firm Trade". In the *blue line* the quality of contracting institutions takes the mean value of the estimated sample, while in the *red line* it takes the value of the 75th percentile. All the other variables of the model are measured at their mean values

Policy Issues

We have examined some of the factors that determine why some firms offshore part of their production process to external suppliers whereas others employ affiliated plants. While issues related to industry characteristics (e.g., capital intensity) or country characteristics (e.g., factor abundance) emerged as important drivers of this internalization decision, perhaps the aspect that deserves most elaboration in terms of policy implications is the issue of contracting institutions.

Therefore, we now move beyond the econometric results shown earlier and discuss in more depth how contracting institutions can shape the development of global value chains. It is argued that different legal jurisdictions across countries could segment markets in much the same ways that transport costs or tariffs do (Rodrik, 2000). For example, when an agent in a country reneges on a contract involving residents of foreign countries, local courts may be unwilling to enforce the contract, especially if such enforcement would adversely affect the local resident (Antràs, 2014). Another complication is related to enforcing a contract when the party having to pay damages does not have assets in the court's country. In general, then, ambiguous practices and uncertainty in contract enforcement can generate distrust between parties of different countries, thus limiting their willingness to engage in cross-border production sharing. While it is true that contractual frictions can undermine any international transaction, they can be particularly acute for transactions in global supply chains because many are related to significant relationship-specific investments. For instance, suppliers may customize their production to the specification of particular buyers. In this case, the outside option of this production might be close to 0 if the buyer decides to renege on the contract. Similarly, when the supplier does not commit to its contractual obligations, the buyer's investments are severely affected, as well as its reputation and ultimately the relationship with its own clients. Therefore, transactions in the global supply chain that typically entail customized intermediate inputs are particularly susceptible to contractual problems.

As mentioned earlier, firms might still locate slices of their value chain in countries with poor contracting institutions by establishing affiliates as a way to exercise more control. But even though this approach may facilitate the internal resolution of potential disputes, adequate contracting institutions might still be necessary. Even a multinational might need to resort to the legal institutions of a host country to solve problems with a subsidiary located there. For instance, the causes for removing a director of a subsidiary, contained in the bylaws of the company, might not apply to specific disputes, and thus the parent company might need to go to the local court of law to resolve the dispute.[28] It is also possible that the subsidiary itself might need to use local suppliers to conduct part of its businesses, and these local suppliers may not respect contracts and local courts may not enforce them; again, this situation will not be attractive for the multinational. Recent evidence from China supports this last claim. Feenstra, Hong, Ma, & Spencer (2012), for example, examine the cross-provincial variation in institutional quality in China to show that foreign firms located in China and engaged in processing trade[29] tend to export more out of provinces with good judicial systems. This implies that some level of contract enforcement might be important for enabling developing countries to join international production networks even when the participation takes place through foreign subsidiaries. Therefore, it is necessary to review the state of contracting institutions in the Latin American region.

[28] For instance, Hong Kong technology developer CDC Corp. sued its own subsidiary, CDC Software Corp., in Atlanta, to block a sale of part of CDC Software businesses to another company. It might have taken CDC Corp. as long as 2 months to hold a meeting and exercise its right to remove the board members that voted to approve the potential operation, so CDC Corp. asked the bankruptcy court in Atlanta to issue an emergency injunction to stop the deal from progressing (*The Wall Street Journal*, 2012). Another example is the Dutch trading card company Upper Deck International, which filed a lawsuit against its own Upper Deck Co. subsidiary in California, claiming that by counterfeiting the Yu-Gi-Oh! card game the subsidiary cost its parent company millions of dollars in legal fees, lost sales, and damaged reputation (Anime News Network, 2011).

[29] In other words, these firms are clearly inserted in international supply chains.

Table 3.3 Governance variables, simple average of countries in sample

Variable	Range	World	LAC	EU-27	Asia-Pacific
(1) No. of procedures for enforcing a contract	–	36.32	38.32	31.64	33.23
(2) Time for enforcing a contract, in days	–	604.14	733.28	540.76	398.92
(3) Cost for enforcing a contract, as % of claim	–	31.64	31.01	21.38	30.53
(4) Legal formalism index[a]	1 to 6	3.66	4.41	3.63	2.97
(5) Index of legal structure and security of property rights[b]	0 to 10	5.89	4.98	7.27	6.72
(6) Index of property rights[b]	0 to 100	49.01	45.83	70.02	52.86
(7) Index of protection of intellectual property rights[b]	0 to 10	5.48	4.51	6.85	6.23
(8) Rule of law index[b]	−2.5 to 2.5	0.05	−0.39	1.12	0.37

Notes: The table shows the simple average of the countries in the sample. The variables are: (1) the number of procedures for enforcing a contract; (2) the time (in days) for enforcing a contract; (3) the cost (as a percentage of the claim) of enforcing a contract from the Doing Business dataset, data for year 2012; (4) an index of legal formalism measuring the number of formal legal procedures necessary to resolve a simple case of collecting on an unpaid check, from Djankov, La Porta, Lopez-de-Silanes, and Shleifer (2003); (5) an index of legal structure and security of property rights, from the Fraser Institute, data for year 2012; (6) an index of property rights from the Heritage Foundation, data for year 2012; (7) an index of protection of intellectual property rights, from the Property Rights Alliance, data for year 2012; (8) an index of rule of law, from Kaufmann, Kraay, & Mastruzzi, 2006

[a]Higher value corresponds to worse governance outcome

[b]Higher value corresponds to better governance outcome

Table 3.3 presents a battery of indicators that proxy the quality of contracting institutions for countries in Latin America as well as in other regions. The table shows the following variables: (1) the number of procedures for enforcing a contract, (2) the time (in days) for enforcing a contract, (3) the cost (as a percentage of the claim) of enforcing a contract, (4) an index of legal formalism measuring the number of formal legal procedures necessary to resolve a simple case of collecting on an unpaid check, (5) an index of legal structure and security of property rights, (6) an index of property rights protection, (7) an index of intellectual property rights protection, and (8) an index of the rule of law.[30,31]

[30] Measures (1) to (3) come from the Doing Business dataset, measure (4) originates from the work by Djankov et al. (2003), and measures (5) to (8) come from the Fraser Institute, the Heritage Foundation, the Property Rights Alliance, and Kaufmann et al. (2006), respectively.

[31] Measures (1) to (4) correspond to the costs of enforcing straightforward contracts; measures (5) to (7) address the concept of property rights, and measure (8) deals with the broader concept of the rule of law. Even though there might be differences between the role of contracting institutions and the role of property rights institutions, there are also many commonalities, since both sets of institutions relate to the protection of individuals from opportunistic behavior (Acemoglu & Johnson, 2005). As such, we include in the table the property rights measures as additional indicators that capture the general level of respect for existing agreements among citizens.

The table clearly indicates that Latin America has a generally subpar record in terms of the quality of contracting institutions, compared with other regions. For instance, while the average time for enforcing a contract in the Asia-Pacific countries is 398 days, the corresponding figure for Latin America is 733 days. Similarly, while the average cost (as a percentage of the claim) for enforcing a contract in Europe is 21 %, the cost in Latin America is 31 %. Similar poorer performances are seen along the property rights index and the rule of law measure. Latin America is outperformed even by the world average in all the variables of the table except for the cost of enforcing a contract. The consistency of these comparisons suggests that the region must improve its institutions charged with regulating and enforcing contractual agreements. An example closer to the ground is presented in Box 3, which illustrates a case in which the issue of contractual uncertainty specifically undermined access to international supply chains.

Box 3: Uncertain Contract Environments and Participation in GVCs

How can uncertain contract environments limit the chances of many firms from participating in global value chains? A case involving a group of Brazilian firms that started as suppliers and subcontractors of Embraer, the Brazilian aircraft producer, might help to answer this question.

Following its privatization in 1994, Embraer went through a process of vertical disintegration in which the firm focused on its core activity as a system integrator while outsourcing most peripheral components. This vertical disintegration promoted the birth of new Brazilian firms that were founded mostly by former Embraer employees. These firms were typically small- and medium-sized and participated almost exclusively as Embraer suppliers. Over time, however, they adopted strategies for joining the global supply chains of other aircraft producers and subsystem manufacturers. In the process, they received support from Apex, the Brazilian Trade and Investment Promotion Agency.

Apex's strategy was to create an export consortium among these firms to enable them to overcome two major constraints. First, many of the activities necessary for accessing international markets, such as participating in international fairs, developing marketing strategies, or solving logistics weaknesses, entail many fixed costs; firms participating in the consortium could share these costs. Second, in the commercial aircraft industry, aircraft producers tend to give preference to suppliers that can provide complete products rather than small parts or partial components; consortium participants could supply a more complex product through the complementary work of each party.

The consortium, called High Technology Aeronautics (HTA), consisted of eight small and medium enterprises. Each member paid an entrance fee and a monthly charge to support the consortium's activities, and each had one vote in the general meetings. According to its statutes, HTA would sign a contract directly with a client and subcontract the production to individual members.

(continued)

Box 3: (continued)

While the idea of the export consortium looked good on paper, it did not work well in practice, particularly in the area of contractual practices. According to Apex, Brazil does not have adequate legal provisions for regulating consortia. Therefore, the agency decided that all of what they termed "exporting consortia" receiving its support—including HTA—should adopt the legal structure of a nonprofit association. This decision became the Achilles' heel of the initiative. In addition to the obvious limitation that this type of association cannot have profit as its main goal, casting the HTA as a non-profit association had other shortcomings. For example, the assets of the association could consist only of the fees paid by its members and other funds and donations, and the associates were not directly liable for the association's obligations. In an attempt to deal with some of these weaknesses, the HTA decided to constitute itself as a private limited liability company, 99 % owned by the nonprofit association. However, this partial remedy was not sufficient to overcome the original limitations.

The flaws of the HTA's design became evident after it proved incapable of entering into contracts with global firms in the industry. For instance, after Pratt & Whitney, a global producer of turbines, contacted HTA, Pratt & Whitney decided to write a contract directly with one of the members of the consortium rather than with HTA. The reason was that Pratt & Whitney did not feel sufficiently secure in entering into a contract with a consortium formed as a nonprofit association that lacked significant assets. In addition, Pratt & Whitney did not know at the outset the identity of the company that would effectively be responsible for the production of the components.

While this example shows the difficulties of legally characterizing associative forms such as a consortium, it also illustrates the more general issue that global firms might be reluctant to engage in partnerships with local suppliers if there is uncertainty and ambiguity in contracting practices.

Source: based on material from Cafaggi et al. (2012) and Joppert Swensson (2012).

Service Offshoring: Grasping the Intangibles

Chapter 2 described the increasing trend of international fragmentation of production not only in goods but also in services. Global production networks originally involved the offshoring of manufactured intermediate inputs, but firms are also increasingly locating business functions abroad that were traditionally performed in-house. These services include computer software development, accounting, auditing and bookkeeping, and database and other information services, which for the most part can be delivered electronically; in other words, they are intangibles. We also showed in Chap. 2 that the performance of Latin America in exporting some of

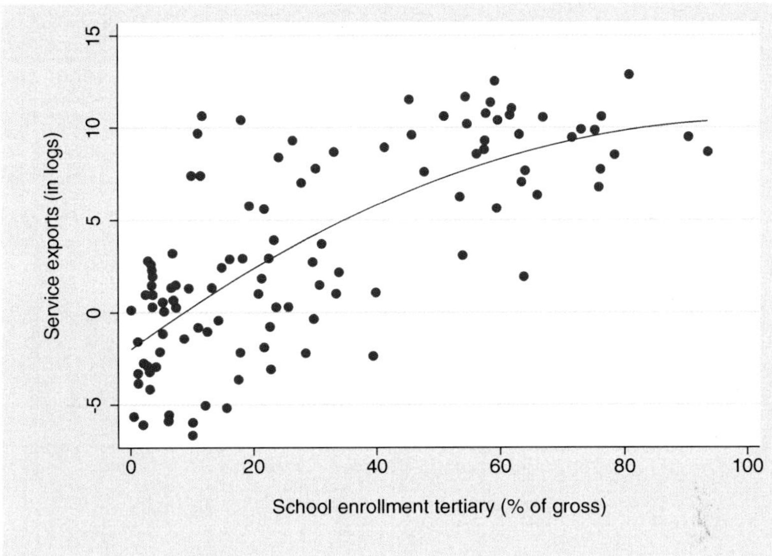

Fig. 3.16 Service exports and human capital. *Source*: Authors' calculations

these services is on average below the norm. In this section we discuss some of the main factors that can improve the prospects of exporting these types of services.

The literature examining trade in services is quite extensive (for a general treatment of the subject, see Mattoo, Stern, & Zanini, 2008), and the list of potential determinants is as varied as the type of services being offshored. For instance, countries endowed with beautiful landscapes are likely to export tourism services, while countries with a long history of financial development are likely to export financial services. Similar to trade in goods, a country's comparative advantage, determined in part by relative endowments, can go a long way in shaping the patterns of specializing in exports of specific services (Deardorff, 1985). Nevertheless, a growing body of empirical studies indicates that at least two factors seem to be important for exporting a wide range of services related to GVCs: an adequate pool of human capital and a satisfactory telecommunication infrastructure that facilitates the electronic delivery of the services (Amin & Mattoo, 2008; Freund & Weinhold, 2002; Lennon, 2006; Lennon, Mirza, & Nicoletti, 2009; Mirza & Nicoletti, 2004; Shingal, 2010).

Figures 3.16 and 3.17 present the correlations between the exports of some GVC-related services and measures of human capital and telecommunication infrastructure, respectively. In particular, we add the exports flows of two service categories: "computer and information services" and "miscellaneous business, professional, and technical services."[32] The latter category includes services related

[32] The source is the Service Trade Database of the United Nations.

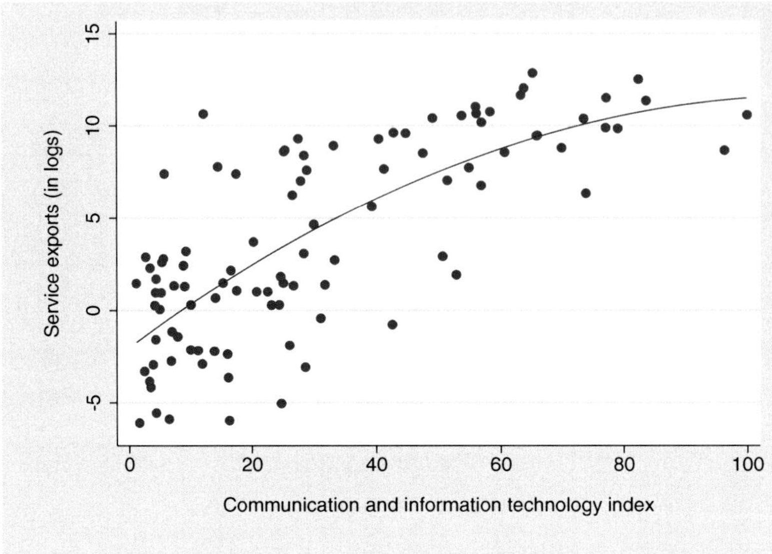

Fig. 3.17 Service exports and ICT. *Source*: Authors' calculations

to business and knowledge process outsourcing. The measures of human capital and telecommunication infrastructure are the country's tertiary education school enrollment and the index of information and communication technology presented earlier in this chapter. This preliminary evidence shows that indeed there is a positive correlation between the exports of these GVC-related services and measures of human capital and telecommunication infrastructure.

However, there is considerable variation in the data, indicating that the relationships between the exports of these services and the explanatory variables are not perfect. The reason is that other factors also affect the prospects of exporting these services. In what follows we perform an econometric analysis that controls for the impact of different determinants. The standard model in this literature is based on a gravity equation that relates bilateral exports of services between two countries to the income per capita and the size of those countries, the quality of the telecommunication infrastructure in both countries, a proxy for the level of human capital in the exporting country, and a vector of bilateral variables that includes the distance between the countries and whether the countries share a common border, language, and colonial ties (for a summary on gravity models for trade in services, see Grover, Gupta, Mattoo, & Sáez, 2012). We follow this specification in a model that also controls for time-invariant country and sector characteristics and also for shocks that may affect all the countries at the same time (for more details, see Appendix B "Specification for the Model of Service Offshoring").

The results, shown in detail in Appendix B "Specification for the Model of Service Offshoring", confirm the existence of the positive relationship seen in Fig. 3.16 between the exports of GVC-related services and human capital.

Interestingly, when we examine the role of different proxies of human capital, including the secondary (and tertiary) school enrollment ratio and the total number of pupils at the secondary level, we obtain the most robust and significant relationship with the last variable. This suggests that while the quality of education may be an important factor, this by itself might not be enough if there is not a sufficiently large pool of individuals with the right skills to supply the market. This finding echoes recent analyses of, for instance, Costa Rica, which argue that even though the country has a good educational system, it needs to increase the quantity of human capital to continue thriving in the information and knowledge-intensive sectors (OECD, 2012).

The second important result from the estimation is that having an adequate ICT infrastructure is also associated with superior performance in service exports. The estimation shows that good ICT is important for both the exporting and the importing countries: such infrastructure facilitates not only sending but also receiving the information at the other end.[33] Another result worth highlighting is the role of languages. The findings imply that countries sharing the same language tend to trade these services 30 % more than countries that do not share the same language.

A final notable result of the estimation is the role of distances. There is a general notion that the growth of Internet penetration in the last two decades has allowed many companies to locate business functions previously performed at home in other countries. The results from our ICT infrastructure measure support this notion. But if the Internet is all that it takes to offshore business services abroad, we should not see any role played by distance when examining the determinants of this type of trade. However, the econometric results indicate that distance generates a negative and significant impact. Other authors have found the same: physical distance reduces the exports of commercial services (Lennon, 2006) as well as finance, IT services, and miscellaneous services (Head, Mayer, & Ries, 2009). The study by Head et al. (2009) is interesting because its year-by-year estimations are consistent with the general notion of the growing importance of the Internet and the diminishing effect of distance from 1996 to 2006. The authors also find that the distance effect does not disappear entirely, but settles after the initial decline. In our own exercise, we also run year-by-year specifications similar to those in Head et al. (2009) and find some support for the decreasing role of distance (see Fig. 3.18).

The fact that distance matters implies that even though many of these services are provided through the Internet, they may need to be tailored to the specific buyer's requirements and monitored for quality. Some of these activities might require face-to-face interactions at some point, and in general they are likely to be more effective if the buyer and the provider are located not too far apart. This has been confirmed by other authors who have analyzed the specific role of Internet penetration in service trade (Freund & Weinhold, 2002).

[33] Similar results are obtained in Mirza and Nicoletti (2004).

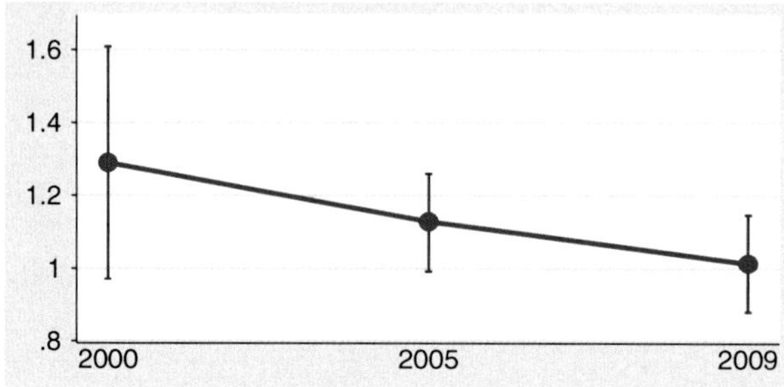

Fig. 3.18 Estimated impact of distance on service exports. *Source*: Authors' calculations. *Note*: The figure shows the elasticities of bilateral exports of services with respect to distance, estimated with the negative binomial model for 3 different years (see Appendix B "Specification for the Model of Service Offshoring"). The *vertical lines* denote the 95 % confidence intervals

Policy Issues

The export of certain business or knowledge-intensive services can demand specific skills that might change quickly over time. The econometric results in this section indicate that with respect to human capital, it is not only the quality but also the quantity of individuals that is important. Sustaining an adequate pool of skills can be challenging. Sometimes the difficulty is education curriculums that do not prepare students with the skills needed for employment in a changing labor market. In many cases, countries have succeeded in overcoming this problem by creating alliances between the private sector, academia, and the public sector. In the Philippines, for example, the Technical Education and Skills Development Agency works in collaboration with the private sector to sustain an adequate pool of professionals in business process outsourcing (BPO) services. Some of the areas in which the agency is involved include surveys to gather information about the required skills, curriculum design, accreditation systems for training institutions, and funding of intensive training programs for college graduates who are not quite ready for the workforce.

The lack of an adequate pool of skills can also be addressed at least temporarily by employing foreign nationals. However, this may be difficult in many countries where stringent restrictions are imposed on the entry of professionals from other countries. Figure 3.19, for example, shows a restrictiveness index for the temporal movement of professionals in accounting and auditing services. Even though, on average, Latin America compares favorably with other regions, many countries impose restrictions that are quite high. In general, greater liberalization of professional and technical services can be an effective way to supply capabilities required to serve specific segments of the offshore services.

The econometric results also show that a common language plays an important role in providing GVC-related services. This represents an opportunity but also a

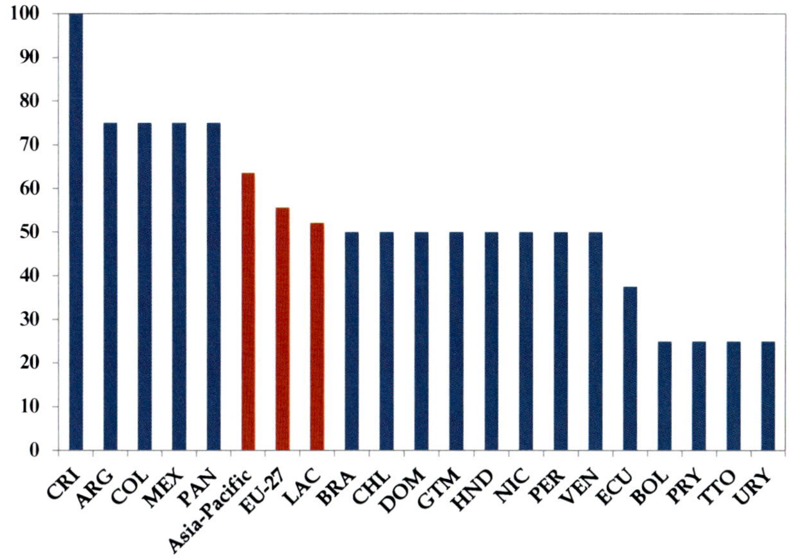

Fig. 3.19 Restrictiveness index for trade in accounting and auditing services, 2008. *Source*: Authors' calculations based on the Services Trade Restrictions Database (WB). *Note*: The figure shows the service trade restriction index for trade in accounting and auditing services. The index goes from 0 to 100, with higher values representing higher restrictions

challenge for many countries in Latin America, particularly for services aimed at the North American market. For instance, there is a growing Spanish-speaking market in the US, with a traditional demand for "call center" services, but which could eventually require IT and specialized business services as well. This is clearly an opportunity. However, the largest market in the US will continue to be the English-speaking segment, and the results from the model imply the importance of developing proficiency in English if this segment is to be targeted.

The fact that proximity plays a significant role in the provision of many services gives Latin America an edge relative to distant countries in Asia or Europe in targeting the US market. The region's advantages are particularly significant for exporting business functions that might require similar time zones or involve specific customization to the client's needs, and for which proximity is an important factor. Box 4 presents two examples in Latin America of firms specialized in exporting customized IT services to the US; in both cases, proximity to clients clearly contributed to their success.

Finally, it has been noted that the countries in Latin America should coordinate efforts to attract more offshore services to the region to encourage potential clients to identify the region as a favorable hub for offshoring (Gereffi, Castillo, & Fernandez-Stark, 2009). Greater collaboration across the region might take the form of cross-fertilization of experiences and ideas, as well as cooperation in disseminating information regarding the region's capacities, attributes, and qualities.

Box 4: Exporting Customized IT Services

It has been well documented that when a product specification cannot be easily codified (for instance, because the product requires customized features), the buyer and supplier engage in frequent face-to-face interactions and high levels of explicit coordination to ensure that the relevant information is properly transmitted (Gereffi et al., 2005). This is the case not only in manufacturing but also in services. Following are two examples of firms in Latin America that had an advantage in exporting customized IT services to the US because proximity facilitated the transmission of such knowledge between the clients and the providers.

<u>Avionix.</u> Embedded software integrates systems from third-party electronics components. In the aeronautics industry this software can be very sophisticated and tends to be customized to a product's particular specifications. For example, the new Boeing 787 Dreamliner requires about 6.5 million lines of tailor-made software code for the plane's avionic and onboard support systems.

In 1998, Avionix opened its first engineering facility in Melbourne, Florida, to develop avionic embedded software. In 2004, the firm opened a second engineering facility in San Jose, Costa Rica. Over the next 3 years, all the engineering operations were moved to the Costa Rica facility. Avionix has completed projects for virtually every aircraft subsystem, including navigation, weather/traffic/terrain surveillance, communication, flight control, cockpit displays, etc. The main clients of Avionix are in the US, for which the firm develops software customized to the client's specifications in a process that requires a continuous flow of communication between Avionix and the client.

According to the company, Costa Rica offers important advantages over other major IT offshoring destinations, such as India. The advantages are most significant for the development of customized software for clients located in the US. For instance, a similar time zone with the US is very important for arranging weekly teleconference status meetings, which are necessary to meet coordination needs.

Proximity is critical for other reasons as well. For example, unlike PC or Web development projects, hardware containing the embedded project is generally developed in parallel with the software. This requires a great deal of communication with the client. Also, multiple revisions of the hardware may need to be shipped offshore to the supplier to support the development of the software, and proximity helps to keep these shipping costs low relative to the more distant competitors, such as India.

<u>Softek.</u> There is a growing trend for outsourcing IT services for functions ranging from software development to monitoring and managing a company's IT systems, including website creation, database analysis, data storage, and testing.

(continued)

Box 4: (continued)

The Mexican firm Softek provides a wide range of IT services, including application-related services, software testing, server and datacom services, and procurement services. While the company's initial clients were located in Latin America, Softek ventured into the US market after realizing the critical importance of proximity to customers in need of swift solutions to business problems.

According to the company, geographic proximity is particularly important for scoping projects and assessing clients' needs. The company targets a market niche of tailor-made software applications and IT services that require direct, agile, and constant communications with the client. The firm's location in Mexico qualifies it for NAFTA's short-term visas, which facilitate quick trips to the US. Such flexibility and agility to respond to client needs is not necessarily offered by large software producers in distant countries, such as India or China. By differentiating its products, targeting the tailor-made software market, and using proximity to its advantage, Softek avoids direct price competition with its counterparts in Asia.

These examples illustrate how the region can successfully compete with lower-cost IT offshoring destinations in Asia by exploiting segments of the offshore services in which there are clear comparative advantages, such as in the tailor-made and customized solutions. These are products in which the exchange of tacit information between the buyer and the supplier requires frequent face-to-face interactions as well as a great deal of coordination. Similar time zones and geographic proximity provide a natural competitive edge for delivering these services.

Sources: the example of Avionix is based on material from Monge-Gonzalez and Zolezzi (2012). The case of Softek is based on material from Brown-Grossman and Domínguez-Villalobos (2012).

Chapter 4
What It Takes to Join an International Value Chain: The Firm-Level Evidence

The previous chapter examined factors affecting global value chain participation that are mostly external to the firm, such as the role of a country's transport infrastructure or the quality of its contracting institutions. Now we turn to determinants of GVC accession that are specific to the firms themselves, such as skills and capabilities. The theme of this chapter is that participation in international production networks typically demands skills and capabilities that often exceed levels found in firms that only serve the domestic market. While firms are responsible for the development of their own capacities, they also face constraints in attaining these capacities that include lack of information and coordination. In this chapter we discuss policy options for reducing these constraints.

No Ordinary Firms

The literature on GVCs has emphasized that firms in global production networks are usually associated with critical firm capabilities. Incentivized by the prospects of receiving a contract from a global buyer, potential suppliers may undertake improvements on their own (Javorcik, 2008). Once they join an international production network they may continue to acquire knowledge and experience from their buyers (Humphrey & Schmitz, 2002; Schmitz, 2006; Schmitz & Knorringa, 2000). As a result of this knowledge, and since they are required to have higher competencies, these firms tend to produce goods of higher quality than other firms in their countries.

An increasing number of case studies have shown that access to a global production network is indeed associated with the acquisition of critical capabilities and high-quality goods. Analyses have been carried out in many sectors, including apparel (Gereffi, 1999), motorcycles (Fujita, 2011), agroindustry (Cafaggi et al., 2012), and the computer industry (Kawakami, 2011). In this section we provide

J.S. Blyde (ed.), *Synchronized Factories: Latin America and the Caribbean in the Era of Global Value Chains*, DOI 10.1007/978-3-319-09991-0_4

additional systematic evidence showing that participation in production networks is associated with improved competencies and higher-quality goods.[1]

The section that follows combines a detailed dataset of multinational companies with plant-level data from Chile to analyze the performance of affiliates of multinationals located in that country that provide inputs to their parent firms in other countries (vertically integrated affiliates). The aim is to determine whether these firms have an edge in capacities and outcomes compared to other Chilean firms. The argument is that suppliers in global production networks need superior capabilities to successfully perform in value chains, and these capabilities should be evident in a number of firm characteristics. Several caveats are in order here. First, the evidence we are presenting is for one country and cannot automatically be applied to other countries. Second, the challenges for acquiring capabilities are likely to differ between affiliates of multinationals and independent suppliers. Again, this requires some caution before generalizing the results to all types of suppliers. We will review below a number of additional analyses developed for other countries and for different types of suppliers and discuss how the results compare to those shown here. Finally, the exercise does not intend to establish causality between the formation of capabilities and participation in GVCs, but only correlations. Additional material presented later in the chapter will examine the nuances behind the relationship between GVCs and the acquisition of capabilities.

We start by analyzing whether vertically linked affiliates have superior capabilities relative to other firms in the country with respect to size, share of skilled labor, and level of total factor productivity.[2] A proper examination of these factors must compare these attributes across firms in similar sectors. To this end we run an econometric model that meets this requirement. The estimation also includes a variable that controls for whether the firm is an affiliate of a multinational company or not. This allows us to separate the potential effect of ownership from the effect of belonging to a GVC. Detailed information regarding the econometric model and the data sources appear in appendix C "Specification for Measuring the Performance of Vertically Linked Affiliates".

We first compare the vertically-linked affiliates with all the other firms in the survey, which include other exporters as well as non-exporters. The results are shown in Fig. 4.1 (dark brown bars). Vertically linked affiliates compare more favorably than the rest of the firms in all three variables: they tend to be larger, employ

[1] This is related to a more general discussion in the trade literature about the productivity effects of exporting. According to this literature, firms may undertake substantial investment to improve performance prior to exporting, and they may also improve their performance (productivity) after entering export markets (see, e.g., Alvarez & López, 2005; Aw, Chung, & Roberts, 2000; Bernard & Jensen, 1999, 2004; Clerides, Lach, & Tybout, 1998; De Loecker, 2013; Fernandes, 2007; Harrison, 1994; Pavcnik, 2002).

[2] In recent trade models, productivity is the single factor that captures the capability of the firm to export successfully (see Arkolakis, 2010; Bernard, Eaton, Jensen, & Kortum, 2003; Chaney, 2008; Melitz, 2003).

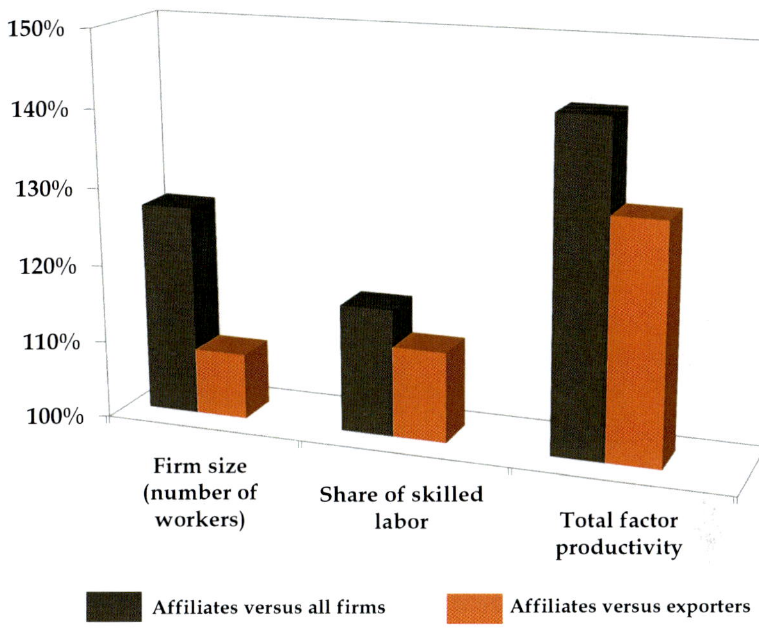

Fig. 4.1 Comparison between vertically-linked affiliates and other firms across various characteristics, Chile. *Source*: Authors' calculations

about 27 % more workers, have 16 % more skilled workers, and have 42 % higher total factor productivity. Then, we compare the vertically linked affiliates with only the exporters (orange bars); as the figure shows, their superiority over the exporters is slightly lower than before, but it remains present in all three variables.

We also compare export outcomes of vertically linked affiliates in terms of the following variables: total value of exports, number of products exported, and average exports per product. Once again, we compare firms in similar sectors (see appendix C "Specification for Measuring the Performance of Vertically Linked Affiliates"). The results are shown in Fig. 4.2: vertically linked affiliates demonstrate stronger export performance than the rest of the exporters. For instance, vertically linked affiliates have around 82 % more exports, export about 17 % more products, and have 32 % more exports per product than the other exporters.[3] The general evidence, then, indicates that the vertically linked affiliates have superior capabilities and outcomes compared to the other exporters.

It is worth mentioning that the effects we found in terms of GVC participation are different from those associated with foreign ownership (see Appendix C "Specification for Measuring the Performance of Vertically Linked Affiliates").

[3] We also compared the two groups in terms of export unit values as a measure of quality and found no significant differences. It has been noted, however, that export unit value is an imperfect measure of quality (Hallak & Schott, 2011).

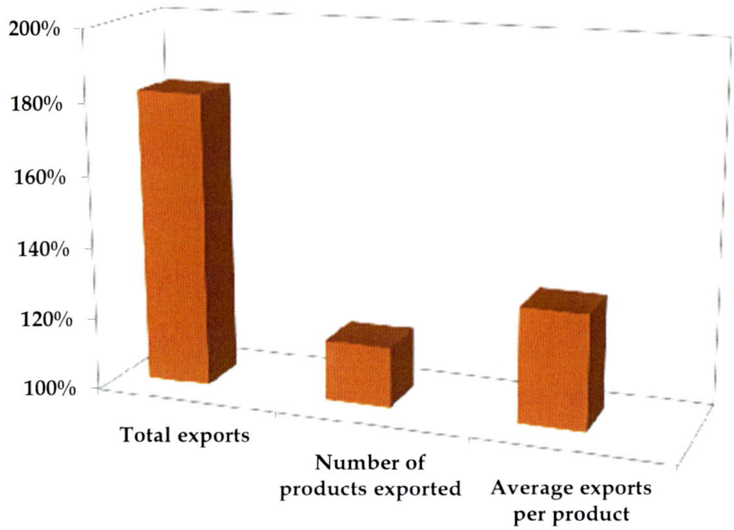

Fig. 4.2 Comparison between vertically linked affiliates and other exporters across various measures of export performance, Chile. *Source*: Authors' calculations

Indeed, we ran an additional exercise (not shown) in which we compared only company affiliates. We found that the affiliates of multinationals that are inserted in GVCs have superior capabilities than the affiliates of multinationals that are not inserted in GVCs. The reason could be that affiliates that provide inputs to their parents in other countries are exposed to higher standards than the affiliates that only serve the domestic market.

While the exercise that we present in this section focused only on one mode of offshoring—vertical FDI—other studies have found similar results: firms participating in international production networks (not only affiliates of multinationals but also local independent suppliers) tend to have superior capabilities and outcomes than other firms. For instance, a study of Italian firms shows that independent local suppliers that serve firms abroad also tend to have greater productivity levels than other firms in the country (Agostino, Giuntam, Nugent, Scalera, & Trivieri, 2011). An increasing number of studies also show that suppliers selling inputs to global firms located in their own countries have improved capabilities relative to other local firms (Gorodnichenko, Svejnar, & Terrell, 2010; Javorcik & Spatareanu, 2009). In one example of this latter set of studies, Iacovone, Smarzynska Javorcik, Keller, and Tybout (2011) described how Walmart provides local manufacturers of consumer goods with a larger market but at the same time puts pressure on these suppliers to improve their products' appeal. Their analysis showed that after Walmart entered Mexico, the high-quality upstream suppliers of merchandise and food expanded their sales and became more productive, whereas the low-quality suppliers experienced reductions in both sales and productivity.

The evidence in this section and the literature in general indicates that firms in developing countries seeking to join international production networks must improve skills and capacities—typically to levels above those of the average local firm—to meet the standards of global players.

In the next section we use case studies to dig deeper into the relationship between the capabilities of firms in Latin America and their ability to join international production networks. The case studies evaluate not only affiliates of multinationals but also independent suppliers. Examining the experience of these firms provides insights into what it takes to become part of an international production network and in what specific characteristics the firms that became engaged in a GVC differ from other firms. By establishing the empirical regularities that make these firms successful members of global supply chains, we can provide additional insights on policy issues that might help other firms achieve similar outcomes.

Empirical Regularities from Case Studies

In this section we summarize the results of ten case studies prepared for this report with the aim of increasing our understanding of the drivers of GVC participation. We use the case studies to highlight common characteristics among firms participating in international supply chains and discuss what these common characteristics tell us about challenges and obstacles involved in GVC participation.

Each case study analyzes a firm in Latin America that successfully joined an international production network by providing intermediate inputs or services to other firms abroad, either as a subsidiary of a MNC or independently through contractual agreements. The case studies encompass the following industries and countries: footwear and auto parts in Argentina, aeronautics and coffee in Brazil, food products in Colombia, software and electronics in Costa Rica, and IT services and aeronautics in Mexico.[4] The methodology for the case studies was informed by an emerging literature on GVCs that emphasizes governance aspects of these chains, and thus the characteristics and power relations across the various participating units (see, for instance, Gereffi, 1999; Gereffi, Humphrey, & Sturgeon, 2005; Humphrey & Schmitz, 2000).

[4] The case studies were developed as part of the IDB research project International Fragmentation of Production and Insertion of Latin America and the Caribbean in Global Production Networks. The corresponding references are the following: González, Hallak, Schott, and Soria (2012); Cafaggi et al. (2012); Meléndez and Uribe (2012); Monge-Gonzalez and Zolezzi (2012); Brown-Grossman and Domínguez-Villalobos (2012).

It is natural to expect differences among the cases; after all, each study analyses the experience of a particular firm in a given country and industry. While each case has its own peculiarities and idiosyncrasies, we found surprising similarities in the characteristics of the firms participating in these networks. We group these similarities into five empirical regularities. We now describe each of these five empirical regularities and use examples from the case studies to illustrate them.[5] Then, we comment on what these empirical regularities reveal in terms of challenges and policy implications.

Empirical Regularity 1: Prior Exposure to International Practices and/or Markets

The first empirical regularity that we observed in almost all the cases is prior international business experience. Typically, the manager, the CEO, or the owner of the firm had some exposure to international practices and/or markets even before the firm was established.[6] Two examples illustrate this point. The first one is from Basso, an Argentine firm that manufactures combustion engines and has become a successful supplier to automakers around the world (see Box 1, Chap. 3). In the beginning, the company sold valves exclusively in the domestic market. It later entered the international markets, largely as the result of the international experience gained by the elder son of one of the company's owners as an electromechanical engineer at one of Basso's steel suppliers in France and then at Renault plants in France and Argentina. These experiences gave him critical technical knowledge not only about valves, engines, and materials, but also about the organization and business practices of global automakers. In particular, working for Renault gave him first-hand knowledge about the relationships global firms expect to have with their suppliers. Later, when he started work in Basso, he introduced changes in the production methods and the organization of the firm that became critical for the company's entry into several international supply chains.

---

[5] Note that this does not intend to create a taxonomy for value chain participation. After all, the evidence is based on only ten cases of firms that are all located in LAC. The purpose of this exercise is to highlight common characteristics that could reveal particular challenges that firms in the region are facing to join GVCs.

[6] This evidence is consistent with other studies that examine the relationship between prior international experience and exports in general. For example, Artopoulos, Friel, and Hallak (2013) describe case studies in which export pioneers had previous experience working and/or living in foreign markets. Molina and Muendler (2013) and Mion and Opromolla (2010) show that firms that hire workers and managers with previous experience in exporting firms are more likely to export.

The second example is Graúna, a Brazilian producer of parts and components for airplanes that has supplied global companies that include Pratt & Whitney, Boeing, Airbus, and Cessna. Graúna was established by ex-employees of Embraer, the Brazilian airplane maker, an experience that gave the new company's executives exposure to international practices and methods. Graúna gained additional expertise by selling inputs and components to Embraer. These associations with Embraer proved instrumental in helping Graúna to eventually join the supply chains of some of the foremost aircraft integrators in the world.[7]

Empirical Regularity 2: Targeting of Market Segments Based on Some Form of Comparative Advantage

The second empirical regularity among the case studies is that firms join international supply chains by targeting segments of the markets where they have a comparative advantage. In some cases, these comparative advantages have been resource based, such as the insertion of Brazilian coffee grower Daterra in the supply chain of Illy, the Italian coffee roster. In other cases, the companies have exploited the relative spatial and cultural proximity with the US to enter segments of industries in which the relationship with the buyer required frequent face-to-face interactions.[8] This was the case, for instance, for software companies in Costa Rica (Avionix) and Mexico (Softek) in targeting tailor-made software to the US market, where their ability to provide rapid and flexible solutions gave them an advantage over giant companies in distant India and China (see Box 4, Chap. 3). Another example of purposely selecting specific market niches where comparative advantages can be exploited is Tosone, an Argentine footwear producer. In this case, the firm explicitly avoided engaging in direct price competition with lower-wage Asian countries by targeting high-quality design-intensive shoes not oriented to the mass market, and where volume and low factor costs were not vital for survival.

Empirical Regularity 3: Painstaking Accumulation of Capabilities and Use of Certifications as Evidence of Proficiency

Once firms target a specific segment of the market, they accumulate capabilities to the point where they receive at least some form of certification as evidence of proficiency. This was the situation in almost every case analyzed, from the resource-based Brazilian coffee grower Daterra, which obtained ISO 14001 certification for

[7] Benefits in these cases may include not only technical knowledge but networking as well.

[8] This is typically refer to as "relational linkages."

expertise in production sustainability, to the highly technical Costa Rican aircraft software developer Avionyx, which obtained a DO-178B certification required by the US Federal Aviation Administration on software safety attributes. In some of the cases, the contract the firm signed with the buyer included support for certification as part of the agreement. In other cases, potential suppliers obtained certifications on their own to raise their profile and thus their potential for joining GVCs. Some firms regarded the certifications as business cards, which they used to introduce themselves to potential clients.

Empirical Regularity 4: Firms Leveraged Resources and Collaborated with Other Peers to Address Common Challenges

Evidence from the case studies indicates that firms seldom join an international production network on their own. Instead, they tend to leverage resources with other firms, particularly as a means for attaining certain capabilities. Sometimes they address information or coordination problems by engaging in various forms of collaboration, such as clusters or business associations. One example is Graúna, the Brazilian subcontractor in the aeronautic industry mentioned earlier. Graúna increased its production scale, financial structure, and technological capacity through a merger with two other companies and a venture capital group. This enabled Graúna to offer the technological and financial capabilities needed by the global aircraft firms. Another example comes from Tosone, the Argentine footwear supplier. In order to service a global buyer in Sweden, Tosone had to offshore part of its own production process to upstream suppliers in Brazil because its own capabilities were not sufficient to comply with the high standards required by the Swedish buyer.

Examples of less formal forms of cooperation provide equally useful insights. In one, auto parts producers in Rafaela, Argentina, formed a group for lobbying the government to improve trade facilitation issues. Another example is the business association of coffee growers in Brazil that collected fees to pay for the fixed costs of participating in international trade fairs.

Empirical Regularity 5: Continuing to Learn and Improving Capabilities Even After Joining a GVC

Another interesting aspect that we observed in many of the case studies is that firms do not stop accumulating capabilities after joining a global network. Indeed, in some cases this process intensified. One example is Hugo Restrepo, the Colombian firm profiled in Box 1, Chap. 1 that provides chili pepper paste to the American company McIlhenny. Even after the two companies signed a long-term agreement, Hugo Restrepo had to continuously acquire key technical knowledge on crop management and production. Indeed, over the course of 15 years after signing the first contract, McIlhenny sent experienced agronomists to Colombia twice a year to check on the crops and to make sure that Hugo Restrepo was incorporating the latest technological innovations.

The second example is Daterra, the Brazilian coffee grower mentioned previously. Daterra began operations in the low-price, low-quality local commodity coffee market, but meticulously accumulated skills to enter the high-price, high-quality supply chain of Illy. Entering Illy's supply chain only marked the beginning of Daterra's road to improving its capabilities. Daterra continued to acquire technical knowledge through its relationship as a supplier of Illy. Indeed, after some years the two firms formed a joint venture in genetic research to develop new varieties of coffee. The exposure of Daterra to this global company allowed the firm to eventually sell to other specialty coffee buyers around the world. Today, Daterra sells less than 2 % of its high-quality coffee to Illy; in 2000 it sold virtually its entire production to that firm.

In this section we have presented five empirical regularities drawn from a group of ten case studies of LAC firms that participated in international supply chains. It is important to mention that these regularities should not be read as necessary conditions to join GVCs. Some firms successfully participated in production networks without having all of these regularities at the same time.

The evidence presented here will certainly not settle the discussion of what it takes to join an international production network successfully, since the analysis looks at only a small sampling of firms. Nevertheless, this evidence does highlight major issues that help determine a firm's successful participation in global supply chains, particularly firms in Latin America and the Caribbean. In the next section we return to each of these empirical regularities and discuss what they reveal in terms of challenges associated with GVC participation, and the lessons they hold for policy makers.

Policy Lessons from the Empirical Regularities

International exposure. The first empirical regularity regarding international exposure reveals a challenge that is all too common in accessing international production networks: information failures. Lack of information is the reason for many failed attempts to meet quality standards demanded by lead firms. This can be the case for domestic producers, for example, which may operate in local environments that tolerate quality defects and business practices that are unacceptable in developed countries. As such, these firms might not know what it takes to comply with the rigorous standards imposed by lead firms in international supply chains, or they might not understand the importance of adhering to those standards (González et al., 2012).

Information problems can be particularly acute in many international supply chains. Suppliers typically need to customize their production to the requirements of particular buyers, while buyers need to convey this information to the suppliers and make sure they are capable of delivering the product with the correct specifications. In other words, the information flows that are typically required for a match between a buyer and a supplier in an international supply chain can be vast, and lack of information can easily keep potential suppliers on the sidelines while buyers rely only on a few known providers. Exposure to international practices and/or markets can certainly facilitate access to information, which may explain why evidence of prior international experience was so widespread in the successful cases summarized in the previous section. The challenge is to identify policy measures that can address the problem of lack of information.

Traditional government actions designed to deal with information problems in the area of international trade fall on the shoulders of export promotion organizations (EPOs). Therefore, an obvious area for public policy relates to efforts for strengthening export promotion. EPOs may offer training for inexperienced firms on export procedures, marketing, and business negotiations. EPOs may provide information on trade opportunities abroad as well as specialized counseling and technical assistance for taking advantage of these opportunities. They may also coordinate, support, and co-finance participation in international trade missions and trade shows, and arrange meetings with potential foreign buyers (Volpe Martincus, 2010). But these actions do not always materialize. Evidence from the case studies, for example, shows that EPOs do not always properly prepare firms before trade fairs; or, the business rounds they generate fail to properly match the capabilities of domestic firms with the requirements of foreign buyers. In general, the effectiveness of the EPO's actions to help firms become part of international supply chains is proportional to their efforts in gathering information regarding the structure, the modes, and the specific conditions of these supply chains.

Another policy option for reducing information gaps is to promote environments that facilitate exchanges of information between players in the industry or across industries. While it is natural that firms compete with each other, successful players often are willing to share their experiences with their peers. For instance, ProChile, the country's EPO, conducts a coaching program in which a group of potential exporters meets with a mentor to share its experience in the international markets. Such information exchanges can be helpful in various ways. Sometimes, potential exporters are not fully aware of the steps or procedures that might be required to attain and maintain quality standards, or they might not even be convinced that such efforts are worth the trouble. Exchanges with successful peers can be an effective way to internalize this information. Similarly, information exchanges can help spur quality upgrades that might serve many different firms, even different industries. For instance, if many firms can benefit from the same type of input modifications or the same quality of upgrades, policy efforts could promote information exchanges between the relevant players that could eventually lead to the desired upgrade (González et al., 2012).

Governments also can help organize exchanges where the information gap is filled by current or retired staff from international buyers. These experts can provide clinics on what buyers expect from their suppliers, in workshops organized by sectors. This was the approach taken by the Department of Trade and Industry in the Philippines through its Product Specialists Program. Another approach is to send representatives of local firms abroad rather than bring specialists to them. This strategy has been used by the Indian Export-Import Bank through its Indian Export Marketing Fund (Egan & Mody, 1992).

Exploit market segments with comparative advantages. Regarding this second empirical regularity, one could argue that firms naturally target market segments where they can survive. But we do not know whether this is always the case, in large part because we lack information about firms that have failed in their attempts to join GVCs. What is revealing from the successful cases that we observe is that they all consist of firms seeking to exploit some clear forms of comparative advantage. The policy discussion here is whether the government should encourage firms to target some sectors or market segments and not others; in other words, whether public support should engage in "targeting."

The issue of targeting as a public policy can be controversial because the government appears to be "picking winners." Moreover, the discussion as to whether public agencies should engage in targeting does not pertain solely to the GVC arena, and thus the issue is not going to be settled here. What the case studies show, however, is that effective policy efforts like the one mentioned above in export promotion require gathering vast amounts of information on different aspects of the GVCs. Gathering this amount of information is not practical without some form of prioritization. Not surprising, therefore, various studies indicate that targeting in both export promotion and investment attraction is more effective than not targeting (for a summary, see Blyde, Pietrobelli, & Volpe, 2014). The guidance that the case studies from this report could provide is that if targeting is going to be part of public policy, it should be aligned to the country's comparative advantages.

Certifications, visibility, and credibility. Support for our third empirical regularity regarding firms meeting international standards as a condition for accessing GVCs can be found in other studies (see Morrison, Pietrobelli, & Rabellotti, 2008). The importance of standards and certifications obviously varies by type of industry and even by products. In general, however, compliance with standards has become an important condition when global firms screen potential suppliers (Humphrey & Schmitz, 2008; Nadvi, 2004; Quadros, 2004). The public sector could help to establish standards or facilitate their implementation by the private sector.

Note that implementing standards and certifications could entail additional production and trade costs to the suppliers, as compliance might require adapting products and/or practices, building administrative systems, auditing, and testing or investing in new technologies. Indeed, some early cross-country evidence suggested a negative relationship between standards and entry into export markets (e.g., Chen, Otsuki, & Wilson, 2006). However, more recent individual country analyses with more disaggregated data indicate that standards are associated with increased exports (Volpe Martincus, Castresana, & Castagnino, 2010). Moreover, the new evidence generally shows that benefits in terms of increased exports tend to outweigh compliance costs (see, for example, Mangelsdorf, Portugal-Perez, & Wilson, 2012; Masakure, Henson, & Cranfield, 2009; Otsuki, 2011).

Compliance might not necessarily be mandatory when implementing quality standards and certifications. A group of firms interested in signaling their ability to deliver higher-quality goods could develop and attain quality labels to increase visibility and overcome information barriers. The public sector could also develop expertise in creating and managing such labels and fostering their implementation by the private sector (González, et al., 2012). Local certifications, however, could have minor or no effects if the global buyers do not know them or are skeptical of their value. Therefore, in developing and implementing standards, links could be formed with standards and certification institutions in developed countries, since these confer greater credibility (Egan & Mody, 1992).

Besides certifications, buyers sometimes look at the credit rating of potential suppliers to determine whether their businesses are sustainable. Often, however, credit ratings are not available. Governments in the region could promote the provision of credit rating services, perhaps with the assistance of international agencies.

A final area related to credibility concerns the reputation of the country. The buyer may assume that the technological capabilities of the supplier or its overall skills reflect the country's development or economic level. Buyers can hold initial negative expectations of a potential supplier if the country's reputation is not good. One way governments can improve their countries' image is by identifying exemplary plants and inviting international buyers to tour them (Egan & Mody, 1992).

Cooperation. The fourth empirical regularity is the cooperative activities firms carry out among themselves to raise capabilities, address common barriers, pay for the fixed costs of certain activities like assisting for an international trade fair, etc. Government support for such cooperation could be particularly important to solve coordination problems. For instance, an assembly plant might not be able to start operations because there are no local suppliers of a particular component; conversely, a potential supplier of that component might not initiate production because there is no local downstream demand for its product and the component may be costly to export (Trindade, 2005). Another example of a coordination problem is that a supplier might not invest in improving its production process without a buyer's commitment to establish a long-term relationship; but the buyer might not support such improvements unless the supplier assures the buyer will have exclusive benefits.

Therefore, cooperation among firms may not materialize for a variety of reasons, and public policy may be useful in making it happen. Some examples follow below. One area relates to mergers and acquisitions (M&As). Acquiring a wide range of skills might be particularly important for firms in certain industries such as aeronautics, which tend to give preference to suppliers that can deliver complete products rather than sub-components.[9] A small firm might not have all the skills to produce a complete product on its own, but it might be able to do so by acquiring another firm and its capabilities. M&As can also be important given recent trends in consolidation, in which buyers are using only the most capable and largest suppliers

[9]There is also more general evidence indicating that in some industries, such as electronics (Sturgeon & Kawakami, 2010) and automobiles (Van Biesebroeck & Sturgeon, 2010), lead firms appear to prefer larger, more capable first-tier suppliers that operate globally.

and eliminating the others (Gereffi & Frederick, 2010; Milberg & Winkler, 2010; Sturgeon & Kawakami, 2010).

The typical problem facing small firms contemplating a merger or acquisition is the lack of sufficient investment capital to carry out the operation, despite the likelihood of large future benefits. Public policies could be designed to fill this intertemporal gap, as shown by the example mentioned above of the Brazilian firm Graúna, which merged with two other companies and a venture capital group. Graúna benefited from a program run by the Brazilian development bank BNDES, which provides temporary capital for small and medium-sized firms.[10] The program has two notable features: first, BNDES always acquires less than 50 % of the shares of the company to avoid taking control of the firm; and second, BNDES exits from the company capital after 4 years, a period that is deemed adequate for the firm to succeed in its business and to buy the shares back from BNDES.

Other countries elsewhere in the world also offer programs to support M&A. One example is the Economic Development Board (EDB), an autonomous government agency in Singapore that offers a mergers and acquisitions scheme that consists on an allowance of 5 % of the value of the acquisition, a tax deduction for the transaction costs, and stamp duty relief on the transfer of shares.

These examples of government designed programs aim at encouraging companies to grow their business and shorten the time needed to acquire capabilities through M&As. Clearly, there is not a one-size-fits-all program; each design might depend on a number of factors, including the country's anti-trust laws. One should also not to expect that M&As can be the panacea at all times. The business world is full of examples of M&As that have failed to live up to expectations, although there is also an increasing body of literature offering advice on how to minimize the chances of M&As going sour (e.g., Papadakis, 2007). In general, however, the empirical research supports the positive effects of M&As. It has been shown, for instance, that after M&As, many firms have been able to use synergies from asset complementarities to introduce new products, improve cash flows and/or increase exports (Beena, 2006; Hoberg & Phillips, 2010; Pulak & Neha, 2012).[11]

Public action can also help to strengthen business associations or create new ones in sectors where they are lacking. Empirical analyses, including some of the evidence reviewed in the previous section, show that industry associations often have helped to address information problems by collecting fees to pay for participation in international trade fairs, producing international publicity, developing joint marketing strategies, creating certification schemes, or forming a united front in the negotiation of raw materials, among others. Wagner (2012), for example, shows that firms that engage in international trade rely more than other firms on business associations, even after controlling for country and industrial sector and after conditioning on productivity.

[10] In particular, the Program for the Capitalization of Technological-Based Companies (CONTEC).

[11] Note that other programs that subsidize SMEs might delay this process of consolidation; therefore, efforts should be made to ensure that if M&A programs are pursued, they are not hampered by potentially incompatible initiatives.

In some cases, however, business associations are weak or are designed for rent seeking rather than constructive work. Therefore, governments could support sectors that wish to improve their organization (Altemburg & Meyer-Stamer, 1999). For example, the Brazilian Specialty Coffee Association (BSCA) received support from the Brazilian Trade and Investment Promotion Agency that enabled it to carry out several important initiatives. These included helping its associated firms participate in international fairs and establish classifications and certifications. These initiatives enabled many coffee growers to overcome the asymmetric information problems that were restricting their participation in the supply chains of international roasters (see Box 1).

Governments can also implement programs to encourage collective action among private firms, such as Chile's Associated Development Programs (Programas Asociativos de Fomento, PROFO), run by CORFO, the country's economic development agency. In this program, resources are transferred to a group of firms instead of to an individual company, in a competitive process in which the firms design and present a common project. Anecdotal evidence indicates that the program helped the

Box 1: Strengthening Business Associations

Brazilian coffee growers and the Illy supply chain. For decades the worldwide coffee business was structured almost exclusively around the commodity model prevailing when coffee was regulated with a target price in the international market and an allocation of export quotas among producing countries. The collapse of the system in 1984 generated economic incentives for the development of a market in which coffee could be differentiated by quality or processes (e.g., organic).

The Italian firm Illy, a medium-sized roaster, went to Brazil, attracted by the high quality of the country's coffee cherries. It quickly discovered that problems in processing the cherries into quality coffee were mainly due to the lack of incentives for producers to invest in high-quality production methods. Illy created an award for the best coffee beans and established a price differential to reward quality. But the company did not teach prospective producers the precise characteristics of superior coffee and how to identify these characteristics. Some of this knowledge is tacit, and its acquisition requires a great deal of practice and learning.

The information the growers needed was ultimately provided by an intermediary: the Brazilian Specialty Coffee Association (BSCA), which received the support of the Brazilian Trade and Investment Promotion Agency. BSCA developed a special classification system, a certification scheme, and a technical training program that enabled many growers to learn how to identify the characteristics of a high-quality coffee. This eventually enabled some of the growers to reach Illy's standards and join its supply chain.

Source: Based on material from Cafaggi et al. (2012).

country's wine industry by supporting the efforts of private firms to build common wineries or create wine-related business associations (Dini, 2009). More formal evaluations also found positive effects among participating firms (Benavente & Crespi, 2003; Maffioli, 2005). Although the program has not focused specifically on the participation of firms in global supply chains, its core aim of reducing the transaction costs in inter-firm collaboration certainly supports this objective.

Firms that lack the full range of the capabilities needed to meet international standards have also experimented with consortium schemes, in which different companies share their skills in an arrangement that is relatively formalized under a legal framework; these schemes sometimes have received government support. The design of the consortium is a fundamental issue in these initiatives. Box 3, Chap. 3, for example, shows that consortia can run into problems if they are not well designed—for instance if the buyer does not know with certainty which consortium member is ultimately responsible for the production process.

On some occasions purely inter-firm collaboration would not be enough. Cooperation between the public and private sector might be required, particularly for providing a specific public good. This was the case in the creation of a customs office in the Argentine city of Rafaela. As seen in Box 1, Chap. 3, this facility, which resulted from the coordinated lobbying efforts of private firms and city officials, was instrumental in creating an improved logistics environment that greatly facilitated the participation of auto parts firms in international supply chains (see Box 1, Chap. 3).[12]

A final policy area associated with promoting complementarities among firms relates to a country's levels of trade protection. An example is the Argentine supplier that offshored part of its own production process to upstream suppliers in Brazil, a practice that firms often use to complement their own capabilities with those of their peers in other countries. Accordingly, governments in the region should be aware of the potentially injurious effect of tariff barriers, import quotas, or non-automatic renewal of import licenses, in limiting the access of local suppliers to high-quality inputs from abroad.

Ongoing learning. The evidence from the case studies indicates that ongoing learning is a widespread practice. Indeed, in some cases, the improvement of capabilities was assisted by the buyer or the lead firm after accession to the GVC.

The buyer may promote learning by supplier firms through different means, such as sending international experts to train local workers (as in the case of Hugo Restrepo and McIlhenny), conducting training in the buyer's plant, or even providing online lessons (Egan & Mody, 1992). This is consistent with a literature on GVCs showing that suppliers in production networks receive training and knowledge from lead firms. This, however, does not suggest that an initial contact between a local supplier and a global buyer is sufficient to develop these capabilities. As the previous empirical regularities indicate, a great deal of preparation from the supplier on its own might be required to gain initial access to an international production network.

[12] For a more general discussion on public policies for promoting more collective actions among private firms and between the public and private sector, see Pietrobelli, Casaburi, and Maffioli (2014).

Additionally, the transmission of knowledge from lead firms to suppliers does not necessarily occur automatically, as it might depend on a host of different factors (see Pietrobelli & Rabellotti, 2011). For instance, lead firms may transfer some knowledge to their suppliers because failing to do so might entail risks for themselves (Humphrey & Schmitz, 2002; Schmitz, 2006; Schmitz & Knorringa, 2000).[13] However, the literature on GVCs stresses that while global firms are likely to support suppliers to improve the production process for the inputs that they are buying, or to improve the quality of those inputs, they do not tend to support actions that would enable the suppliers to carry out activities that are close to the global firm's core competencies, and thus potentially bypass them in the supply chain, or even enter the market as competitors (Egan & Mody, 1992; Humphrey & Schmitz, 2002; Kaplinsky, 2005).[14]

Nevertheless, the overall issue that emerges from this empirical regularity of long-term learning is that the ability to succeed as a member of an international supply chain might depend on the supplier engaging in a continuous process of adaptation to the changing conditions of a supply chain. This point is reinforced by two trends in GVC practices: the constant assessment of alternative sourcing points and the process of consolidation.

For example, a recent survey conducted by the University of Michigan and the Supply Chain Management Review at 164 companies from around the world indicates that lead firms increasingly reassess possibilities for optimizing their supply chains.[15] Sixty-five percent of these companies indicated that they constantly rethink existing sourcing points by evaluating current and potential suppliers. They do so partly in response to changing economic conditions in the sourcing countries, such as variations in salaries, fluctuations in exchange rates, or modifications in taxes and regulations, which force lead firms to re-optimize their sourcing strategies. Another reason is changing trends in global supply chain strategies and the constant introduction of new practices. The introduction of new practices often means that suppliers constantly must adapt and develop new capabilities and strengths. Box 2 presents concrete examples of new supply chain practices increasingly implemented by lead firms around the world that demand superior capabilities from suppliers. All this means that writing an initial contract with a lead firm does not necessarily guarantee a long-term relationship in an international production network. Suppliers must constantly adapt to new supply chain requirements or risk being replaced by other suppliers.[16]

---

[13] For example, the arrival of a component with the incorrect specifications can shut down entire production lines until all the correct inputs have been assembled, thus delaying production of the final product.

[14] In the GVC jargon, this has been referred to as the willingness of the lead firms to support their suppliers in actions leading to "process" and "product" upgrading, but much less to "functional" upgrading (Humphrey & Schmitz, 2000, 2002).

[15] Eighth Annual Global Survey of Supply Chain Progress.

[16] Note that constant adaptation to new market conditions is also important for firms engaged in final goods trade.

Box 2: Adapting to Changing Supply Chain Strategies
The increasing importance of supply chains for many firms has given rise to a supply chain management field that aims to optimize supply chain structures through the efficient integration of suppliers, factories, warehouses, and stores to ensure that the merchandise is produced and distributed in the right quantities, to the right locations, and at the right time, while minimizing total system costs.

The supply chain management field is constantly evolving, and new strategies are introduced and applied by many corporations. Lead firms use many of the strategies to manage uncertainty or to cope with supply chain disruptions. Very often these strategies require that suppliers develop greater capabilities to adapt to more demanding environments. In Chap. 3, for example, we saw how just-in-time delivery services put great demands on suppliers and on the logistics systems of their countries. Below are three additional examples of supply chain strategies increasingly implemented by lead firms that require top performance from their suppliers.

<u>Postponement.</u> Lead firms occasionally must delay the final customization of a semi-finished good until the exact customer specifications are fully known; this strategy is known as postponement. Consider, for example, a company A that sells T-shirts in its own stores but outsources the manufacturing process to suppliers in other countries. Under a traditional arrangement, the T-shirts are produced by the suppliers according to predetermined demand forecasts. Once they are completed they are shipped to company A's stores. Suppose that due to the forecast analysis, all the T-shirts are dyed green. If demand suddenly changes to red, company A's stores are now stuck with a product that nobody wants and that can't be changed. Under a postponement arrangement, however, suppliers keep stocks of undyed T-shirts in their facilities until company A tells them which color they should be dyed. Postponement, therefore, reduces the chances of unwanted merchandise due to changing market demands. Note, however, that this arrangement requires more capabilities on the part of the supplier. For one thing, the burden of inventory holdings is shifted to the suppliers, which must warehouse an inventory of undyed T-shirts. In addition, they need a more agile production system, capable of stopping at a semi-finished stage and resuming quickly once the final specification is known.

<u>Supply chain risk mitigation.</u> The 2011 earthquake and tsunami in Japan clearly demonstrated how natural disasters can disrupt global supply chains. Many Toyota, Honda, and Nissan suppliers had to shut down plants, which significantly reduced production. Honda and Nissan, for instance, saw their domestic production fall by more than half. While the natural disaster in Japan was clearly a rare event, many other kinds of incidents frequently occur that can bring supply chains to a halt. Examples are machine breakdowns, contamination, strikes, and political instability. Accordingly, lead firms increasingly engage in strategies to mitigate potential supply chain disruptions.

(continued)

Box 2: (continued)

One such strategy is to build resilience across the supply chain by creating redundancy. For instance, lead firms employ redundant suppliers that are geographically diversified, so if a disaster hits a supplier in one location, the same input can be sourced from a supplier in another location. Clearly, increasing redundancy represents a pure cost increase for the lead firm, but these costs tend to be considered an insurance premium. The redundancy strategy may also take the form of requiring a supplier to increase reserves or to develop plans for disruptions in internal operations. In these cases, the supplier must hold excess inventory or design contingency plans. In this way, supply chain risk mitigation strategies tend to demand higher capabilities from all the members of the chain, including the suppliers.

Cash-to-cash cycle. The time required to convert raw materials or inventory purchases into sales revenue is called the cash-to-cash cycle. This is generally related to inventory turn: the higher the inventory turn, the quicker the cash conversion. For instance, if a lead firm has to pay its suppliers immediately after receiving intermediate inputs, and then holds inventory for days before its own sales are completed, the firm will not be able to use this cash for other purposes during this period. At the other extreme, if the firm sells the final product before paying its suppliers, in effect it enjoys free inventory and may even earn interest by investing cash while awaiting the payment date. Supply chain management strategies related to inventory turn are typically geared towards reducing the period between the date of investing in inventory purchases and the date of collecting cash from the customers.

One way lead firms can reduce the cash-to-cash cycle is simply by delaying payment to their suppliers until cash from their own sales is collected; this is illustrated in Fig. 4.3, with the example of five companies. The blue bars measure the average number of days it takes for each of these companies to pay its suppliers, while the red bars indicate the average number of days the companies hold inventory before completing their own sales. In all the cases, the blue bars are higher than the red bars, meaning that the suppliers are financing the lead firms when they hold inventory. Once again, this practice requires capable suppliers with working capital sufficient to carry them through long periods of time before collecting cash from selling their intermediate goods.

The three practices shown in this box illustrate how suppliers are addressing increasing challenges through the use of agile and adaptable production processes as well as adequate financial capabilities.

(continued)

Box 2: (continued)

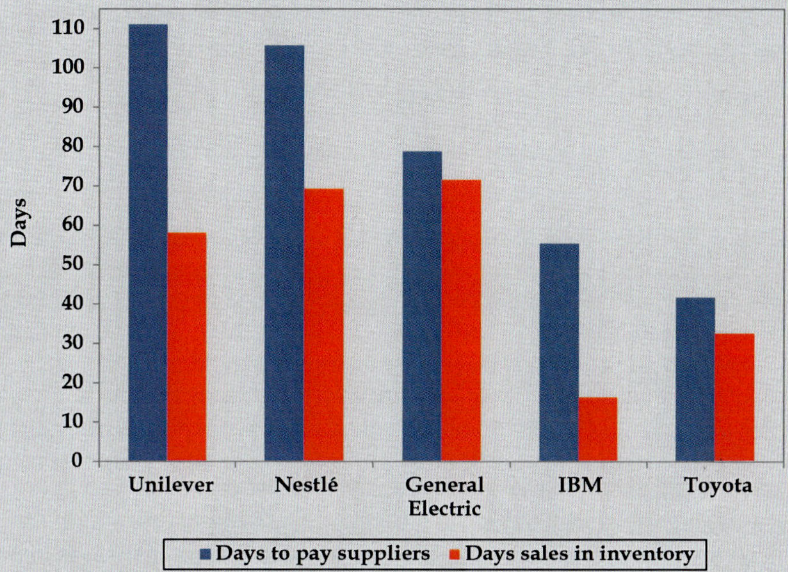

Fig. 4.3 Key indicators of cash-to-cash cycle in selected firms (2012). *Source*: Authors' calculations based on the companies' annual reports, 2012

A second trend, which has been ongoing for more than a decade and which was exacerbated after the global financial crisis of 2008, is the consolidation of GVCs. While buyers are always looking for information about good suppliers in case a need arises, these same buyers are increasingly reducing the number of their suppliers and forging closer arrangements with the most capable performers. By working more closely with fewer suppliers, buyers can visit the suppliers' plants more frequently, make direct assessments of problems, and help to reduce various business uncertainties, all of which ultimately lower overall costs (Egan & Mody, 1992). While consolidation can be a threat to current suppliers, it can also be seen as an incentive to continue to improve performance and join a selected group of suppliers.[17]

The most important message to take away from this last empirical regularity is that supplier firms cannot regard the job of improving capabilities as a one-time effort. They must continue to learn and upgrade their capabilities even after they initially break into the network. This might have implications for public policy too, although at

[17] For potential suppliers, however, consolidation may imply that the window of opportunity to break into a network might be smaller today than in the past.

a broader scale. For instance, providing public support in the form of a sector-specific public good or to solve a coordination failure does not mean that the same sector might not require another specific public good down the road, or might not face a new coordination problem in the future. This kind of support should be continuous.

Local Linkages

Participating in international production networks is not limited to firms that export intermediate goods or services to companies in other countries. Firms in developing countries might also take advantage of the increasing fragmentation of production by becoming upstream suppliers to international companies (e.g., multinationals) located in their home countries, and which themselves are inserted in GVCs. While this could be the most reasonable strategy for many small and medium firms in developing countries, it does not constitute a way of sidestepping issues discussed earlier regarding firms' skills, capabilities, and product quality. As illustrated by the example of the Brazilian coffee growers inserted in Illy's supply chain (see Box 1), issues regarding firms' capabilities remain important even if the supplier does not export directly. Nevertheless, it is reasonable to expect that the challenges of joining an international production network are reduced when the hassles of exporting directly are taken out of the equation. This is particularly the case for small and medium firms.

Fostering linkages between local upstream suppliers and international firms located in the same country can be important even for countries deeply engaged in international production networks, such as Mexico. For instance, even though thousands of firms in Mexico directly export through supply chains to the US, there is a general perception that the insertion has been mostly in assembly operations, and that additional Mexican value should be incorporated in the international production networks in which the country participates. Box 3 presents statistical evidence supporting this perception.

Countries in various parts of the world have been pursuing programs to foster backward linkages between global firms located in their territories and local suppliers. In this section we take a look at some of these programs, which are generally designed to address information and coordination failures.[18] Experiences from different countries illustrate how these issues were addressed.

[18] Multinationals might not have sufficient information about the existence of potential suppliers and/or their capabilities, which may result in selection bias and reliance on previously known suppliers. On the other hand, potential suppliers might not have the information needed to improve their capabilities or to access the resources needed to contact potential multinationals. Coordination problems might also inhibit backward linkages: multinationals might not transfer knowledge to potential suppliers, for fear that they might go off to serve other firms and take the knowledge with them. For their part, potential suppliers might not engage in costly relationship-specific investments, for fear the relationship will be short-lived.

The Costa Rican program Linkages for Exports (Encadenamientos para la Exportación)[19] was created in 2001 to increase the domestic value added from high-tech multinational companies and help SMEs become local suppliers of these companies and subsequently direct exporters by expanding their technological capacity. The program, which is administered by PROCOMER, the country's national trade promotion organization, is a business matchmaking service based on the multinational firms' demands. In the program, the needs of these companies for inputs and raw materials are identified and then matched with local suppliers that can meet the required production, technical, and quality specifications and product characteristics. The program also seeks to create business opportunities through small projects jointly carried out by local SME suppliers and multinational firms to help the former become global suppliers. By reducing the potentially high costs of identifying local suppliers, the program primarily addresses a market failure related to information problems (see Monge-González, Rivera, & Rosales-Tijerino, 2010). Linkages for Exports has mainly focused on SMEs with more capabilities, fewer technical assistance needs, and thus a higher likelihood of becoming successful providers of multinational companies (see Monge-González & Rodríguez-Álvarez, 2013).

Over the period 2001–2012, Linkages for Exports created 1,355 linkages between more than 400 local companies (up from 23 in 2003) and 301 exporters, primarily multinational firms. During the same period, the annual number of backward linkages sponsored by the program increased from fewer than 10 to almost 250, and sales jumped from US$800,000 to US$12 million. The number of products sold by domestic companies averaged 1.5 in most recent years compared with one in the first half of the 2000s. Figure 4.4 shows the year-to-year evolution of some of these variables, which suggests that the program has been an effective matchmaking mechanism. Interviews with both SMEs and multinational companies confirm this positive view regarding the program's matchmaking function (see Monge-González et al., 2010; Vargas Madrigal, Céspedes, Gonzalez et al., 2010).

In a recent econometric evaluation, the program was shown to have had a positive impact on the real wages, employment, and export status of participating firms. Furthermore, firms continue to receive benefits from the knowledge acquired through their commercial relationships with multinational corporations, beyond the year they join the program. The evidence also shows that firms receiving more services from the program have received the greater benefits, which supports the idea that the level of support is important (see Monge-González & Rodríguez-Álvarez, 2013).

Despite these positive effects, Linkages for Exports appears to have a limited scope. For instance, the purchases associated with participation in the program accounted (on average) for a very small share of the total local purchases by multinational companies in Costa Rica over the period 2001–2011; in 2007 it was less than 1 %. Further, less than 20 % of the linkages under the program were actually incorporated into the multinational companies' high-technology final products, suggesting that most of the linkages involve inputs of low technological content

[19] Formerly known as "Costa Rica Provee."

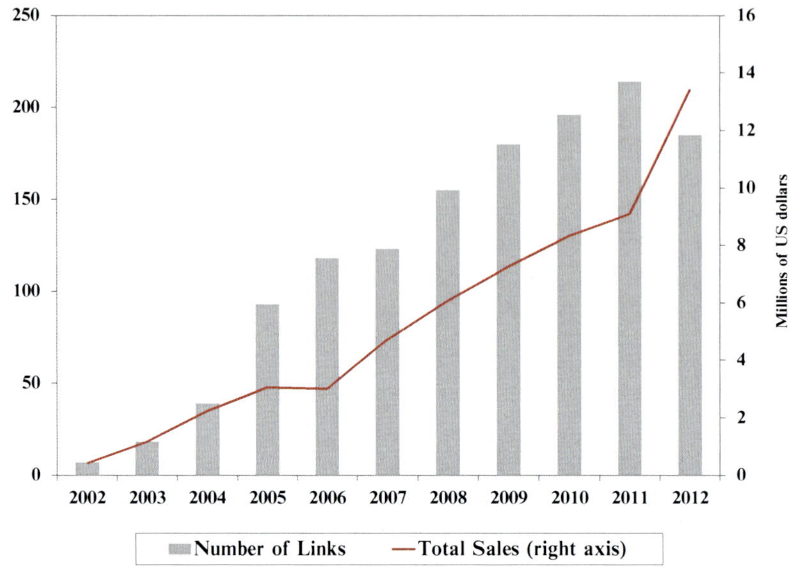

Fig. 4.4 Linkages for exports. Number of links and sales, 2002–2012. *Source*: Authors' calculation based on data from PROCOMER and Encadenamientos para la Exportación

(see Monge-González et al., 2010; Vargas Madrigal et al., 2010). More generally, there is a perception that even though the program is a valuable first step, it is far from making a substantial contribution; linkages between multinational and domestic firms are still weak, and spillovers associated with backward linkages are still limited (see, e.g., Monge-González et al., 2010; OECD, 2012; Paus & Gallagher, 2008).

Three potential factors might explain the program's relatively limited contribution. First, the resources devoted to the program seem modest. For instance, the unit running the program has only seven employees (one director and six staff tasked with business matchmaking) and an annual budget of US$300,000 over the last 5 years. Even though the recent evaluation indicates positive results, these resources seem too small to significantly change the country's linkage capability. The second factor could be that Linkages for Exports has mostly concentrated on correcting the market failure associated with information obstacles through the matchmaking process. But in many cases, addressing this initial information problem might not be enough. Lack of technical know-how, absorptive capacity, certifications, human resource training, and difficulties in accessing financing have been identified as other obstacles in Costa Rica to expanding sales to multinationals (see Beltrán & Gutiérrez, 2007; Monge-González et al., 2010; Paus & Gallagher, 2008). Finally, it has been argued that Linkages for Exports could be better connected to other public programs dealing with other market failures (see Monge-González & Rodríguez-Álvarez, 2013). The government of Costa Rica has taken a series of steps towards correcting this situation. First, the directorate in charge of Linkages for Exports has begun to provide assistance to develop suppliers. Second, a Commission of Linkages for

Exports was established in 2010 to improve coordination of programs administered by member public and private organizations (see Dobles Madrigal, 2012a, 2012b).[20]

We now review other international experiences with local linkage programs that have gone beyond the simple matchmaking process.

Countries around the world, and particularly those that have attracted large amounts of FDI, have implemented programs targeted at supporting local firms in their efforts to become suppliers of MNCs and participate in GVCs. A well-known example is Ireland's National Linkage Program (NLP), which was established in 1985 and managed initially by the country's Industrial Development Agency. Prior to the program, the government's efforts to encourage backward linkages were focused on a database and a liaison service to match MNCs with potential domestic suppliers. However, a government study found that these efforts had been weak and failed to close the technical and managerial gap between MNCs and local suppliers (Battat, Frank, & Shen, 1996). Therefore, the NLP was designed to go beyond helping MNCs find potential suppliers within Ireland to also help build the capacity and capability of these local suppliers. The program initially assessed the ability of companies to improve their technical, financial, and managerial capabilities, and then provided assistance to selected suppliers on specific development areas, including operational management and control, quality systems, finance, and marketing. The NLP is considered to have been a successful initiative. Fewer than 10 years after its creation, more than 200 MNCs and 80 suppliers had participated in the program, and more than 80 % of the suppliers had received ISO 9000 certifications (Battat et al., 1996). Eventually, the NLP program evolved from an initiative that exclusively supported linking local firms with MNCs in Ireland to a broader program helping incorporate Irish companies into GVCs.

Another example of a linkage program was Singapore's Local Industry Upgrading Program (LIUP), which begin in 1986 and was administered by the country's Economic Development Board. The distinctive feature of this program was that multinational companies trained the local firms in return for government incentives. As such, the LIUP went beyond matchmaking to foster partnerships between specific multinational companies and potential suppliers. The multinational companies were encouraged to choose local subcontractors and help them improve efficiency. An employee from the multinational company was seconded to the local supplier, and the program paid the employee's salary. Local suppliers were selected on the basis of merit in an assessment that evaluated the strength of their core competencies and their capacity and critical mass to grow. By the mid-1990s the LIUP had already reported positive results. According to studies carried out by the LIUP and reported in Battat et al. (1996), the productivity of the suppliers in the early years of the program increased by 17 % and the value added per worker rose by 13.7 %.

[20] These member organizations are the Ministry of Foreign Trade; the Ministry of Economy, Industry, and Commerce; the Ministry of Science and Technology; the Coalition of Development Initiatives; the Chamber of Industries of Costa Rica; the Chamber of Exporters of Costa Rica; the Association of Free Trade Zone Companies; the National Council for Scientific and Technological Research; and the Foreign Trade Promoter.

In 1994 the program included 32 buyer companies and 180 SME suppliers (Battat et al., 1996). The program continued to expand over the decade, and by 1999 the number of suppliers benefiting from the program had risen to 670. Eventually, LIUP was subsumed in a more general partnership program, and in 2012 received a budget of US$250 million over 5 years.

The experience of Malaysia is particularly interesting because it provides elements of success as well as failure. An early initiative created in 1988 with the Vendor Development Program was aimed at assisting local SMEs to become suppliers of MNCs and other large companies in the country. For the most part, the program was restricted to SMEs owned by indigenous people.[21] As a result of selecting SMEs on the basis of non-economic criteria, many suppliers failed to meet the needs of the MNCs (UNCTAD, 2011). For example, in 1996 54 anchor companies had signed up with the program, but only 27 had commercial relations with vendors (Karikomi, 1998). The largest anchor company, the national car maker Proton, had 17 vendors under the program, but they represented only 12 % of the company's vendors (Suyderhoud, 1999). The main concern was the low quality of the products the vendors provided (UNCTAD, 2011).

In the mid-1990s, the Industrial Linkages Programme (ILP) was launched. Unlike its predecessor, the new program provided for more merit-based selection criteria, a more active role of the MNCs in the selection of suppliers, and more assistance for the supplier to access finance and build capability. The program, administered by the Small and Medium Enterprise Corporation Malaysia, supports a range of supplier activities, including engaging in strategic alliances with multinational firms, training their employees, developing new products, and auditing factories to ensure the quality of their products. The program's main policy tool is a series of tax relief measures for both the suppliers and the multinationals. For example, suppliers are allowed to deduct expenditures from their income tax that they incurred in ILP activities, such as employee training, product development and testing, and factory auditing. If the company receives pioneer status, it is given a 100 % exemption for 5 years on income and a tax investment allowance of 60 % on qualifying capital expenditures incurred within the same period. Pioneer status can be achieved if the firm manufactures products contained in the List of Promoted Activities and Products and supplies its products to MNCs or large companies (UNCTAD, 2011). For its part, the participating MNC is allowed to deduct expenses incurred in supporting the supplier. The program seems to have fared better than its predecessor. By 2007, for example, 906 SMEs were registered under the ILP, and 128 of them were linked to MNCs and other large companies (UNCTAD, 2011).

In the Latin American region, Mexico has long supported the creation of business linkages between MNCs and local suppliers. In the 1970s, for example, the Mexican government created an information exchange system called the Sub-contracting Exchanges (Bolsas de Subcontratación), in which a database of businesses was made

[21] The Bumiputera is the term used to describe the Malay race and other indigenous people of Southeast Asia. In 1970, the Malaysian government started implementing policies in different areas to favor this ethnic group.

available to multinational companies seeking local suppliers. Another initiative was the Productive Linkage Centers (Centros de Articulación Productiva), which helped foreign firms identify and select potential suppliers, mainly through buyer–supplier matchmaking services. However, matchmaking mechanisms proved to be of limited effectiveness in fostering successful linkages compared to other initiatives with a more comprehensive range of services (see UNCTAD, 2010). Therefore, Mexico has also tried out other initiatives beyond simple matchmaking, an interesting example being a set of initiatives in the Guadalajara electronics cluster. Mexico has attracted substantial foreign direct investment in the electronics sector since the early 1990s, particularly in the State of Jalisco and the city of Guadalajara. The cluster has been supported by a set of policies to promote the emergence of favorable spillovers from these foreign direct investments and the upgrading of local firms into more sophisticated segments and niches of the electronics value chain (see Dussel, 2010; Dussel, Palacios, & Woo, 2003; ECLAC, 2008; Padilla-Pérez, 2005, 2008; Padilla-Pérez, Cordero, Hernández, & Romero, 2008; Palacios, 2008).

In Chile, a supplier development program was launched in 1998 by the country's development agency, CORFO. The program was not specifically directed at fostering participation in global supply chains, since buyers did not have to be multinationals or exporters. Nevertheless, the initiative was designed in the same spirit as other linkage programs that are related to GVCs. For example, it resembles the LIUP in Singapore in creating linkages between anchor firms and suppliers. In the case of both programs, an anchor firm presents a proposal to help improve the capability of a group of suppliers, and an initial diagnosis carried out by an independent consultant determines the needs for upgrading. The anchor firm then carries out the action plan. The program finances up to 50 % of the costs of the upgrading process, and the anchor firm covers the rest. A recent impact evaluation found that the suppliers that participated in the program increased their sales, employment, and salaries relative to a control group (Arráiz, Henríquez, & Stucchi, 2012).[22]

It is difficult to determine the effectiveness of these programs due to a lack of rigorous impact evaluations in many cases. Nevertheless, their experiences and evolution provide general lessons regarding program design. First, programs based exclusively on matchmaking services seem to have had more limited effects in fostering linkages between lead firms and local suppliers than programs that also provide complementary support to the suppliers. It is difficult to generalize about the type of complementary support required, since each industry and country has different needs. Nevertheless, judging from the experiences examined here, programs based on bundling matchmaking services together with some form of employee training seems to have been generally effective.

A corollary of the first lesson is the need for a proper articulation of linkage programs with other initiatives. For example, many countries have SME development policies, which may include training schemes. Coordination with such initiatives might result in more effective programs to foster linkages.

[22] Pietrobelli and Staritz (2013) offer an insightful typology of interventions in GVCs.

Second, most successful linkage programs are based on merit-based selection criteria. Selecting the supplier using non-economic criteria may not only waste valuable resources but also jeopardize the sustainability of the program and discourage further FDI flows into the country. To ensure that the linkages are mutually beneficial, merit-based selection can be based on criteria designed by the government and also by the MNCs, as in the Malaysian ILP program. This calls for the involvement of MNCs from early on in the process.

Third, the assistance should be based on an objective diagnosis and auditing of the supplier so that its specific shortcomings can be identified and areas needing improvement can be addressed. The specific assistance might vary depending on the design of the program. Examples include soft loans provided directly to the suppliers, co-financing, tax relief to the suppliers and/or the MNCs, or contributions to the salary of an MNC's employee seconded to the supplier, as in the Singapore LIUP program. Finally, before committing large amounts of resources for a full-fledged program, a pilot program may be undertaken to fine-tune objectives, strategies, targets, and action plans. After the program is initiated, periodical reviews should be conducted to provide feedback for future policy design (see Axèle & Delane, 2008; IFC, 2008; Potter, 2001; UNCTAD, 2010). In addition, the program should reach a minimum scale to ensure that it makes a difference.

Box 3: Mexico's Insertion in Global Supply Chains: The Challenge of Adding Mexican Value

Mexico has outperformed most of its Latin American peers when it comes to participating in global supply chains, particularly with North America (see Chap. 2). Proximity, low trade barriers, and low factor prices relative to the US and Canada, among other factors, have made Mexico an attractive destination for firms in the North seeking to engage in cross-border production sharing. Accordingly, Mexico stands apart in Latin America in the ability of its firms to join international production networks.

Mexico has also been pursuing policies for many years to foster such international linkages. The Maquiladora program, for instance, started in the mid-1960s to allow imports from the US to enter duty-free as long as the output from the Maquiladora firms was exported back to the US. The program later incorporated other tax benefits. The Program of Temporary Imports to Produce Export Goods was another major initiative that had objectives similar to the Maquiladora program. In 2006 both programs were combined to form the Manufacturing Industry, Maquiladora and Export Services Program (IMMEX). IMMEX permits the temporary import of inputs, raw materials, parts and components, and machinery and equipment free of duty for use in a production process, as long as the final product is exported. The program also allows for exemption from the value-added tax. Today, Mexico's processing exports through the IMMEX program represent around 63 % of the country's total exports.

(continued)

Box 3: (continued)

Despite all these efforts, there is a general perception that Mexico's insertion in supply chains has been mostly in assembly operations and that efforts should be made to incorporate additional domestic value in the international production networks in which the country participates. For example, combining input-output tables with trade data, De La Cruz, Koopman, and Wang (2011) show that the domestic value added embodied in Mexico's processing exports is only 23 %.[23] To provide further insights on this issue we conducted an analysis based on plant-level data that enables us to track the evolution of the share of domestic value added over time in processing exports. An increase in this measure, for example, might signal that more segments of the supply chains are moving into Mexico.

We use the IMMEX census conducted by Mexico's National Institute of Statistics and Geography, which provides information for all the plants that participate in the IMMEX program. The census covers 6,400 establishments, of which approximately 5,200 are engaged in manufacturing. We examine monthly data covering the period July 2007 to January 2013.[24]

We first calculate the overall share of domestic value added in total processing exports at the country level as the weighted average of the share of each establishment.[25,26] Figure 4.5 shows the result. While there are various episodes with noticeable changes, in general there is a decreasing trend.

---

[23] This share of domestic value is much lower than the 56 % share implied by our analysis in Chap. 2. Note, however, that the share of domestic value added of 23 % is only for processing exports. According to De La Cruz et al. (2011), the share of domestic value added for all the exports of Mexico is 45 %, a value much closer to our results but still somewhat smaller. Computations regarding trade in value added can differ greatly depending on the assumptions made and the trade data and input-output tables employed in the analysis. Our results for Mexico in Chap. 2 are closer to the 52 % reported by Koopman, Wang, and Wei (2014) because the assumptions and the databases that we use are more similar to that analysis, as explained in appendix A "Trade in Value Added and Set of Countries".

[24] We are grateful to INEGI's staff for kindly running our statistical and econometric codes in their computers.

[25] The weight is the participation of each establishment's processing exports in the total processing exports of the country.

[26] The IMMEX census does not provide information on the value of processing exports; however, there is information regarding the domestic value added incorporated in the processing exports, as well as regarding the value of the foreign inputs used in them. Therefore, we proxy the value of the processing exports by adding these two variables. We then calculate the share of domestic value added for each establishment as the ratio of the domestic value added incorporated in the processing exports over the sum of the domestic value added and the value of the foreign inputs.

(continued)

Box 3: (continued)

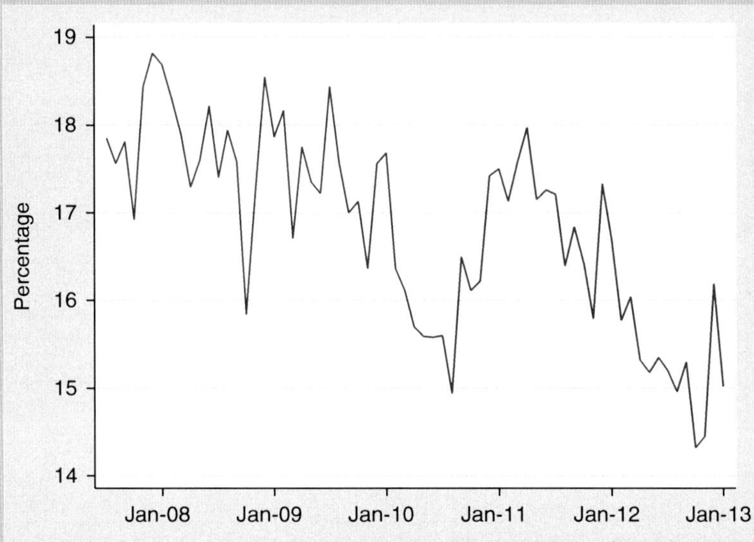

Fig. 4.5 Mexico's share of domestic value added in processing exports. *Source*: Authors' calculation based on the IMMEX census, with support from INEGI

A decline in the overall share of domestic value added of the country, however, does not necessarily mean that the firms are reducing the local value added incorporated in their exports. A decline could result from changes in the participation of each establishment in the total exports of the country. For instance, if establishments with large domestic value added were losing participation in the total level of processing exports while the establishments with low value added were gaining participation, we would see a decline in the overall share of domestic value added.

To analyze whether the drop in overall share of domestic value added is due to within-firm reduction in the share of domestic value added, or to changes in the firm's participation in total processing exports (including firm entry and exit), we follow Kee and Tang (2012) and estimate an equation that relates the share of the domestic value added of each establishment against firm and year variables. A within-firm decline in the share of domestic value added will be captured by a decreasing estimated coefficient for the year variable. We repeat this exercise after recalculating the share of domestic value added using real instead of nominal series.[27]

[27] We use INEGI's monthly production price index to deflate the domestic value added using July 2007 as the baseline date. For the value of foreign inputs we first convert the imports from pesos to US dollars using the monthly nominal exchange rate. Then, we con-

(continued)

Box 3: (continued)

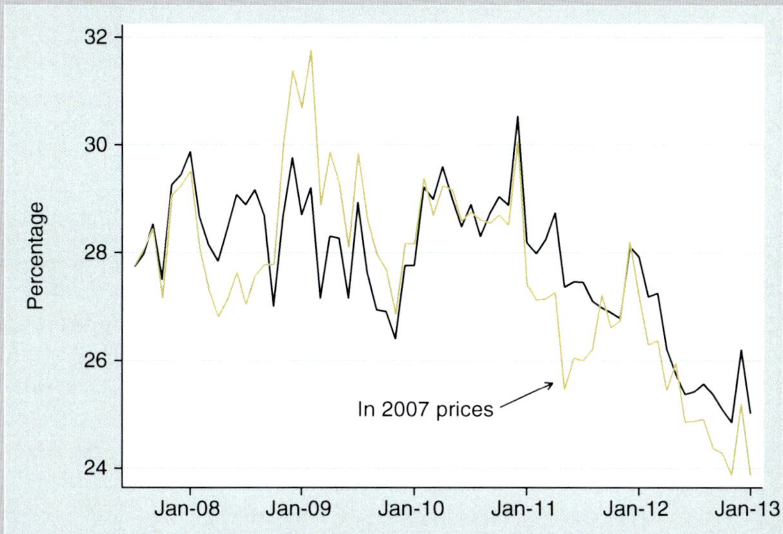

Fig. 4.6 Within-firm evolution of share in domestic value added. *Source*: Authors' calculation based on the IMMEX census, with support from INEGI

In Fig. 4.6, the within-firm changes in the shares of domestic value added are represented by the black line. The brown line presents the results when using July 2007 prices. A declining trend is evident in both cases.

Both figures in this box generally indicate that the share of domestic value added in the country's processing exports has declined during the last 5 years, and that this decline is not the result of market share reallocations. The typical firm engaged in processing exports has reduced its domestic value added by about 3 % points during this period. While certainly this is not a large decline, it is clear that the share of domestic value added is not increasing, a finding that suggests that in recent years, Mexico has not been able to incorporate additional local content in the international supply chains in which the country participates. However, the finding is only a general trend and does not necessarily apply to all the sectors of the economy. Further research will be needed to explore the evolution of the Mexican domestic value added at more detailed sectorial levels and to pin down the precise forces behind these trends.

---

vert them back into pesos using the nominal exchange rate of July 2007, which gives us a series for imports in July 2007 prices. We then recalculate the share of domestic value added for each establishment, as mentioned in the previous footnote.

Exploit Synergies Through a Coordinated Approach

In this chapter we have presented examples of policies aimed at alleviating information and coordination problems that affect participation in GVCs. Certainly these are not the only policies, and many others have been proposed.[28] Examining every policy is beyond the scope of this chapter. The aim of this section is to emphasize the importance of coordinating policies and programs in order to take advantage of potential complementarities and synergies among them.

The rationale for pursuing a coordinated approach is rooted in the notion that accession to international production networks might be hampered by multiple market failures, and the possibility that suboptimal outcomes might arise when market failures in different areas are not addressed in a structured and consistent way (Blyde et al., 2014). Interventions should then be coordinated to take advantage of their complementarities.

Of course, this is easier said than done. Coordination of policies might be hard to achieve, particularly when different agencies are involved. Differences among agencies in terms of mandates, strategic views, agendas, or bureaucratic processes reduce possibilities for coordination. But this does not mean that all efforts are doomed to fail. Certain institutional arrangements might encourage more coordination than others. Examples of such institutional arrangements are presented now, even though they are not all strictly related to participation in GVCs.

One example is a centralized organization that performs several different tasks. Here, the problem of coordination is addressed by outright integration. This path has been taken by several countries that have merged their export and investment promotion organizations into a single agency to better exploit complementarities that could arise from addressing information and coordination problems. Examples can be found in Australia (AUSTRADE), Korea (KOTRA), Colombia (PROEXPORT), Germany (GTAI), and Finland (FINPRO).

Another alternative for achieving coordination is the cross-membership of officials of the relevant agencies in their respective boards. For instance, a representative from TEKES, the Finnish innovation promotion agency, is a member of FINPRO's board (Volpe Martincus, 2010).

Another approach would be to create a body, within the government, charged with coordinating the efforts of various agencies, an approach that some countries have taken as a way to foster competitiveness. Such coordinating bodies could consist of representatives of different agencies, meet on a regular basis, and be chaired by a high-ranking official—even the president—to ensure relevance. A new body does not necessarily need to be created exclusively for GVCs, particularly if the government can employ an existing focal point that already incorporates the relevant agencies.

Other alternatives are also possible. In each case, the optimal institutional arrangement would ultimately be determined by factors specific to individual countries.

[28] Pietrobelli and Staritz (2013) offer an insightful typology of interventions in GVCs.

Chapter 5
Conclusions

Terms such as global value chains, globalization of production, and slicing the value added chain have emerged in recent years to describe the co-participation of countries in the design, production, and distribution of a good or service. Some may argue that beyond the semantics and the sometimes catchy terminology, there is not much LAC can learn about policy issues on this topic; after all, the region has been providing raw inputs and natural resource intensive goods to other countries for decades.

LAC is not new to supply chains, but the region has largely missed the recent surge in the international fragmentation of production. While LAC has indeed been a long-time participant in some forms of international production networks, mainly as a supplier of raw materials and basic inputs, the region has not been able to capitalize on the recent surge of production fragmentation in which goods previously produced in one country are sliced up and co-produced in many parts of the world. Experiments with global sourcing started in the 1970s and 1980s by a few firms in the electronics and car industries, as well as by a handful of retailers. Today, fragmentation of production is employed by many companies around the world and by many industries. This new economic reality could create new opportunities for LAC to diversify its presently limited export base.

Global value chains raise the stakes of addressing long-standing policy challenges, such as those related to transportation and logistics. Taking advantage of the new trends in the international organization of production means addressing new challenges and raising the profile of some of the old ones. Take the issue of transport and logistics infrastructure. After the long period of trade liberalization that started in the late 1980s, most LAC countries understand that future gains from trade are likely to be found in non-tariff-related areas, particularly in improving transport infrastructure. The main argument for making progress on the transportation agenda has been the region's high dependence on exports based on natural resources, which tend to have very high weight-to-value ratios. As freight costs are directly proportional to weight-to-value ratios, exporters of natural resource-intensive goods pay relatively more to transport their goods than exporters of lighter-

J.S. Blyde (ed.), *Synchronized Factories: Latin America and the Caribbean in the Era of Global Value Chains*, DOI 10.1007/978-3-319-09991-0_5

weight goods. As such, the former are also relatively more affected by inadequate transport infrastructure that can easily wipe out the rents that countries can extract from their natural resources. This reasoning has underscored the urgency of addressing shortcomings in the region's transport infrastructure. The importance of this argument has certainly not changed; LAC will remain tied to the exploitation of natural resources for many years to come. But participation in GVCs raises the importance of the transport and logistics infrastructure agenda to a new level. For example, firms fragmenting production internationally must reduce the risks associated with the uncertainty and delays in the arrival of any single component to avoid the risk of disrupting the production of the final goods. Accordingly, these firms seek to work with suppliers in locations with adequate transport and logistics infrastructure. Similarly, modern supply chain practices, such as just-in-time delivery services or postponement (the practice of delaying the final customization of a semi-finished good) increasingly require that suppliers commit to swift deliveries with minimum disruptions, which is akin to having good transportation and logistics systems. The importance of an adequate logistics infrastructure is higher for distant countries than for nearby countries as a means of offsetting the impact of distance. This lesson is particularly important for countries in LAC as they seek to join supply chains in Asia or Europe, or develop supply chains within their own region, where distances may exceed those in Asia or Europe. As a result, the importance of addressing limitations in the transport and logistics industries, while already high on the "to-do lists" of many policy makers of the region, has only increased its priority status with the emergence of international supply chains.

Maintaining low levels of protection and furthering integration in the region has become even more important, with the international fragmentation of production. The relevance of low levels of trade protection has also increased with the advent of GVCs. For instance, gains from tariff reductions are magnified when goods cross borders many times, as is often the case in international production networks. Also, as research in this report indicates, to successfully target GVCs—particularly in developed countries—many potential suppliers in LAC will need to import high-quality inputs from other countries to complement their own production. In this way, high levels of protection at home will damage their ability to complement their own skills with the skills and capacities of suppliers in other countries.

A more integrated economic space for the Americas—a long-time aspiration—also becomes more relevant in an era of production networks. Take, for instance, the myriad of trade agreements in LAC, most of which use different rules of origin. When an exporter produces only one good, and most intermediate inputs are sourced domestically, the costs of complying with multiple rules of origin virtually do not exist. But as firms seek to fragment their production among different countries in different trade agreements, the costs of dealing with multiple origins can be prohibitive. Deepening integration in LAC will allow firms to take advantage of the differences in factor prices across countries, enabling them to freely choose the location for each bundle of production according to each nation's comparative advantage.

True, the region might not embark on a deep integration agreement of a continental size in the foreseeable future, but it can still move towards deeper integration—for example, by fostering the convergence of many of the trade agreements currently in place.

A more integrated region does not have to be viewed solely as an instrument to develop supply chains originating in Latin America. Deeper integration in LAC does not exclusively favor the development of supply chains among Latin American countries. A deeply integrated region could also serve as a platform to enhance trade and investment ties with third countries. For instance, exploiting production complementarities within the bloc will help LAC countries reach other markets with more competitive goods. Likewise, a more integrated economic space will encourage the attraction of investment and production blocks from outside LAC, which will subsequently be sliced and shared among the countries of the region.

Tariff escalation is still common in many parts of the world, which limits LAC countries' access to higher value-added segments of supply chains. In the area of trade policy, gaining access to supply chains in other regions will require addressing the still widespread practice of countries imposing low duties on raw inputs and materials and higher duties on higher value-added segments of the supply chain—the so-called tariff escalation problem. The existing scheme, which is still common in many developed countries, clearly generates disincentives for countries in LAC to move beyond the supply of raw materials and join supply chains in developed countries, particularly with higher value-added content.

Contracting institutions can be a source of comparative advantage, particularly for countries seeking to join international supply chains. The emergence of global value chains has brought to the forefront issues that policy makers had often overlooked previously. One of them is the notion that the quality of contracting institutions can shape the geographical location of fragmented production and thus the capacity of the country to join international production networks. Ambiguous practices and uncertainty in contract enforcement can generate distrust between parties of different countries, limiting their willingness to engage in cross-border transactions. While contractual frictions can certainly undermine any international transaction, including the exports of final goods, they can be particularly harmful for transactions in global supply chains, where suppliers must often customize their production to the specifications of particular buyers, and where the parameters governing such specifications are typically set up in contractual agreements. Research in this report shows that global firms can be reluctant to form partnerships with local suppliers located in countries where there is uncertainty and ambiguity in contracting practices.

One could argue that the lack of contract enforcement is not necessarily a relevant issue because many global firms open their own affiliates in the host country where they operate, rather than rely on dubious contracts with local suppliers. This is not true. For one thing, evidence shows that in some industries, offshoring takes place almost exclusively through independent local suppliers rather than through FDI; local firms in countries with weak contracting institutions will not have opportunities to become suppliers in those industries. For another thing, even if multinationals resolve potential quarrels with their own affiliates internally, they may still need adequate contracting institutions in the host countries where they operate. For instance, the affiliate might need to tap local suppliers to pursue part of its businesses; therefore, a location where local suppliers do not respect contracts, and where local courts do not enforce them, will hardly be an attractive location for doing business. In this report we have presented evidence that LAC has subpar contracting institutions when compared to other regions, making this a clear area for policy action.

Service offshoring also represents an opportunity for export diversification. Global firms co-locate in other countries not only bits of production processes, but also an array of different services that were traditionally performed in-house, such as accounting, auditing, bookkeeping, research and development, and design, among others. Research in this report indicates that even though most of these services can be delivered electronically, proximity continues to be important. This creates an opportunity for LAC vis-à-vis Asia or Europe, particularly for targeting the US market with business functions that tend to require similar time zones or that involve specific customization to the client's needs and for which proximity is an important factor.

Exporting GVC-related services requires not only adequate skills but also a sufficiently large pool of skilled individuals. The export of certain business or knowledge-intensive services might demand specific skills that can change quickly over time. This report presents results that indicate that not only the quality but also the quantity of skilled individuals is important. But sustaining an adequate pool of skills can be challenging. For instance, educational curriculums might not keep up with rapid changes in business practices, thus generating mismatches between demand for specific capabilities and the skills acquired in the educational system. Many countries have successfully addressed this problem by forming alliances between the private sector, academia, and the public sector to ensure that students are taught the skills that employers need. The lack of an adequate pool of skills can also be addressed, at least temporarily, by employing foreign individuals, a policy that requires reducing restrictions on the entry of professionals from other countries.

Access to global supply chains can be seriously hampered by information deficiencies. It is already well established in the literature that international trade transactions can be hampered by information problems. The lack of adequate information is at the root of many failed attempts to export final goods, but it can be particularly problematic for exporting inputs in international production networks. The information flows typically required to match a buyer and a supplier in an international supply chain can be vast: many suppliers need to customize their production to the requirements of particular buyers, while buyers need to convey this information to the suppliers and make sure they are capable of delivering the product with the correct specifications. As a result, lack of information can easily keep potential suppliers on the sidelines, with buyers relying on a few known providers.

Public policy can help reduce information problems and improve visibility and credibility. Policies for addressing information problems in international trade traditionally fall on the shoulders of export promotion organizations (EPOs). As evidence in this report shows, however, EPOs are not always able to understand the complexities of many supply chains. In general, the effectiveness of EPOs' actions in helping firms become part of GVCs is proportional to their success in gathering information regarding the structure of supply chains, their modes of operation, and their specific conditions.

Another policy option to reduce information gaps consists of promoting environments that facilitate exchanges of information between players in the industry or across industries. Programs could consist of some form of coaching, whereby a group of potential exporters meets with firms that have achieved success in the international markets. Alternatively, the government could help organize exchanges where the information gap is filled by current or retired staff from international buyers. Yet another approach is for representatives of the local firms to go abroad to visit the facilities of global firms.

Some information gaps can also be addressed by improving visibility through certifications. It is well known that global firms screen potential suppliers for compliance with relevant standards in their respective supply chains. The public sector could assist in promoting the establishment of local certification agencies. Local certifications, however, could have minor or no effects if the global buyers do not know about them or are skeptical of their value; therefore, establishing links with standards and certification institutions in developed countries might also be required.

Firms in LAC that cannot join global supply chains on their own would benefit from policies that promote collaboration or consolidation among themselves. Evidence from this report indicates that firms seldom join international production networks on their own. Instead, these firms often leverage resources with other firms to achieve certain capabilities, address common barriers, or pay for the fixed costs of activities, such as attending an international trade fair. One area for potential public action, then, is to help create mechanisms whereby firms can cooperate, such as business associations. Since some existing business associations are weak or are designed for rent seeking, governments could support sectors that want to improve their organization or help create new associations when common interests may extend beyond sectors.

Governments can also support the consolidation of interested firms. Evidence presented in this report, for example, indicates that government-designed programs for mergers and acquisitions have been helpful in encouraging companies to grow their businesses and shorten the time to acquire capabilities.

In some situations, purely inter-firm collaboration will not be enough. Cooperation between the public and private sectors might be required, particularly when a specific public good or the resolution of some coordination problem facilitates access to a GVC.

Some local firms, particularly many SMEs, will not be able to join GVCs by exporting directly. But they can still access GVCs by serving global firms located in their own countries. Instead of dealing with the hassles of exporting on their own, firms—and particularly SMEs—could join global supply chains and take advantage of the increasing fragmentation of production by becoming upstream suppliers of international companies located in their home countries, which themselves are inserted in GVCs. Countries in various parts of the world have been pursuing programs to foster such linkages between global firms located in their territories and their local suppliers. A review of some of these experiences suggests the following general lessons: (i) programs based exclusively on matchmaking services seem to have more limited effects than programs that also provide complementary support to the suppliers, such as training; (ii) most successful linkage programs are founded on merit-based selection criteria; (iii) any assistance to the supplier should be based on transparent diagnosis and auditing processes; and (iv) a pilot program may be the best way to start, followed by periodical reviews to fine tune objectives, strategies, targets, and action plans.

Exploit synergies through a coordinated approach. As shown in many parts of this report and also in this summary chapter, accession to international production networks might be hampered by multiple shortcomings and market failures. In this respect, it is important to note that suboptimal outcomes might arise when market failures in different areas are not addressed in a structured and consistent way. This requires that interventions be coordinated as much as possible so as to take advantage of potential complementarities. As multiple government agencies with different mandates, strategic views, and agendas might be responsible for the different policies, some form of coordination among these agencies would be desirable. One option is to create a body within the government, charged with coordinating the efforts of various agencies. In some countries these bodies have arisen to foster competitiveness. The design and architecture of such a body could remain flexible, incorporating relevant agencies as needed; it would be unreasonable to expect governments to be able to identify all possible market failures affecting GVC insertion in all the sectors of the economy. A more realistic approach would be to forge a clear channel of communication with the private sector for airing concerns and presenting proposals to agencies operating within such a government body.

Appendix A

Trade in Value Added and Set of Countries

An international input-output table was used to develop the various indicators of trade in value added shown in Chap. 2. The table details the relationships among all the countries included in the table. For example, the rows in the table not only provide the quantity of the domestic intermediate inputs used in the production of a given product in a given country, but also indicate the amount of intermediate inputs used that originated in each of the other countries.

The international input-output table is obtained after linking national input-output tables using bilateral trade flow statistics and import matrices. Once the international input-output table is constructed, the matrix of technical coefficients is obtained and then inverted to get the matrix of direct and indirect requirements, also known as the Leontief matrix. The Leontief matrix makes it possible to quantify how much value added from a country is used in the production of the goods (and consequently on the exports) of another country. For example, the inverse matrix yields the value added of a country A embodied in the exports of country B, which is generated not only when B directly imports inputs from A, but also when B imports inputs from C that incorporate inputs from A.

The international input-output table constructed for this report used data from the Global Trade Analysis Project (GTAP). The GTAP data come from three sources: (1) balance of payments statistics of the World Bank and International Monetary Fund, (2) bilateral trade flows from the United Nations' COMTRADE database, and (3) national input-output tables gathered from national sources. GTAP then reconciles these three databases to obtain national input output tables that are consistent.

We use the last two available datasets from GTAP—version 7, which corresponds to the year 2003, and version 8, for the year 2007. The last version includes 129 countries (regions) and 57 sectors. All the indicators shown in Chap. 2 were constructed by calculating the indicators separately for GTAP 7 and GTAP 8 and then taking the average of the two values. Data for Honduras and El Salvador are not

J.S. Blyde (ed.), *Synchronized Factories: Latin America and the Caribbean in the Era of Global Value Chains*, DOI 10.1007/978-3-319-09991-0

included in GTAP 7; therefore, for these countries we only use GTAP 8. For Mexico, the values of foreign value added using GTAP 8 were found to be implausibly low relative to other well-known analyses of trade in value added (e.g., De La Cruz, Koopman, & Wang, 2011; Koopman, Wang, & Wei, 2010). Accordingly, for this country we use only GTAP 7.

Additionally, given the size of the production related to the maquiladora activity in Mexico, and because the technical coefficients of the maquiladora production tend to be different from the rest of the economy, for Mexico we supplement the GTAP data with additional input-output tables: a table for the maquiladora production and a table for the remainder of the economy. Both tables were obtained from the Instituto Nacional de Geografía y Estadística (INEGI). Trade data from the Bank of Mexico detailing the trade flows associated with the maquiladora activity and the trade flows from the rest of the economy were also used.

The construction of the international input-output table used in this report as well as of the various indicators presented in Chap. 2 closely follows the methodology presented in Koopman, Wang, and Wei (2014).

Comparator Groups

Asia-Pacific: Australia, Brunei, Cambodia, China, Hong Kong, Indonesia, Japan, Malaysia, Myanmar, New Zealand, Philippines, Singapore, South Korea, Taiwan, Thailand, Vietnam.

EU-27: Austria, Belgium, Bulgaria, Cyprus, Czech Republic, Denmark, Estonia, Finland, France, Germany, Greece, Hungary, Ireland, Italy, Latvia, Lithuania, Luxembourg, Malta, Netherlands, Poland, Portugal, Romania, Slovenia, Spain, Sweden, United Kingdom.

FDI Dataset

Dun & Bradstreet (D&B) is a company that provides information about businesses and corporations around the world; this information is mainly used in credit and investment decisions, market research, business-to-business marketing, and supply chain management. D&B collects the information for the Worldbase dataset from a broad spectrum of sources, including public registries, partner firms, telephone company data, print directory records, news and media sources, and websites. Computer and manual validation checks and reviews are used to ensure quality control.

The Worldbase dataset for the year 2011 includes about 85 million public and private companies—13 million, if services are excluded. Most of these companies are stand-alone businesses with no formal linkages to other companies. About one million establishments are subsidiaries or branches of a corporate linkage; of this group, around 140,000 have corporate linkages that cross borders.[1] This is the group with which we work.[2]

While the Worldbase dataset extends over more than 200 countries and territories, it is not possible to know with certainty the degree to which the data capture the global population of multinationals around the world. It is known, for example, that some types of family relationships that may occur between companies are not linked in the D&B dataset because the relationship does not involve legal or financial responsibility. These are the cases in which one company owns part of, or has a minority interest (less than 50 %) in, another company, or where there is a joint venture involving a 50/50 split in the ownership.

Nevertheless, D&B uses an extensive set of checks and controls to maximize the coverage and quality of the data. For instance, D&B typically combines a top-down approach with a bottom-up process. The top-down approach starts when D&B contacts a knowledgeable source at the parent company or one of its high-level affiliates to ascertain the proper family tree structure. This implies that once a multinational enters the database, all of the establishments in its ownership hierarchy also enter the database regardless of their location. The process minimizes the likelihood that affiliates and branches are underrepresented in developing countries relative to industrial countries. This top-down approach is complemented with a bottom-up process in which a subsidiary/parent company or a branch/headquarter linkage is collected at the country level during regular revisions.

Alfaro and Charlton (2009) present a number of tests to validate the coverage of the Worldbase dataset and argue that it is one of the most complete sources of information for capturing the global population of multinational firms at the plant level. We repeat one of these exercises here, which consists of comparing the number of affiliates of US multinationals in other countries according to D&B and according to the US Direct Investment Abroad dataset from the US Bureau of Economic Analysis. Figure A.1 shows the total number of US affiliates by country according to both datasets. The correlation between the two datasets is 0.96, a reassuring finding. The picture shows that the distribution of affiliates across countries is remarkably similar in both datasets.

---

[1] A corporate linkage occurs when one business location has financial and legal responsibility for another business location. In the D&B dataset, a corporate linkage occurs between a subsidiary and its parent or between a branch and its headquarters. A subsidiary is a corporation that is more than 50 %owned by another corporation. A parent is a corporation that owns more than 50 % of another corporation. A headquarter is a business establishment that has branches reporting to it and is financially responsible for those branches. A branch is a secondary location of its headquarters with no legal responsibility for the headquarters' debts.

[2] D&B data have marketable and non-marketable records. Non-marketable records are firms that have been delisted from the database or whose information is under revision or incomplete (e.g., lacking the business name, physical mailing address, or sector code). We have access only to the marketable records.

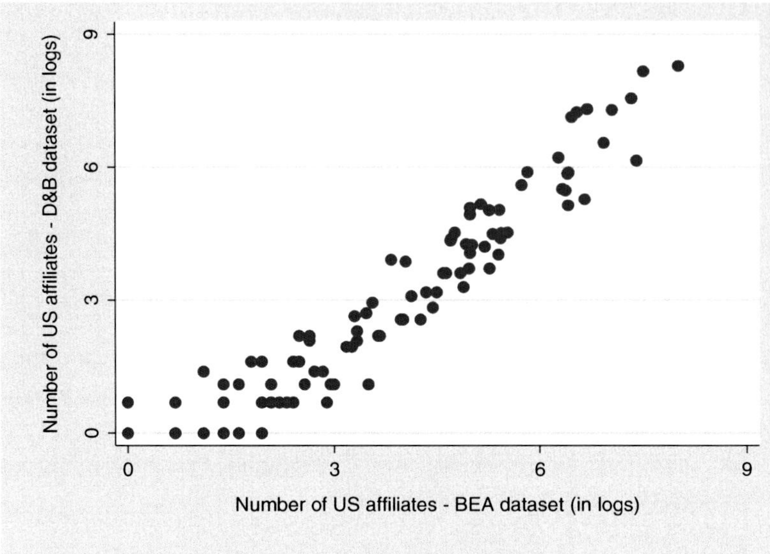

Fig. A.1 Total number of US affiliates by country, according to D&B and BEA databases. *Source*: Authors' calculations based on data from Dun & Bradstreet and BEA

Appendix B

Specification for the Model of Vertical FDI and Logistics Infrastructure

We employ an augmented gravity model of the following form:

$$Y_{ijk} = \theta + D_i + D_j + D_k + \delta X_{ij} + \theta f_{ij} \cdot s_k + \varepsilon_{ijk}$$

where Y_{ijk} is a measure of vertical FDI consisting of the number of vertical affiliates from parent country i that are located in host country j in sector k; D_i, D_j, and D_k are fixed effects for parent country i, host country j, and sector k, respectively; X_{ij} is a vector of bilateral variables including common border, common language, common colonial ties, bilateral distance, a dummy variable for free trade agreement, and the ratio of the parent country's skills to the host country's skills, where country skill is the average years of schooling in the population aged 25 and over; f_{ij} captures the quality of the logistics infrastructure in countries i and j; and s_k is a measure of the dependence of sector k upon logistics services. The formulation follows other formulations in its use of individual country fixed effects to estimate trade equations (Eaton & Kortum, 2001, 2002; Feenstra, 2004) and FDI equations (Head & Ries, 2008). For detailed sources of all the datasets, see Blyde and Molina (2013).

Column 1 of Table B.1 presents the results with a least square estimation and column 2 presents the results with a quasi-maximum likelihood estimator (QMLE); in particular, the negative binomial model that has the advantage of incorporating the zero value observations that are dropped in the least squares because of the linear-in-logs specification. In column 3 we include a more stringent set of fixed effects to control for other potential factors that may influence the decision of a multinational in country i to establish a subsidiary in country j. In particular, we add a parent-host country fixed effect in addition to the previous fixed effects.

J.S. Blyde (ed.), *Synchronized Factories: Latin America and the Caribbean in the Era of Global Value Chains*, DOI 10.1007/978-3-319-09991-0

This set of fixed effects, however, is too demanding for the QMLE iterative techniques to converge. Accordingly, we only present the results with the least-squares estimation. In columns 4 and 5 we re-estimate the regression in column 3 across two groups of countries, which we define by the median distance between the parent and the host country: in column 4 the pair of countries have bilateral distance below the median, and in column 5 the bilateral distances are above the median.

The Effects of Economic Integration Agreements: Estimation and Data Sources

We employ the following specification, based on the gravity equation:

$$Y_{ijt} = D_{ij} + D_{it} + D_{jt} + D_t + \delta EIA_{ijt} + \varepsilon_{ijt} \tag{B.1}$$

where Y_{ijt} is a measure of vertical FDI; D_{ij} is a country-pair fixed effect; D_{it} is a parent country-year fixed effect; D_{jt} is a host country-year fixed effect; D_t is a year fixed effect; and EIA_{ijt} is a dummy variable that takes the value of one if there is an economic integration agreement (EIA) between the parent and the host country in year t, and zero otherwise. The dependent variable Y_{ijt} is the (log of the) number of vertically integrated foreign subsidiaries located in host country j from parent country i in year t.

In estimating Eq. (B.1), we use differencing to eliminate the country-pair fixed effects. This allows us to ameliorate potential problems associated with serial correlation of unobservables and possible "close to" unit-root processes of the dependent variable. We therefore estimate the following baseline equation:

$$\Delta_5 Y_{ijt} = \alpha\, \Delta_5 EIA_{ijt} + D_{it}^{'} + D_{jt}^{'} + \varepsilon_{ijt}^{'} \tag{B.2}$$

where $\Delta_5 Y_{ijt} = \ln Y_{ijt} - \ln Y_{ijt-5}$; $\Delta_5 EIA_{ijt} = EIA_{ijt} - EIA_{ijt-5}$; $D_{it}^{'} = D_{it} - D_{it-5}$; $D_{jt}^{'} = D_{jt} - D_{jt-5}$ and $\varepsilon_{ijt}^{'} = \varepsilon_{ijt} - \varepsilon_{ijt-5}$. Note that we use 5-year differences instead of annual differences. The reasons are both economic and econometric. First, the adjustment of dependent and independent variables is likely to take longer than 1 year (e.g., Anderson & Yotov, 2012; Baier, Bergstrand, & Feng, 2013). Thus, for instance, EIAs take a number of years to fully enter into force, as trade tends to be liberalized gradually over time. The same holds for investment decisions. Second, while first-differencing to eliminate fixed effects generally magnifies the importance of measurement error biases (e.g., Arellano, 2003), this is less of a concern when longer differences are taken, as here (e.g., Griliches & Hauman, 1986).

The source of the data on the vertically integrated foreign subsidiaries is the Worldbase dataset from Dun & Bradstreet. A description of these data can be found in Appendix A "FDI Dataset". The data on preferential integration agreements were compiled by Scott Baier and Jeffrey Bergstrand and cover the period 1960–2005. A distinguishing feature of this dataset is that it contains information on the type of agreement. Agreements are defined according to the following categories: preferential

Table B.1 Estimation results

Regressor	(1) Vertical subsidiaries	(2) Vertical subsidiaries	(3) Vertical subsidiaries	(4) Vertical subsidiaries between proximate countries	(5) Vertical subsidiaries between distant countries
Contiguity	0.3051*** (0.0786)	0.4861*** (0.1704)			
Common language	0.1922*** (0.0626)	0.5404*** (0.1069)			
Colonial ties	0.1071 (0.0794)	0.5284*** (0.1140)			
Skill difference	1.0537*** (0.1819)	−1.4130 (3.9196)			
PTA	−0.0406 (0.0745)	0.3282** (0.1436)			
Distance	−0.3085*** (0.0313)	−0.7400*** (0.0581)			
Logistics infrastructure	0.6915*** (0.1136)	0.5476*** (0.2057)			
×Time-sensitiveness	0.0710*** (0.0114)	0.0568*** (0.0210)	0.0712*** (0.0141)	0.0568*** (0.0168)	0.0795*** (0.0165)
Parent country fixed effect	Yes	Yes	Yes	Yes	Yes
Host country fixed effect	Yes	Yes	Yes	Yes	Yes
Sector fixed effect	Yes	Yes	Yes	Yes	Yes
Parent-host country fixed effect	No	No	Yes	Yes	Yes
Observations	8611	305760	4339	4369	8708
R^2	0.49	–	0.50	0.50	0.50

Notes: The dependent variable in column (2) is the number of subsidiaries in country i from country j in sector k. The dependent variable in columns (1), (3), (4) and (5) is the log of number of subsidiaries in country i from country j in sector k. Column (2) is estimated using a negative binomial model. Columns (1), (3), (4) and (5) are estimated using least squares. Robust standard errors clustered by country pairs reported in parentheses

***; **; *Significant at the 1%, 5% and 10% level respectively trade agreements, free trade agreements, customs unions, common markets, and economic unions. Accordingly, we can explore whether deeper forms of integration exhibit larger impacts than shallower agreements. For simplicity, we follow Johnson and Noguera (2012b) and regroup the agreements in only three categories: (i) preferential trade agreements; (ii) free trade agreements; and (iii) deep integration agreements covering customs unions, common markets, and economic unions.

Table B.2 presents ordinary least squares (OLS) of Eq. (B.2), along with two alternative specifications of this equation, i.e., with no fixed effects and with just year fixed effects for the period 1980–2005. In the right panel of Table B.2, we report the respective estimates when we differentiate the data over 10 years instead of 5 years, thereby allowing for a longer adjustment period. These estimates are also positive and significant and larger in magnitude than the original ones.

In Table B.3 we go through several robustness checks. First, there is a substantial number of country pairs without vertical FDI activity. To account for the potential selection bias associated with these zero observations, we estimate separate cross-sectional probits for each sample year using religion as the exclusion restriction, compute and include the implied Mills ratio in Eq. (B.1), and then differentiate this equation to arrive at an alternative specification of Eq. (B.2) (e.g., Baier et al., 2013). Second, whereas the main specification accounts for time-varying country-level variables, unobserved time-varying country-pair factors such as changing investment costs unrelated to the agreements are not controlled for. In the third column we resort to another alternative specification of Eq. (B.2) to account for these unobserved factors. More precisely, we specify a random growth model, whereby we include country-pair fixed effects in Eq. (B.2) and proceed with the estimation by differentiating them away. Third, we address potential reverse causality. In particular, we test the exogeneity of EIAs by including both lagged and lead changes in this variable (i.e., changes between $t-10$ and $t-5$ and between t and $t+5$, respectively). In addition, we conduct a placebo exercise along similar lines. We assign country-pair EIA status in 1995, 2000, and 2005 to the respective observations in 1975, 1980, and 1985, and re-estimate Eq. (B.2) on this alternative sample. Putting it differently, we regress the current bilateral number of vertically integrated foreign subsidiaries on future EIAs.

In the upper panel of Table B.4 we investigate whether deeper forms of integration induce more cross-border production sharing than shallower integration agreements. In so doing, we group agreements in three categories: preferential trade agreements (PTAs), free trade agreements (FTAs), and deep integration agreements covering customs unions, common markets, and economic unions (CUs, CMs, and EUs) (e.g., Johnson & Noguera, 2012b).

The lower panel of Table B.4 presents the channels through which the increase in vertically linked subsidiaries arises. We estimate the impact of EIAs on the number of parents, number of sectors, number of affiliates per parent, and number of affiliates per sector, based on Eq. (B.2). For more details of the entire analysis, see Blyde, Graziano, and Volpe (2013).

Table B.2 Baseline estimates

	Five years			Ten years		
	(1)	(2)	(3)	(4)	(5)	(6)
EIA	0.218*** (0.033)	0.210*** (0.032)	0.082*** (0.031)	0.366*** (0.067)	0.351*** (0.065)	0.196*** (0.060)
Year fixed effect	No	Yes	No	No	Yes	No
Host country-year fixed effect	No	No	Yes	No	No	Yes
Investing country-year fixed effect	No	No	Yes	No	No	Yes
Number of observations	9,271	9,271	9,271	4,391	4,391	4,391

***, **, * significant at the 1%, 5% and 10% level respectively

Table B.3 Robustness checks

	Baseline	Selection	Second differences	Lag and lead	Placebo
	(1)	(2)	(3)	(4)	(5)
EIA	0.082*** (0.031)	0.062** (0.030)	0.054* (0.030)	0.102** (0.040)	–0.019 (0.040)
Lagged EIA				0.077** (0.037)	
Forwarded EIA				–0.007 (0.027)	
Inverse Mill's ratio		0.725*** (0.111)			
Year fixed effect	No	No	No	No	No
Host country-year fixed effect	Yes	Yes	Yes	Yes	Yes
Investing country-year fixed effect	Yes	Yes	Yes	Yes	Yes
Number of observations	5,733	5,429	5,072	4,265	1,854

***, **, * significant at the 1%, 5% and 10% level respectively

Table B.4 Deepness of agreement and channels

Heterogeneous effects by type of agreement	
PTA	0.041 (0.046)
FTA	0.090*** (0.032)
CU, CM, EU	0.120*** (0.040)
Year fixed effect	No
Host country-year fixed effect	Yes
Investing country-year fixed effect	Yes
Number of observations	5,733
Channels	
Number of parents	0.069** (0.030)
Number of sectors	0.087*** (0.031)
Number of subsidiaries per parent	0.013** (0.005)
Number of subsidiaries per sector	−0.004(0.010)
Year fixed effect	No
Host country-year fixed effect	Yes
Investing country-year fixed effect	Yes
Number of observations	5,733

***, **, * significant at the 1%, 5% and 10% level respectively

Specification for the Model of Intra-firm Trade

To examine the factors that affect the internalization decision we employ the following framework that follows very closely the work in Bernard, Jensen, Redding, and Schott (2010) as well as Nunn and Trefler (2008):

$$X_{ci} = \beta_0 + \beta_1 r_i + \beta_2 G_c + \beta_3 r_i G_c + \beta_4 k_i + \beta_5 Z_c + \beta_6 k_i Z_c + \beta_7 s_i + \beta_8 H_c + \beta_9 s_i H_c + \beta_{10} P_c + \varepsilon_{fpc}$$

where X_{ci} is a measure of intra-firm exports in industry i from country c to the United States; r_i, k_i, and s_i are measures of contractibility, capital intensity, and skill intensity of industry i, respectively; G_c, Z_c, H_c, and P_c are measures of the legal contractual framework, physical capital abundance, human capital abundance, and total population in exporting country c; and ε is the error term. We examine both the extensive and the intensive margins of trade. For the extensive margin, the dependent variable takes the form of a dummy that is equal to one if there are positive intra-firm exports of country c in industry I, and zero otherwise. In this case, the equation is estimated using a probit model. In the case of the intensive margin, the dependent variable is the share of intra-firm exports of country c in industry i. This regression is estimated using least squares. For detailed sources of all the datasets, see Blyde (2013).

Data on intra-firm exports to the US are taken from the US Related Party Trade database from the US Census Bureau. We choose the year 2005 to match as close as possible the time frame available for most of the covariates. Additionally, we work at the six-digit NAICS level of disaggregation because this matches exactly the level of disaggregation of all the covariates in the model that capture industry characteristics. Following Nunn and Trefler (2008), we use Nunn's measure of industry contract intensity. Nunn defines contract intensity as when the production of a good requires the use of highly specialized and customized inputs. The more specialized and customized the input is, the more specific the relationship is and the more contract-intense the production of the good becomes. To facilitate the interpretation of the results, we follow Nunn and Trefler (2008) and use one minus the fraction of inputs that are relationship-specific as the variable of interest in the regression. The higher the value of this variable, the less contract-intensive is the industry.

Capital intensity in industry i (k_i) is measured by the capital-to-labor ratio of the industry, while skill intensity (s_i) is measured by the ratio of non-producer workers to total workers. These data are taken from the NBER-CES Manufacturing Industry Database, which are available at the six-digit NAICS level for the year 2005. Physical capital abundance in country c (Z_c) is an updated version of the Hall and Jones (1999) measure of physical capital per worker. The update is constructed using the Penn World Tables dataset for the year 2005. Total population is also taken from the Penn World Tables. Following a standard practice in the development literature, we use as a proxy of human capital abundance in country c (H_c) the average years of schooling attained in the population older than 25. The data are available for the year 2005 from the Barro-Lee dataset. Similar to Bernard et al. (2010) we employ the Kaufmann, Kraay, and Mastruzzi (2006) measures of governance to assess the quality of the country contractual environment. We also employ the index of Rule of Law because this is the measure that most closely captures the state of the legal contractual framework of the country as suggested by the theory. We use the data for the year 2005.

We also include two additional covariates in the model to measure the role of trade costs. Even though the theory is silent with respect to these costs, they might have an important impact on the location decision of the firms. We specifically include a dummy variable equal to one if the exporting country has a preferential trade agreement with the US and zero otherwise. This measure intends to capture the role of market access on intra-firm trade. The second variable is a measure of transport costs, consisting of the ad valorem freight rate associated to the exports from country c to the US in industry i. The freight rates are calculated using the US imports of the Merchandise dataset from the US Census Bureau, which includes the customs import value of all import transactions in the US as well as their associated freight charges in the 10-digit Harmonized System (HS). The dataset is converted to six-digit NAICS using a concordance table taken from the World Integrated Trade Solution of the World Bank. The data is for the year 2005.

In the chapter we present results for the exports of all goods and for the exports of intermediates only. To eliminate the exports of final goods from the total flows of exports we employ the Bureau of Economic Analysis (BEA) 2002 Import Matrix and Input-Output table, which are disaggregated at the six-digit NAICS level.

Table B.5 Estimation results

	Probit	OLS
Regressor	(1)	(2)
Contract intensity$_i$	0.1235*** (0.0229)	0.0813*** (0.0264)
Governance$_c$	0.0694*** (0.0233)	0.0238 (0.0163)
×Contract intensity$_i$	0.0697*** (0.0259)	−0.0643*** (0.0215)
Capital intensity$_i$	−0.0176 (0.0238)	0.1739*** (0.0189)
Capital abundance$_c$	0.0719*** (0.0180)	0.0364** (0.0169)
×Capital intensity$_i$	0.0346 (0.0223)	−0.0058 (0.0114)
Skill intensity$_i$	0.1131** (0.0497)	0.1205*** (0.0359)
Human capital abundance$_c$	0.0261 (0.0642)	−0.0808 (0.0667)
×Skill intensity$_i$	0.2958** (0.1431)	−0.2431** (0.1115)
Population$_c$	0.1082*** (0.0079)	−0.0230*** (0.0086)
PTA$_c$	0.1704*** (0.0428)	−0.0267 (0.0602)
Freights$_{ic}$	−0.0386*** (0.0051)	−0.0653*** (0.0056)
Observations	19103	12995
R^2		0.09
Pseudo R^2	0.18	

Notes: Column (1): Probit regression results. Numbers are marginal effects. Dependent variable indicates whether the exports of country *c* in industry *i* to the US are intra-firm. Column (2): OLS regression results. Dependent variable is the share of exports of country *c* in industry *i* to the US that is intra-firm; only positive values are included. Contract intensity is Nunn's measure of contract intensity in industry *i*. Governance is the index of rule of law from Kaufmann et al. (2006). Capital intensity is the capital labor ratio in industry *i*. Capital abundance is the log of physical capital per worker in country *c*. Skill intensity is the ratio of non-production workers to total workers in industry *i*. Human capital abundance is the log of average years of schooling attained in country *c*. Population is the log of total population in country *c*. PTA is a dummy equal to one if country *c* has a preferential trade agreement with the US. Freights is the ad valorem freight rate of the exports in industry *i* from country *c* to the US. Robust standard errors adjusted for clustering at the country level are in parentheses

***; **; *Significant at the 1%, 5%, and 10% levels, respectively

This information shows the share of imports used as intermediate inputs and the share of imports used for final consumption for each import at the six-digit NAICS level. We multiply the share of imports used as an intermediate with the flows of related and non-related party trade to eliminate the exports of final goods in each category. Then, we recalculate the ratio of related to total (related + non-related) exports.

Column 1 of Table B.5 presents the results of the probit estimation for the extensive margin, and column 2 presents the results of the least squares for the intensive margin. Several additional regressions are also run to check for the robustness of the results. The tests consist of: (i) dropping sectors that are intensive in foreign-owned firms; (ii) excluding the export flows associated with final goods; (iii) estimating a Heckman two-stage selection model to control for the possibility that the observations are not randomly selected; and (iv) adding industry and country fixed effects to control for other potential determinants of the internalization decision that are not explicitly included in the model. All the findings remain qualitatively similar to those in Table B.5. See Blyde (2013) for details.

Specification for the Model of Service Offshoring

The standard empirical model behind the determinants of services trade is a gravity equation that often takes the following functional form (see Grover, Gupta, Mattoo, & Sáez, 2012):

$$S_{ijkt} = \beta_1 G_{it} + \beta_2 G_{jt} + \beta_3 P_{it} + \beta_4 P_{jt} + X_{ij} \cdot \varnothing + \beta_5 I_{it} + \beta_6 I_{jt} + \beta_7 E_{it} + \theta_i + \theta_j + \theta_k + \theta_t + \varepsilon_{ijkt}$$

where S_{ijkt} is the log of exports of services from country i to country j of the type k in year t; G_{it} and G_{jt} are the logs of GDP per capita for countries i and j, respectively; P_{it} and P_{jt} are the logs of total population for countries i and j, respectively; X_{ij} is a vector of bilateral variables that includes the log of bilateral distance and dummy variables for whether or not they share a common border, language, and colonial ties; I_{it} and I_{jt} are proxies for the quality of the telecommunication infrastructure in countries i and j, respectively; E_{it} is the level of human capital in the exporting country; and θ_i, θ_j, θ_k, and θ_t are exporting country fixed effects, importing country fixed effects, sector fixed effects, and time effects, respectively.

Service trade data was collected from the OECD database. We take the bilateral imports of 35 OECD countries from 136 exporting countries during the period 2000–2009. We use bilateral trade in services of two categories: "computing and information services" and "miscellaneous business, professional, and technical services."

GDP, population, school enrollment, and number of pupils in secondary education were obtained from the World Development Indicators. The distance, language, colony, and contiguity variables were obtained from the CEPII database. ICT is an index of information and communication technology used in the analysis of logistics infrastructure in Chap. 3. The index combines hard indicators following the core measures on ICT infrastructure suggested by The Partnership on Measuring ICT for Development: fixed telephone lines per 100 inhabitants, mobile cellular telephone subscriptions per 100 inhabitants, terrestrial mobile wireless subscriptions per 100 inhabitants, dedicated mobile data subscriptions per 100 inhabitants, fixed (wired) Internet subscriptions per 100 inhabitants, fixed (wired) broadband Internet subscriptions per 100 inhabitants, and the international Internet bandwidth per Internet user.

The model is estimated using least squares and a quasi-maximum likelihood estimator (QMLE)—specifically, the negative binomial model. The last estimator is employed to account for the presence of zero value observations. The results are presented in Table B.6.

Table B.6 Estimation results

Variables	Least squares (1)	Negative binomial (2)
GDP per capita$_i$	0.3986** (0.1704)	0.6957*** (0.1668)
GDP per capita$_j$	0.2735** (0.1231)	0.5601*** (0.1236)
Population$_i$	1.2985 (1.3908)	3.6061*** (1.3654)
Population$_j$	−3.7276*** (0.7877)	−2.8239*** (0.9449)
ICT$_i$	0.1063**(0.0423)	0.5570** (0.2789)
ICT$_j$	0.0609*** (0.0127)	0.2491*** (0.0762)
Education$_i$	0.8164**(0.3230)	0.9543*** (0.3287)
Distance$_{ij}$	−0.9859*** (0.0303)	−1.0576*** (0.0308)
Language$_{ij}$	0.1319* (0.0758)	0.2986*** (0.0898)
Colony$_{ij}$	0.4953*** (0.0618)	0.4172*** (0.0822)
Contiguity$_{ij}$	0.0647 (0.0621)	0.2059***(0.0659)
Exporter fixed effect	Yes	Yes
Importer fixed effect	Yes	Yes
Sector fixed effect	Yes	Yes
Year fixed effect	Yes	Yes
Observations	7,862	10,634
R^2	0.82	

Robust standard errors in parentheses

***; **; *significant at the 1%, 5%, and 10% levels, respectively

Appendix C

Specification for Measuring the Performance of Vertically Linked Affiliates

To compare firm characteristics—specifically size (employment), share of skilled workers, and total factor productivity across firms of similar sectors—we run the following specification:

$$Y_{ikt} = \theta + \beta V_i + \gamma F_i + D_k + D_t + \varepsilon_{ikt} \tag{C.1}$$

Where Y_{ikt} is either the log of employment, the log of the share of skilled workers, or an index of total factor productivity of plant i in sector k in year t; V_i is a dummy variable that takes the value of one if the plant is a vertically linked affiliate and zero otherwise; F_i is a dummy variable equal to one if plant i is a subsidiary of a multinational company (the share of foreign owned capital is greater than 50 %) and zero otherwise; and D_k and D_t are sector and year fixed effects, respectively. The sector in this specification is defined at the four-digit ISIC rev 3 level.

To compare total export values, total number of products, and average export per product across firms of similar sectors, we employ the same specification as in Eq. (C.1) but substitute the dependent variable on the left-hand side with the appropriate export outcome measures.

We merge three datasets for this analysis. First, we employ a worldwide dataset of multinationals, the Worldbase dataset from Dunn & Bradstreet (see Appendix A "FDI Dataset" for a description of this dataset). The second dataset consists of transaction-level data from the Chilean national customs authority (Servicio National de Aduana) for all the manufacturing firms. Trade transactions in this dataset are identified at the eight-digit HS level, and each record includes a firm identifier, the destination country, the export value of the transaction, and its unit value in US dollars. These data provide the basis for comparing unit values and other export performance indicators across firms. Finally, we employ plant-level data from the annual manufacturing survey, ENIA (Encuesta Nacional Industrial Anual), conducted by

J.S. Blyde (ed.), *Synchronized Factories: Latin America and the Caribbean in the Era of Global Value Chains*, DOI 10.1007/978-3-319-09991-0

the National Institute of Statistics, INE. The survey covers all manufacturing firms in the country with more than 10 employees. Capital stocks are constructed using the perpetual inventory method for each plant, and a measure of the plant's total factor productivity is constructed using multifactor superlative index numbers, as in Bernard, Jensen, and Schott (2006b). Using this manufacturing survey allows us to compare vertically linked affiliates with the other plants in terms of the firm characteristics described above.

The ENIA survey includes an average of 5,400 plants per year, of which 1,400 are exporters. We analyze in detail the export transactions of these 1,400 plants after merging the ENIA survey with the customs data. Using the Worldbase dataset, we identify from this group of exporters 73 plants that are vertically linked to multinationals in other countries. We compare these 73 plants against the other plants (for total labor, share of skilled labor, and TFP) and exporters (for export outcomes) in the sample. The data are available for the 1997–2006 period. The main results are reported in Tables C.1 and C.2.

Table C.1 Regressions on establishment characteristics

	Productivity		Labor		Share of skilled workers	
	(1)	(2)	(3)	(4)	(5)	(6)
Comparison with all firms						
Dummy vertical affiliate	0.3635*** (0.0383)	0.3528*** (0.0384)	0.2355*** (0.0389)	0.2392*** (0.0392)	0.1542*** (0.0108)	0.1518*** (0.0109)
Dummy foreign ownership	0.0164 (0.0233)	0.0177 (0.0233)	0.6511*** (0.0237)	0.6578*** (0.0239)	0.0324*** (0.0066)	0.0327*** (0.0066)
Observations	57,680	57,680	65,178	65,178	65,178	65,178
R^2	0.04	0.07	0.16	0.17	0.11	0.13
Comparison with exporters						
Dummy vertical affiliate	0.2739*** (0.0404)	0.2665*** (0.0411)	0.0729 (0.0471)	0.0813* (0.0486)	0.1107*** (0.0108)	0.1101*** (0.0109)
Dummy foreign ownership	−0.0060 (0.0266)	−0.0015 (0.0273)	0.3438*** (0.0312)	0.3464*** (0.0324)	0.0425*** (0.0072)	0.0432*** (0.0073)
Observations	16,343	16,343	18,134	18,134	18,134	18,134
R^2	0.09	0.14	0.17	0.19	0.21	0.25
Comparison with non-exporters						
Dummy vertical affiliate	0.4375*** (0.0535)	0.4454*** (0.0539)	0.9186*** (0.0436)	0.9282*** (0.0442)	0.1328*** (0.0149)	0.1250*** (0.0151)
Dummy foreign ownership	−0.0021 (0.0437)	−0.0197 (0.0441)	0.2804*** (0.0350)	0.2825*** (0.0356)	0.0490*** (0.0119)	0.0542*** (0.0121)
Observations	42,343	42,343	48,201	48,201	48,201	48,201
R^2	0.05	0.08	0.13	0.15	0.11	0.13
Sector fixed effect	Yes	No	Yes	No	Yes	No
Year fixed effect	Yes	No	Yes	No	Yes	No
Sector-year fixed effect	No	Yes	No	Yes	No	Yes

Notes: The dependent variable in columns (1) and (2) is a measure of total factor productivity based on the multifactor superlative index number; the dependent variable in columns (3) and (4) is the log of the firm's labor force; the dependent variable in columns (5) and (6) is the share of skilled workers in total workers.. The sector is defined at the four-digit ISIC rev 3 level

***; **; *significant at the 1%, 5%, and 10% levels, respectively

Table C.2 Regressions on exports, number of products, and average exports per product

	Exports		Number of products		Average exports per product	
	(1)	(2)	(3)	(4)	(5)	(6)
Dummy vertical affiliate	0.5912*** (0.1450)	0.5990*** (0.1514)	0.1669*** (0.0606)	0.1559*** (0.0629)	0.2401*** (0.0769)	0.2785*** (0.0790)
Dummy foreign ownership	1.1782*** (0.0959)	1.1446*** (0.1004)	0.3128*** (0.0401)	0.3139*** (0.0418)	0.3818*** (0.0509)	0.3588*** (0.0524)
Sector fixed effect	Yes	No	Yes	No	Yes	No
Year fixed effect	Yes	No	Yes	No	Yes	No
Sector-year fixed effect	No	Yes	No	Yes	No	Yes
Observations	8,000	8,000	8,000	8,000	8,000	8,000
R^2	0.32	0.35	0.15	0.20	0.37	0.42

Notes: The dependent variables are the log of exports (columns 1 and 2), log of the number of products (columns 3 and 4), and log of the average exports per product (columns 5 and 6) at the firm, sector, and year level. Sector is defined at the four-digit ISIC rev 3 level
***; **; *significant at the 1%, 5%, and 10% levels, respectively

References

Acemoglu, D., & Johnson, S. (2005). Unbundling institutions. *Journal of Political Economy, 113*, 5.

Acemoglu, D., Johnson, S., & Mitton, T. (2009). Determinants of vertical integration: Financial development and contracting costs. *Journal of Finance, 64*(3), 1251–1290.

ACI (Airports Council International). (2008). *Airport economics survey*. Geneva: Airports Council International.

Agostino, M., Giuntam, A., Nugent, J. B., Scalera, D., & Trivieri, F. (2011) *Firm productivity, organizational choice and global value chain*. Orkestra working paper series in territorial competitiveness, number 2011-R09.

Aguerro, C., & Mastrini, G. (2009). *La regulación de las telecomunicaciones y el desarrollo de la banda ancha. Implicancias para la región andina*. Unpublished document, Association for Progressive Communications.

Aldana, A., & Vallejo, A. (2010). Telecomunicaciones, convergencia y regulación. *Revista de economía institucional, 12*, 23.

Alfaro, L., & Charlton, A. (2009). Intra-industry foreign direct investment. *American Economic Review, 99*(5), 2096–2119.

Alfaro, L., & Chen, M. (2011). *Surviving the global financial crisis: Foreign ownership and establishment performance*. NBER working papers 17141, National Bureau of Economic Research.

Altemburg, T., & Meyer-Stamer, J. (1999). How to promote clusters. Policy experiences from Latin America. *World Development, 27*(9), 1693–1713.

Alvarez, R., & López, R. (2005). Exporting and performance: Evidence from Chilean plants. *Canadian Journal of Economics, 38*(4), 1385–1400.

Amin, M., & Mattoo, A. (2008). *Human capital and the changing structure of the Indian economy*. Policy research working paper 4576. Washington, DC: World Bank.

Anderson, J. E., & Yotov, Y. V. (2012). *Gold standard gravity*. NBER working papers 17835, National Bureau of Economic Research.

Antràs, P. (2003). Firms, contracts and trade structure. *Quarterly Journal of Economics, 118*(4), 1375–1418.

Antràs, P. (2014). Grossman-Hart (1986) Goes global: Incomplete contracts, property rights, and the International Organization of Production. *Journal of Law, Economics, and Organization, 30*(1), 118–175.

Antràs, P., & Helpman, E. (2004). Global sourcing. *Journal of Political Economy, 112*, 552–580.

Antràs, P., & Helpman, E. (2008). Contractual frictions and global sourcing. In E. Helpman, D. Marin, & T. Verdier (Eds.), *The organization of firms in a global economy*. Cambridge: Harvard University Press.

J.S. Blyde (ed.), *Synchronized Factories: Latin America and the Caribbean in the Era of Global Value Chains*, DOI 10.1007/978-3-319-09991-0

Arellano, M. (2003). *Panel data econometrics: Advanced texts in econometrics*. Oxford: Oxford University Press.

Arkolakis, C. (2010). Market penetration costs and the new consumers margin in international trade. *Journal of Political Economy, 118*, 6.

Arráiz, I., Henríquez, F., & Stucchi, R. (2012). Supplier development programs and firm performance: Evidence from Chile. *Small Business Economics, 41*, 1.

Artopoulos, A., Friel, D., & Hallak, J. C. (2013). Export emergence of differentiated goods from developing countries: Export pioneers and business practices in Argentina. *Journal of Development Economics, 105*, 19–35.

Augier, P., Gasiorek, M., & Tong, C. L. (2005). The impact of rules of origin on trade flows. *Economic Policy, 20*, 43.

Aw, B., Chung, S., & Roberts, M. (2000). Productivity and turnover in the export market: Micro-level evidence from the Republic of Korea and Taiwan (China). *World Bank Economic Review, 14*, 65–90.

Axèle, G., & Delane, B. (2008). *Policies promoting MNEs linkages in host economies: A comparison between Brazil and Malaysia*. Paper presented in the Global Forum on International Investment VII. Paris: OECD.

Baier, S., Bergstrand, J., & Feng, M. (2013). *Economic integration agreements and the margins of international trade*. Clemson University and University of Notre Dame, mimeo.

Baldwin, R. (2006). *Globalization: The great unbundling(s)*. Unpublished document, Graduate Institute of International Studies, Geneva.

Baldwin, R. (2011). *Trade and industrialization after globalization 2nd unbundling: How building and joining a supply chain is different and why it matters*. NBER working paper series no. 17716.

Baldwin, R. (2012). *Global suppiy chains: Why they emerged, why they matter, and where they are going*. CEPR discussion paper series no. 9103.

Baldwin, R., & Taglioni, D. (2011). *Gravity chains: Estimating bilateral trade flows when parts and components trade is important*. European Central Bank, working paper no. 1401.

Baldwin, R., & Venables, A. (2013). Spiders and snakes: Offshoring and agglomeration in the global economy. *Journal of International Economics, 90*, 2.

Battat, J., Frank, I., & Shen, X. (1996). *Suppliers to multinationals*. Foreign Investment Advisory Services, occasional paper 6.

Beena, S. (2006). *Mergers and acquisitions in the Indian pharmaceutical industry: Nature, structure and performance*. MPRA paper 8144.

Beltrán, C., & Gutiérrez, A. (2007). *La Vinculación de Suplidores Domésticos con Multinacionales en Costa Rica*. Unpublished, Department of Economics, University of Costa Rica.

Benavente, J. M., & Crespi, G. (2003). *The impact of an associative strategy (the PROFO Program) on small and medium enterprises in Chile*. SPRU working paper series 88, SPRU—Science and Technology Policy Research, University of Sussex.

Bernard, A., Eaton, J., Jensen, B., & Kortum, S. (2003). Plants and productivity in international trade. *American Economic Review, 93*, 4.

Bernard, A. B., & Jensen, B. (1999). Exceptional exporter performance: Cause, effect, or both? *Journal of International Economics, 47*(1), 1–25.

Bernard, A. B., & Jensen, B. (2004). Exporting and productivity in the USA. *Oxford Review of Economic Policy, 20*, 3.

Bernard, A. B., Jensen, B., Redding, S., & Schott, P. K. (2010). Intra-firm trade and product contractibility. *American Economic Review, Papers and Proceedings, 100*(5), 444–448.

Bernard, A., Jensen, J. B., & Schott, P. (2006b). Trade costs, firms and productivity. *Journal of Monetary Economics, 53*, 917–937.

Bhagwati, J. (2013). Dawn of a new system. *Finance and Development*. International Monetary Fund.

Black, S. E., & Strahan, P. E. (2002). Entrepreneurship and bank credit availability. *Journal of Finance, 57*(6), 2807–2833.

Blyde, J. (2013). *On the determinants of the internalization decision*. Unpublished document, Inter-American Development Bank, Washington, DC.

Blyde, J., Graziano, A., & Volpe, C. (2013). *Economic integration agreements and production fragmentation: Evidence on the extensive margin*. Unpublished document, Inter-American Development Bank, Washington, DC.

Blyde, J., & Molina, D. (2013). *Logistics infrastructure and the international location of fragmented production*. Unpublished document, Inter-American Development Bank, Washington, DC.

Blyde, J., Pietrobelli, C., & Volpe, C. (2014). *Internationalization for productive development*. Unpublished document, Inter-American Development Bank, Washington, DC.

Brown-Grossman, F., & Domínguez-Villalobos, L. (2012). *Can Mexico set up in the aerospace and the software and IT global value chains as a high-value-added player?* Inter-American Development Bank working paper no. 372, Washington, DC.

Buckley, P. J., & Casson, M. (1976). *The future of the multinational enterprise*. London: Macmillan.

Cafaggi, F., Macedo, R., Swensson, L., Andreotti, T., Piterman, C., de Almeida, L., et al. (2012). *Accessing the global value chain in a changing institutional environment: Comparing aeronautics and coffee*. Inter-American Development Bank working paper no. 370, Washington, DC.

Carluccio, J., & Fally, T. (2012). Global sourcing under imperfect capital markets. *Review of Economics and Statistics, 94*, 3.

Caves, R. E. (1975). *Diversification, foreign investment and scale in North American manufacturing industries*. Ottawa: Economic Council of Canada.

CEPAL. (2012). *Boletín Marítimo #49, Comisión Económica para América Latina y el Caribe*. Santiago, Chile: Naciones Unidas.

Chaney, T. (2008). Distorted gravity: The intensive and extensive margins of international trade. *American Economic Review, 98*, 4.

Chen, M. X., Otsuki, T., & Wilson, S. (2006). *Do standards matter for export success?* World Bank Working Research Policy working paper 3809, Washington, DC.

Clark, X., Dollar, D., & Micco, A. (2004). Port efficiency, maritime transport costs, and bilateral trade. *Journal of Development Economics, 75*, 417–450.

Clark, D., Schaur, G., & Kozlova, V. (2012). *Supply chain uncertainty as a trade barrier*. Unpublished document.

Clerides, S., Lach, S., & Tybout, J. (1998). Is learning by exporting important? Micro-dynamic evidence from Colombia, Mexico and Morocco. *Quarterly Journal of Economics, 113*, 903–947.

Corcos, G., Delphine, I., Mion, G., & Verdier, T. (2009). *The determinants of intra-firm trade*. CEPR working paper no. 7530.

Corden, W. M. (1984). Booming sector and Dutch disease economics: Survey and consolidation. *Oxford Economic Papers, 36*, 3.

Costinot, A., Oldenski, L., & Rauch, J. (2011). Adaptation and the boundary of multinational firms. *The Review of Economics and Statistics, 93*(1), 298–308.

Curran, L., & Zignago, S. (2012). EU enlargement and the evolution of European production networks. *Research in International Business and Finance, 26*, 2.

De La Cruz, J., Koopman, R., & Wang, Z. (2011). *Estimating foreign value-added in Mexico's manufacturing exports*. US International Trade Commission working paper no. 2011-04A.

De Laiglesia, J. (2007). Telecomunicaciones en América Latina: ¿pueden las multinacionales cerrar la brecha? *Percepciones* 52. OECD.

De Loecker, J. (2013). Detecting learning by exporting. *American Economic Journal: Microeconomics, 5*, 3.

Deardorff, A. (1985). Comparative advantage and international trade and investment in services. In R. M. Stern (Ed.), *Trade and investment in services: Canada/US perspectives*. Toronto: Ontario Economic Council.

Deardorff, A. V. (2001a). Fragmentation across cones. In S. W. Arndt & H. Kierzkowski (Eds.), *Fragmentation: New production patterns in the world economy*. Oxford: Oxford University Press.

Deardorff, A. V. (2001b). Fragmentation in simple trade models. *The North American Journal of Economics and Finance, 12*(2), 121–137.

Dedrick, J., Kraemer, K. L., & Linden, G. (2008). *Who profits from innovation in global value chains? A study of the iPod and Notebook PCs*. UC Irvine. Paper prepared for the Sloan Industry Studies Annual Conference.

Dini, M. (2009). Capital social y programas asociativos: reflexión sobre instrumentos y estrategias de fomento de CORFO. In O. Muñoz Gomá (Ed.), *El Desarrollo Productivo en Chile*. Catalonia, Chile: CORFO, FLACSO.

Djankov, S., La Porta, R., Lopez-de-Silanes, F., & Shleifer, A. (2003). Courts. *The Quarterly Journal of Economics, 118*, 453–517.

Dobles Madrigal, R. (2012a). Comisión de Encadenamientos para la Exportación. *Informe Anual*. PROCOMER, San José, Costa Rica.

Dobles Madrigal, R. (2012b). *Encadenamientos para la exportación*. PROCOMER, San José, Costa Rica.

Dolan, C., & Humphrey, J. (2000). Governance and trade in fresh vegetables: The impact of UK supermarkets on the African horticulture industry. *Journal of Development Studies, 37*, 2.

Drewry. (2010). *Container terminal capacity and performance benchmarks*. London: Author.

Dussel, P. E. (2010). *Mexico's economic relationship with China: A case study of the PC industry in Jalisco, Mexico*. UNAM, Centro de Estudios China-Mexico, n.1, Mexico. Retrieved from http://www.uea.ac.uk/polopoly_fs/1.113471!5%20JALISCO.pdf

Dussel, P. E., Palacios, L. J., & Woo, G. (2003). *La industria electrónica en México: problemática, perspectivas y propuestas*. Guadalajara, México: Universidad de Guadalajara.

Eaton, J., & Kortum, S. (2001). Trade in capital goods. *European Economic Review, 45*, 1195–1235.

Eaton, J., & Kortum, S. (2002). Technology, geography, and trade. *Econometrica, 70*(5), 1741–1779.

ECLAC. (2008). *Structural change and productivity growth 20 years later. Old problems, new opportunities*. Santiago, Chile: United Nations.

Egan, M. L., & Mody, A. (1992). Buyer-seller links in export development. *World Development, 20*, 3.

Estevadeordal, A., & Suominen, K. (2006). Mapping and measuring rules of origin around the world. In O. Cadot, A. Estevadeordal, A. Suwa-Eisenmann, & T. Verdier (Eds.), *The origin of goods: Rules of origin in regional trade agreements*. Oxford: Oxford University Press.

Estevadeordal, A., & Suominen, K. (2008). What are the effects of rules of origin on trade? In A. Estevaderodal & K. Suominen (Eds.), *Gatekeepers of global commerce: Rules of origin and international economic integration*. New York: Inter-American Development Bank.

Evans, C., & Harrigan, J. (2005). Distance, time and specialization: Lean retailing in general equilibrium. *American Economic Review, 95*, 292–313.

Feenstra, R. C. (1998). Integration of trade and disintegration of production in the global economy. *Journal of Economic Perspectives, 12*(4), 31–50.

Feenstra, R. (2004). *Advanced international trade: Theory and evidence*. Princeton: Princeton University Press.

Feenstra, R., Hong, C., Ma, H., & Spencer, B. J. (2012). *Contractual versus non-contractual trade: The role of institutions in China*. National Bureau of Economic Research working paper 17728.

Feenstra, R., & Kee, H. L. (2004). On the measurement of product variety in trade. *American Economic Review, 94*, 2.

Fernandes, A. M. (2007). Trade policy, trade volumes and plant-level productivity in Colombian manufacturing industries. *Journal of International Economics, 71*, 1.

Findlay, R., & Jones, R. (2001). Input trade and the location of production. *American Economic Review, 91*(2), 29–33.

Freund, C., & Weinhold, D. (2002). The internet and international trade in services. *American Economic Review, 92*, 2.

Fujita, M. (2011). Value chain dynamics and local supplier's capability building: An analysis of the Vietnamese Motorcycle Industry. In M. Kawakami & T. Sturgeon (Eds.), *The dynamics of local learning in global value chains: Experiences from East Asia*. Basingstoke: Palgrave Macmillan, IDE-Jetro.

Fukao, K., Ishido, H., & Ito, K. (2003). Vertical Intra-industry and Foreign direct Investment in East Asia. *Journal of the Japanese and International Economies, 17*, 468–506.

Fung, K. C., Garcia-Herrero, A., & Siu, A. (2009). *Production sharing in Latin America and East Asia*. BBVA working paper no. 0901.

Gereffi, G. (1999). International trade and industrial upgrading in the apparel commodity chain. *Journal of International Economics, 48*, 1.

Gereffi, G., Castillo, M., & Fernandez-Stark, K. (2009). *The offshore services industry: A new opportunity for Latin America*. IDB policy brief no. 101.

Gereffi, G., & Frederick, S. (2010). The global apparel value chain, trade and the crisis: Challenges and opportunities for developing countries. In O. Cattaneo, G. Gereffi, & C. Staritz (Eds.), *Global value chains in a postcrisis world: A development perspective*. Washington, DC: The World Bank.

Gereffi, G., Humphrey, J., & Sturgeon, T. (2005). The governance of global value chains. *Review of International Political Economy, 12*, 1.

Giuliani, E., Pietrobelli, C., & Rabellotti, R. (2005). Upgrading in global value chains: Lessons from Latin American clusters. *World Development, 33*, 4.

González, A., Hallak, J. C., Schott, P., & Soria, T. (2012). *Insertion of Argentine firms in global value chains not oriented to the mass market: The cases of high-end footwear and the Basso Group*. Inter-American Development Bank working paper no. 375, Washington, DC.

Gorodnichenko, Y., Svejnar, J., & Terrell, K. (2010). Globalization and innovation in emerging markets. *American Economic Journal: Macroeconomics, 2*, 2.

Griliches, Z., & Hauman, J. (1986). Errors in variables in panel data. *Journal of Econometrics, 31*, 1.

Grossman, G., & Rossi-Hansberg, E. (2008). Trade in tasks: A simple theory of offshoring. *American Economic Review, 98*(5), 1978–1997.

Grover, A., Gupta, P., Mattoo, A., & Sáez, S. (2012). Service exports: Are the drivers different for developing countries? In A. Grover, A. Mattoo, & S. Sáez (Eds.), *Exporting services. A developing country perspective*. Washington, DC: The World Bank.

Hackett Group. (2012). *Supply chain optimization study*. Atlanta.

Hall, R. E., & Jones, C. I. (1999). Why do some countries produce so much more output per worker than others? *The Quarterly Journal of Economics, 114*(1), 83–116.

Hallak, J. C., & Schott, P. (2011). Estimating cross-country differences in product quality. *Quarterly Journal of Economics, 126*(1), 417–474.

Harrison, A. (1994). Productivity, imperfect competition and trade reform: Theory and evidence. *Journal of International Economics, 36*, 53–73.

Hayakawa, K. (2012). *Impact of diagonal cumulation rule on FTA utilization: Evidence from bilateral and multilateral FTAs between Japan and Thailand*. IDE discussion paper no. 372.

Head, K., Mayer, T., & Ries, J. (2009). How remote is the offshoring thread? *European Economic Review, 53*, 429–444.

Head, K., & Ries, J. (2008). FDI as an outcome of the market for corporate control: Theory and evidence. *Journal of International Economics, 74*(1), 2–20.

Helpman, E. (1984). A simple theory of trade with multinational corporations. *Journal of Political Economy, 92*, 451–471.

Helpman, E., & Krugman, P. (1985). *Market structure and foreign trade*. Cambridge: MIT Press.

Hiratsuka, D. (2011). *Production networks in the Asia-Pacific region: Facts and policy implications*. Unpublished document, IDE-JETRO.

Hoberg, G., & Phillips, G. (2010). Product market synergies and competition in mergers and acquisitions: A text-based analysis. *The Review of Financial Studies, 23*, 10.

Horstmann, I. J., & Markusen, J. R. (1987). Strategic investments and the development of multinationals. *International Economic Review, 28*, 109–121.

Hummels, D. (2007). Transportation costs and international trade in the second era of globalization. *Journal of Economic Perspectives, 21*, 3.

Hummels, D., Ishii, J., & Yi, K.-M. (2001). The nature and growth of vertical specialization in world trade. *Journal of International Economics, 54*, 1.

Hummels, D., & Klenow, P. J. (2005). The variety and quality of a nation's exports. *American Economic Review, 95*(3), 704–723.

Hummels, D., Rapoport, D., & Yi, K-M. (1998). Vertical specialization and the changing nature of world trade. *Economic Policy Review*. Federal Reserve Bank of New York.

Hummels, D., & Schaur, G. (2012). *Time as a trade barrier*. National Bureau of Economic Research working paper 17758.

Humphrey, J. (2004). *Upgrading in global value chains*. ILO working paper no. 28. Geneva: Policy Integration Department, World Commission on the Social Dimension of Globalization, International Labor Office.

Humphrey, J., & Schmitz, H. (2000). *Governance and upgrading: Linking industrial cluster and global value chain research*. IDS working paper no. 120. Brighton: Institute of Development Studies, University of Sussex.

Humphrey, J., & Schmitz, H. (2002). *Developing country firms in the world economy: Governance and upgrading in global value chains*. INEF report no. 61. Duisburg: University of Duisburg.

Humphrey, J., & Schmitz, H. (2008). Inter-firm relationships in global value chains: Trends in chain governance and their policy implications. *International Journal of Technological Learning, Innovation and Development, 1*, 3.

Iacovone, L., Smarzynska Javorcik, B., Keller, W., & Tybout, J. R. (2011). *Supplier responses to Wal-Mart's invasion of Mexico*. National Bureau of Economic research working paper 17204.

IFC. (2008). Linkages programs to develop small and medium enterprises. *Monitor*. Washington, DC: International Financial Corporation, World Bank Group.

Ishii, J., & Yi, K.-M. (1997). *The growth of world trade*. Federal Reserve Bank of New York research paper, no. 9718.

Javorcik, B. S. (2008). Can survey evidence shed light on spillovers from foreign direct investment? *The World Bank Research Observer, 23*, 2.

Javorcik, B. S., & Spatareanu, M. (2009). Tough love: Do Czech suppliers learn from their relationships with multinationals? *Scandinavian Journal of Economics, 111*, 4.

Johnson, R. C., & Noguera, G. (2012). Accounting for intermediates: Production sharing and trade in value added. *Journal of International Economics, 86*, 224–236.

Johnson, R. C., & Noguera, G. (2012b). *Fragmentation and trade in value added over four decades*. National Bureau of Economic research working paper 18186.

Jones, R. W., & Kierzkowski, H. (1990). The role of services in production and international trade: A theoretical framework. In R. Jones & A. Krueger (Eds.), *The political economy of international trade*. Oxford: Basil Blackwell.

Jones, R. W., & Kierzkowski, H. (2000). Globalization and the consequences of international fragmentation. In R. Dornbush, G. Calvo, & M. Obstfeld (eds.), *Money, factor mobility and trade: A festschrift in honor of Robert A. Mundell*. Cambridge, MA: MIT Press.

Jones, R. W., & Kierzkowski, H. (2001). A framework for fragmentation. In S. W. Arndt & H. Kierzkowski (Eds.), *Fragmentation: New production patterns in the world economy*. Oxford: Oxford University Press.

Jones, R. W., Kierzkowski, H., & Leonard, G. (2002). Fragmentation and intra-industry trade. In P. J. Lloyd & H. H. Lee (Eds.), *Frontiers of research in intra-industry trade*. Basingstoke: Palgrave Macmillan.

Joppert Swensson, L. (2012). *Contractual networks and the access of small and medium enterprises to global value chains: The case of the Brazilian aircraft industry*. Unpublished document.

Kaplinsky, R. (2005). *Globalization, poverty and inequality: Between a rock and a hard place*. Cambridge: Polity Press.

Karikomi, S. (1998). *The development strategy for SMEs in Malaysia*. IDE APEC Study Center, working paper series 97/98, no. 4.

Karkkainen, A. (2008). EU-15 foreign direct investment in the new member states. Eurostat, *Statistics in Focus*, 71.

Kaufmann, D., Kraay, A., & Mastruzzi, M. (2006). *Governance matters V: Aggregate and individual governance indicators for 1996–2005*. Policy Research working paper series 4012. The World Bank.

Kawakami, M. (2011). Inter-firm dynamics in notebook PC value chains and the rise of Taiwanese original design manufacturing firms. In M. Kawakami & T. Sturgeon (Eds.), *The dynamics of local learning in global value chains: Experiences from East Asia*. Basingstoke: Palgrave Macmillan, IDE-Jetro.

Kee, H. L., & Tang, H. (2012). *Domestic value added in Chinese exports: Firm-level evidence*. Unpublished document.

Kimura, F. (2006). International production and distribution networks in East Asia: Eighteen facts, mechanics, and policy implications. *Asian Economic Policy Review, 1*, 326–344.

Kimura, F., & Obashi, A. (2011). *Production networks in East Asia: What we know so far*. ADBI working paper 320. Tokyo: Asian Development Bank Institute.

Koopman, R., Wang, Z., & Wei, S. J. (2008). *How much of Chinese exports is really made in China? Assessing domestic value-added when processing trade is pervasive*. National Bureau of Economic Research working paper no. 14109.

Koopman, R., Wang, Z., & Wei, S. J. (2010). *Give credit where credit is due: Tracing value added in global production chains*. National Bureau of Economic Research working paper 16426.

Koopman, R., Wang, Z., & Wei, S.-J. (2014). Tracing value-added and double counting in gross exports. *American Economic Review, 104*(2), 459–494.

KPMG. (2012). *The death of outsourcing*. KPMG International.

Krugman, P. (1995). *Growing world trade: Causes and consequences*. Brookings papers on economic activity 1.

Larrain, F., Sachs, J., & Warner, A. (1999). *A structural analysis of Chile's long-term growth: History, prospects and policy implications*. Paper prepared for the Government of Chile, Santiago.

Lawrence, R. Z. (1996). *Regionalism, multilateralism and deeper integration*. Washington, DC: Brooking Institution Press.

Leamer, E. E. (1996). *In search of Stolper-Samuelson effects on U.S. wages*. National Bureau of Economic Research working paper 5427.

Leamer, E. E., Maul, H., Rodriguez, S., & Schott, P. K. (1999). Does natural resource abundance increase Latin American income inequality? *Journal of Development Economics, 59*, 1.

Lederman, D., & Maloney, W. (2003). *Trade structure and growth*. Policy Research working paper series 3025, The World Bank.

Lennon, C. (2006). *Trade in services and trade in goods: Differences and complementarities*. Unpublished document.

Lennon, C., Mirza, D., & Nicoletti, G. (2009). Complementarity of inputs across countries in services trade. *Annals of Economics and Statistics, 93–94*, 183.

Limão, N., & Venables, A. J. (2002). Infrastructure, geographical disadvantage, transport costs and trade. *World Bank Economic Review, 2001*(15), 451–479.

Lipsey, R. E. (1978). The creation of microdata sets for enterprises and establishments. *Annales de l'INSEE, 30–31*, 395–422.

Maffioli, A. (2005). *The formation of network and public intervention: Theory and evidence from the Chilean experience*. ISLA working paper 23, Università Bocconi.

Mangelsdorf, A., Portugal-Perez, A., & Wilson, J. S. (2012). Food standards and exports: Evidence from China. *World Trade Review, 11*, 3.

Markusen, J. R. (1984). Multinationals, multi–plant economies, and the gains from trade. *Journal of International Economics, 16*(3–4), 205–226.

Markusen, J. R. (1997). *Trade versus Investment Liberalization*. National Bureau of Economic Research working paper 6231.

Masakure, O., Henson, S., & Cranfield, J. (2009). Standards and export performance in developing countries: Evidence from Pakistan. *The Journal of International Trade and Economic Development, 18*, 3.

Maskus, K. (2012). *Private rights and public problems: The global economics of intellectual property in the 21st century*. Washington, DC: Peterson Institute of International Economics.

Mattoo, A., Stern, R., & Zanini, G. (2008). *A handbook of international trade in services*. Oxford: Oxford University Press.

Meléndez, M., & Uribe, M. J. (2012). *International product fragmentation and the insertion of Latin America and the Caribbean in global production networks: Colombian case studies*. IDB working paper no. 374. Washington, DC: Inter-American Development Bank.

Melitz, M. (2003). The impact of trade on intra-industry reallocations and aggregate industry productivity. *Econometrica, 71*, 6.

Mesquita Moreira, M., Blyde, J., Volpe, C., & Molina, D. (2013). *Too far to export? Domestic transport costs and regional disparities in Latin America and the Caribbean*. Washington, DC: Inter-American Development Bank.

Micco, A., & Serebrisky, T. (2006). Competition regimes and air transport costs: The effects of open skies agreements. *Journal of International Economics, 70*, 1.

Milberg, W., & Winkler, D. (2010). Trade, crisis, and recovery: Restructuring global value chains. In O. Cattaneo, G. Gereffi, & C. Staritz (Eds.), *Global value chains in a postcrisis world: A development perspective*. Washington, DC: The World Bank.

Mion, G., & Opromolla, L. (2010). *Managers' mobility, trade status and wages*. CEPR discussion paper no. 8230. London, UK: Centre for Economic Policy.

Miroudot, S., & Ragousssis, A. (2009). *Vertical trade, trade costs and FDI*. OECD Trade Policy working paper no. 89.

Mirza, D., & Nicoletti, G. (2004). *What is so special about trade in services?* Research paper 2004/02. Nottingham: Leverhulme Centre for Research on Globalisation and Economic Policy, University of Nottingham.

MIT. (2012). *U.S. re-shoring: A turning point*. Prepared by MIT Forum for Supply Chain Innovation and Supply Chain Digest.

Molina, D., & Muendler, M. (2013). *Preparing to export*. National Bureau of Economic Research working paper 18962.

Monge-González, R., Rivera, L., & Rosales-Tijerino, J. (2010). *Productive development policies in Costa Rica: Market failures, government failures and policy outcomes*. IDB working paper series no. IDB-WP-157.

Monge-González, R., & Rodríguez-Álvarez, J. A. (2013). *Impact evaluation of innovation and linkage development programs in Costa Rica: The cases of Propyme and CR Provee*. Unpublished document.

Monge-Gonzalez, R., & Zolezzi, S. (2012). *Insertion of Costa Rica in global value chains: A case study*. Inter-American Development Bank working paper no. 373, Washington, DC.

Moreira, M. M., Volpe, C., & Blyde, J. (2008). *Unclogging the arteries: the impact of transport costs on Latin American and Caribbean trade, special report on integration and trade*. Washington, DC: Inter-American Development Bank.

Morrison, A., Pietrobelli, C., & Rabellotti, R. (2008). Global value chains and technological capabilities: A framework to study learning and innovation in developing countries. *Oxford Development Studies, 36*, 1.

Nadvi, K. (2004). The effect of global standards on local producers: A Pakistani case study. In H. Schmitz (Ed.), *Local enterprises in the global economy: Issues of governance and upgrading*. Cheltenham: Edward Elgar.

Navas-Alemán, L. (2011). The impact of operating in multiple value chains for upgrading: The case of the Brazilian furniture and footwear industries. *World Development, 39*, 8.

Ng, F., & Yeats, A. (1999). *Production sharing in East Asia—Who does what for whom and why?* World Bank Staff paper. Washington, DC: World Bank.

Nunn, N., & Trefler, D. (2008). The boundaries of the multinational firm: An empirical analysis. In E. Helpman, D. Marin, & T. Verdier (Eds.), *The organization of firms in a global economy*. Cambridge: Harvard University Press.

OECD. (2005). *Measuring globalization: OECD handbook of economic globalization indicators*. Paris: OECD.

OECD. (2012). *Attracting knowledge-intensive FDI to Costa Rica: Challenges and policy options*. Paris: OECD Development Centre.

Otsuki, T. (2011). *Effect of international standards certification on firm-level exports: An application of the control function approach*. OSIPP discussion paper 11E005, Osaka School of International Public Policy, Osaka University.

Padilla-Pérez, R. (2005). *Estudio sectorial de la industria electrónica en México*. Mexico: Autonomous Technological Institute of Mexico (ITAM).

Padilla-Pérez, R. (2008). A regional approach to study technology transfer through foreign direct investment: The electronics industry in two Mexican regions. *Research Policy, 37*, 849–860.

Padilla-Pérez, R., Cordero, M., Hernández, R., & Romero, I. (2008). *Evolución reciente y retos de la industria manufacturera de exportación en Centroamérica, México y República Dominicana: una perspectiva regional y sectorial*. CEPAL Estudios y perspectivas, No. 95, Mexico City, ECLAC.

Pages, C. (Ed.). (2010). *The age of productivity: Transforming economies from the bottom up*. Washington, DC: Inter-American Development Bank.

Palacios, L. J. J. (2008). *Alianzas público-privadas y escalamiento industrial. El caso del complejo de Alta tecnología de Jalisco, México*. CEPAL Estudios y perspectivas, No. 98, México.

Papadakis, V. (2007). Growth through mergers and acquisitions: How it won't be a loser's game. *Business Strategy Series, 8*, 1.

Park, I., & Park, S. (2009). *Consolidation and Harmonization of Regional Trade Agreements (RTAs): A path toward global free trade*. MPRA paper no. 14217.

Paus, E., & Gallagher, K. P. (2008). Missing links: Foreign investment and industrial development in Costa Rica and Mexico. *Studies in Comparative International Development, 43*, 53–80.

Pavcnik, N. (2002). Trade liberalization, exit, and productivity improvements: Evidence from Chilean plants. *Review of Economic Studies, 69*, 245–276.

Pietrobelli, C., Casaburi, G., & Maffioli, A. (2014). *Policies to promote inter-firm linkages and coordination*. Unpublished document, Inter-American Development Bank, Washington, DC.

Pietrobelli, C., & Rabellotti, R. (2007). *Upgrading to compete. Global value chains, SMEs and clusters in Latin America*. Cambridge: Harvard University Press.

Pietrobelli, C., & Rabellotti, R. (2011). Global value chains meet innovation systems: Are there learning opportunities for developing countries? *World Development, 39*, 7.

Pietrobelli, C., & Staritz, C. (2013). *Challenges for global value chain interventions in Latin America*. Technical note no. IDB-TN-548. Washington, DC: Inter-American Development Bank.

Pipkin, S. (2011). Local means in value chain ends: Dynamics of products and social upgrading in apparel manufacturing in Guatemala and Colombia. *World Development, 39*, 12.

Poon, T. S.-C. (2004). Beyond the global production networks: A case of further upgrading of Taiwan's information technology industry. *International Journal of Technology and Globalization, 1*, 1.

Potter, J. (2001). *Embedding foreign direct investment*. Paris: OECD.

Pulak, M., & Neha, J. (2012). Mergers, acquisitions and export competitiveness: Experience of India manufacturing sector. *Journal of Competitiveness, 4*, 1.

Quadros, R. (2004). Global quality standards and technological upgrading in the Brazilian Auto-components Industry. In H. Schmitz (Ed.), *Local enterprises in the global economy: Issues of governance and upgrading*. Cheltenham: Edward Elgar.

Razo, C., & Rojas Mejia, F. (2007). *Del monopolio de Estado a la convergencia tecnológica: evolución y retos de la regulación de telecomunicaciones en América Latina*. Serie Desarrollo Productivo, No. 185, CEPAL, Chile.

Rodrik, D. (2000). How far will international economic integration go? *Journal of Economic Perspectives, 14*(1), 177–186.

Rozas, P. (2002). *Competencia y conflictos regulatorios en la industria de telecomunicaciones en America Latina*. Serie Gestión Pública, No. 25. Chile: CEPAL.

Sanchez, R., & Wilmsmeier, G. (2009). *Liner shipping networks and market concentration*. Santiago: CEPAL. Mimeo.

Schmitz, H. (2006). Learning and earning in global garment and footwear chains. *The European Journal of Development Research, 18*, 4.

Schmitz, H., & Knorringa, P. (2000). Learning from global buyers. *Journal of Development Studies, 37*, 177–205.

Serebrisky, T., Schwartz, J., Pachón, M. C., & Ricover, A. (2011). *Making a small market thrive: Recommendations for efficiency gains in the Latin American air cargo market*. World Bank transport paper, TP-35, Washington, DC.

Shingal, A. (2010). *How much do agreements matter for service trade?* Unpublished document.

Staples, B., & Harris, J. (2009). *Origin and beyond: Trade facilitation disaster or trade facilitation opportunity?* Asian Development Bank Institute working paper no. 171.

Sturgeon, T. (2002). Modular production networks: A new American model of industrial organization. *Industrial and Corporate Change, 11*, 3.

Sturgeon, T. (2008). *From commodity chains to value chains: interdisciplinary theory building in an age of globalization*. Industrial Performance Center, MIT, Working paper 08-001.

Sturgeon, T., & Florida, R. (2004). Globalization, deverticalization, and employment in the motor vehicle industry. In M. Kenny & R. Florida (Eds.), *Locating global advantage: Industry dynamics in a globalizing economy*. Palo Alto: Stanford University Press.

Sturgeon, T., & Kawakami, M. (2010). Global value chains in the electronics industry: Was the crisis a window of opportunity for developing countries? In O. Cattaneo, G. Gereffi, & C. Staritz (Eds.), *Global value chains in a Postcrisis world: A development perspective*. Washington, DC: The World Bank.

Sturgeon, T., Nielsen, P., Linden, G., Gereffi, G., & Brown, C. (2012). *Direct measure of global value chain: collecting product- and firm-level statistics on value added and business function outsourcing and offshoring*. MIT-IPC Working paper 12-001.

Suyderhoud, J. P. (1999). *The Malaysian economic development challenge: Can productivity growth co-exist with income redistribution?* K. J. Luke working paper no. 00-15.

Tempest, R. (1996, September 22). Barbie and the world economy. *Los Angeles Times*.

Tewari, M. (1999). Successful adjustment in Indian industry: The case of Ludhiana's Woolen Knitwear Cluster. *World Development, 26*, 9.

Tomiura, E. (2007). Foreign outsourcing, exporting and FDI: A productivity comparison at the firm level. *Journal of International Economics, 72*, 113–127.

Trindade, V. (2005). The big push, industrialization and international trade: The role of exports. *Journal of Development Economics, 78*, 22–48.

UNCTAD. (2010). *Creating business linkages: A policy perspective*. Geneva: United Nations.

UNCTAD. (2011). *Best practices in investment for development. How to create and benefit from FDI-SME linkages: Lessons from Malaysia and Singapore*. Geneva: United Nations.

Van Biesebroeck, J., & Sturgeon, T. (2010). Effects of the 2008-09 crisis on the automotive industry in developing countries: A global perspective. In O. Cattaneo, G. Gereffi, & C. Staritz (Eds.), *Global value chains in a postcrisis world: A development perspective*. Washington, DC: The World Bank.

Vargas Madrigal, T., Céspedes, O., Gonzalez, C., & Ramírez, F. (2010). *Evaluación de Impacto del Proyecto para Desarrollar Suplidores para Empresas Multinacionales de Alta Tecnología en Costa Rica*. Unpublished document, Multilateral Investment Fund, Washington, DC.

Volpe Martincus, C. (2010). *Odyssey in international markets. An assessment of the effectiveness of export promotion in Latin America and the Caribbean*. Special report on integration and trade. Washington, DC: Inter-American Development Bank.

Volpe Martincus, C., Castresana, S., & Castagnino, T. (2010). ISO standards: A certificate to expand exports? Firm-level evidence from Argentina. *Review of International Economics, 18*, 5.

Wagner, R. (2012). *The collective action of global entrepreneurs*. Unpublished document.

Williamson, O. E. (1975). *Markets, hierarchies: Analysis, antitrust implications*. New York: Free Press.

Williamson, O. E. (1985). *The economic institutions of capitalism*. New York: Free Press.

WTO. (2008). *Understanding the WTO*. Geneva: World Trade Organization.

WTO. (2011). The WTO and preferential trade agreements: From co-existence to coherence. *World Trade Report*. Geneva, Switzerland.

Yeats, A. (2001). Just how big is global production sharing? In S. W. Arndt & H. Kierzkowski (Eds.), *Fragmentation: New production patterns in the world economy*. Oxford: Oxford University Press.